AN 'ANTIQUARIAN CRAZE'

The life, times and work in archaeology
of Patrick Lyons R.I.C.
(1861-1954)

Dear Sir, I thank you most heartily for a kind letter. It brings to me pleasant memories over the span of 60 years — memories of my comrade the cultured, gentle & virtuous H. R. Goulden. I did not meet him in Mayo — but we had been stationed together previously. It is disappointing to me that he did not rise higher in the R.I.C — but in that service inferior men having "push" & "cheek" took the lead. Save mentally the loss was not as much as it seems — for life for a promoted man in the higher ranks was unpleasant.

As for myself, though I passed the "P.O." I did not ambition beyond N.C. Rank. Fate led me in 1897 to find an ogham (pronounced ouam) inscription. This led me into a connexion with the late Sir John Rhys, Professor of Celtic at Oxford University — which diverted my attention from official advancement & made my antiquarian craze is

An 'antiquarian craze'

The life, times and work in archaeology of
Patrick Lyons R.I.C.
(1861-1954)

MÁIRE LOHAN

DUBLIN: BY ÉAMONN DE BÚRCA
FOR EDMUND BURKE PUBLISHER 2008

© Máire Lohan 2008

ISBN 978 0 946130 45 0

First published in 2008
by
EDMUND BURKE PUBLISHER

All rights reserved. The material in this publication is protected by copyright law. Except as may be permitted by law, no part of the material may be reproduced (including by storage in a retrieval system) or transmitted in any form or by any means; adapted; rented or lent without the written permission of the copyright owners.

This publication has received support from the Heritage Council under the 2008 Publications Grant Scheme.

Design and typeset by Susan Waine in 11pt on 13.5pt Quadraat and Frutiger

EDMUND BURKE PUBLISHER,
Cloonagashel,
27, Priory Drive,
Blackrock,
Co. Dublin.

Frontispiece.
Excerpt from Patrick Lyons' letter dated 8 February 1953 to J.R.W. Goulden.
Document: Lyons Collection, N.U.I.Galway.

Contents

List of Plates	vii
List of Illustrations	ix
Acknowledgements	xi
Glossary	xiii
Introduction	1
Chapter 1: Early Life	3
Chapter 2: Career in the Royal Irish Constabulary	11
Chapter 3: The 'antiquarian craze'	44
Chapter 4: Lyons in Clonmel	144
References	160
Appendices:	
1. Photographic collection in Hardiman Library, N.U.I. Galway	164
2. Published works of Patrick Lyons	177
Bibliography	179
Index	185

LIST OF PLATES

1. Patrick Lyons, aged 85, at Tooracurra, Co. Waterford, in 1946. — 6
2. Kilsheelan motte, Co. Tipperary c.1910. — 8
3. Site of the Royal Irish Constabulary barracks at Lisronagh, Clonmel, in 2005. — 9
4. Photograph of a young man, possibly Patrick Lyons. — 13
5. Undated photograph of "The Stone Man" in Foxhall Church near Legan, Co. Longford. — 14
6. Castletown-Geoghegan motte and bailey, Co. Westmeath. — 17
7. Wren Boys in Ballyhaunis, 26 December 1906. — 19
8. 'A typical Co. Mayo cottage' c.1906. — 21
9. Tulsk Fort, Co. Roscommon c.1910. — 24
10. St. Patrick's Stone, Carrowkeel, Ballyhaunis, Co. Mayo c.1907. — 26
11. Ancient roadway at Athenry, Co. Galway, in 1916. — 29
12. 'Dolmen or perched blocks' near Derrydonnell castle, Athenry c.1913. — 30
13. Dunmore Castle, Co. Galway from east c.1914. — 31
14. Pillar stones at Rosgallive, Mallaranny, Co. Mayo c.1917. — 35
15. Megalith in Drumgollagh, Ballycroy, Co. Mayo c.1916. — 38
16. A threatening notice on a wall in Lisduff, Ballyhaunis, in 1910. — 42
17. Megalith at Feamore, near Ballyhaunis, c.1916. — 47
18. Cross-inscribed gravestone at Meelick, near Swinford, Co. Mayo, in 1910. — 49
19. Pilllar stones at Ballyglass, Kiltullagh, Co. Roscommon, in 1908. — 51
20. Holed pillar stone on Kiltullagh hill in 2005. — 53
21. Uniformed R.I.C. men on earthwork at Ballybride, Co. Roscommon, in 1915. — 56
22. Lisronagh Castle, Clonmel, Co. Tipperary, in 2001. — 58
23. Ogham stone in Kilmannin, Co. Mayo, in 1906. — 59
24. Standing stone at Coolnaha, Ballyhaunis c.1907. — 61
25. Re-erected Kilmovee ogham stone, near Ballyhaunis, in 1908. — 62
26. Undated photograph of Island (Bracklaghboy) ogham stone, near Ballyhaunis. — 64
27. Island ogham stone in 2005. — 65
28. Kilmovee ogham in its finding place in wall of well, in 1908. — 66
29. Cross-inscribed pillar stone at Kildun, Ballycroy, Co. Mayo c.1917. — 68
30. Tubberkevna, Kiltamagh, Co. Mayo c.1910. — 70
31. St. Dominic's well in Cahergal, near Newport, Co Mayo, in 1916. — 70
32. Wheel of Flatley's gig-mill at Cullentra, near Ballyhaunis c.1906. — 73
33. Under-millstone near site of ancient mill at Kilgrariff Brook, near Ballyhaunis, c.1907. — 75
34. Back of millstone in Dhine Brook, near Ballyhaunis c.1907. — 75
35. Ancient gig mill near Bagnelstown, Co. Carlow c.1918. — 77
36. A fortified homestead at Portaghard, Co. Mayo c.1910. — 82
37. Rathmore at Rathcroghan c. 1910. — 86
38. Aerial photograph of Rathmore. — 87
39. Earthwork at Carnabreckna, near Tulsk, Co. Roscommon, in 1914. — 89

40. Aerial photograph of conjoined earthwork at Carnfree near Tulsk, Co. Roscommon. 92
41. Earthwork at Creeve, Co. Roscommon, in 1915. 96
42. Earthwork at Knockfarnaght, near Lahardane, Co. Mayo, in 1916. 97
43. Earthwork at Bohola, near Kiltamagh, Co. Mayo c.1907. 100
44. The Turoe Stone, Bullaun, near Loughrea, Co.Galway. 101
45. 'Cist' discovered by Lyons at the rath of Feerwore, Co. Galway, in 1915. 102
46. Souterrain in Ballygurrane, near Athenry, Co. Galway, in 1915. 106
47. Athenry town wall c.1913 showing tower on eastern wall from SW. 109
48. Athenry town wall c.1913 showing the tower at junction of E and SE walls. 109
49. Athenry town wall in 2006 showing the tower at junction of E and SE walls. 110
50. East window of Athenry Dominican Priory c.1913. 112
51. West wall of Athenry Dominican Priory showing defacement c.1913. 113
52. Athenry Dominican Priory c.1913 showing the aisle and part of the nave. 114
53. Ruined 'altar tomb' in Athenry Dominican Priory c.1913. 115
54. Athenry Castle from NW c.1913. 117
55. Barbican of Athenry Castle c.1913. 118
56. Elevated doorway on E wall of Athenry Castle c.1913. 118
57. Inside of S window on 1st floor of Athenry Castle c.1913. 118
58. SE angle of Athenry Castle c.1913. 119
59. Athenry Castle in 2006 showing restored SE corner of castle wall. 119
60. Window in chancel of St. Mary's Collegiate Church in 1913. 119
61. Athenry town wall showing ditch close to eastern gate site c.1913. 120
62. Tower and outer ramparts of Athenry town wall c.1913. 120
63. Athenry North gate c.1913. 120
64. Athenry Market Cross c.1913. 121
65. The Spinner. 124
66. Wren Boys at Ballyhaunis in 1906. 125
67. Wren Boys at Newport in 1916. 125
68. Wren Boys at Newport in 1917. 125
69. 'Tinkers' camp at Spaddagh, near Ballyhaunis, in 1906. 128
70. Wearing 'morning dress' at 'Tinkers' camp at Spaddagh, near Ballyhaunis in 1906. 129
71. Pattern at Lady's Well, Baunmore, Athenry c.1915. 131
72. Ancient boat in R.I.C. yard, Ballyhaunis c.1906. 134
73. Aerial photograph of earthwork at Ratra, Castlerea, Co. Roscommon. 137
74. Earthwork at Moate, Ballyhaunis c.1907. 137
75. Rathgorgin Castle c.1913 showing details of stonework. 140
76. Rathgorgin Castle c.1913. 141
77. Relig Vreedha, Thurles, Co. Tipperary c.1910. 145
78. Sheela-an-gig removed from a wall at Blue Anchor Lane, Clonmel, in 1944. 148
79. 'Pieta' discovered near the Franciscan Friary, Clonmel, in 1951. 155

LIST OF ILLUSTRATIONS

	Excerpt from Patrick Lyons' letter dated 8 February 1953 to J.R.W. Goulden.	Title Page
Fig. 1.	Map of Lisronagh and locality.	6
Fig. 2.	Royal Irish Constabulary recruits at class.	10
Fig. 3.	Lyons' Service Record -extracted from the Royal Irish Constabulary Register.	13
Fig. 4.	R.I.C. performing eviction duty.	15
Fig. 5.	Sketch of Liam Mellowes.	33
Fig. 6.	Location map and description of the pillar stones at Kiltullagh/Ballyglass in 1908.	52
Fig. 7.	Lyons' description of the finding of the Ogham stone at Rusheen West in 1908.	61
Fig. 8.	Drawing by Westropp to illustrate Knox's paper on millstones.	74
Fig. 9.	Lyons' plan and section of Rath Brenainn, Co. Roscommon.	91
Fig. 10.	Lyons' plan and section of the 'Altered Dumha' at Carnfree, Co. Roscommon.	94
Fig. 11.	Aerial photograph of linear earthworks in Rathcroghan complex in 1982.	96
Fig. 12.	Map of medieval sites in Athenry as published by Rynne in *More Irish country towns*.	108
Fig. 13.	Lyons' drawing of an earthwork at Runnamoat, Co. Roscommon.	139
Fig. 14.	The Stone of Formach, Tooracurra, Ballymacarbery, Co. Waterford.	150
Fig. 15	Patrick Lyons in 1950, aged 89.	153

ACKNOWLEDGEMENTS

I am indebted to many people whose help and information enabled me to write this book.

I am deeply grateful to Professor John Waddell, Department of Archaeology, N.U.I.Galway for his constant advice and encouragement. My thanks to Siobháin de hÓir, former librarian of the Royal Society of Antiquaries of Ireland, who drew my attention to the Knox/Lyons material archived there. My sincere thanks to Gerry Cribbin (since deceased) for providing details of Lyons' life in Ballyhaunis. Sincere thanks also to Colonel Eoghan Ó Néill for sharing his memories of Patrick Lyons with me. Thanks are also due to Patrick Holland for sharing with me the information he had gathered concerning Lyons' time in Clonmel.

My thanks to the Council of the Royal Society of Antiquaries of Ireland who kindly gave me permission to copy the notebooks of H.T. Knox; to Chris Corlett for his assistance and advice regarding the Knox/Lyons photographs archived there; to librarians Colette Ellison and Nicole Arnaud for all their help.

Grateful thanks are due to Dónal Kivlehan of the Garda Archive/Museum for extracting Patrick Lyons' service record from the Royal Irish Constabulary register for me and providing details of life in the ranks of the constabulary.

My thanks to the curator and staff of the Tipperary South County Museum in Clonmel for allowing me access to the Lyons material there and for providing me with reproductions of photographs.

Thanks to Emer Ní Cheallaigh, Department of Irish Folklore, University College, Dublin for assistance regarding Lyons' correspondence with the Irish Folklore Commission.

My thanks to Sinéad Armstrong-Anthony for her map of Lisronagh and surrounding area. Thanks are also due to Michael Kelly, Island, Ballyhaunis for his photograph of the Island ogham stone.

For their assistance with my research, I am very grateful to the staff of the following institutions: National Library and National Photographic Archive; Hardiman Library and Department of Archaeology library at N.U.I.Galway; Mss. Library, T.C.D.; National Library of Wales; Military Archives; Military Museum, Kickham Barracks, Clonmel; Galway City and County Library; Mayo County Library (Castlebar) and South Mayo Family Research Centre; Longford County Library; Tipperary County Library (Clonmel and Thurles); Westmeath County Library (Athlone and Mullingar). Thanks are also due to the staff of the *Clonmel Nationalist* for providing facilities to view editions of the newspaper relating to Patrick Lyons' time in Clonmel.

Grateful thanks to my brother John Carroll for his linguistic assistance and to Sinéad Armstrong-Anthony for reading the draft and for her insightful comments; last but not least, to my husband David for photographic, computer and printing assistance and for putting up for so long with 'the other man' in my life.

Glossary

Crannóg – small defended artificial island (usually a homestead) built on brushwood or stones in a lake.

Fenian – from the Irish *na Fianna*, a legendary warrior band led by Fionn MacCumhaill; hence, member of the Fenian Brotherhood, a revolutionary organization founded in New York in 1859 with the ultimate aim of achieving an Irish Republic by physical force.

Land League – political organization (National Land League of Mayo) set up by Michael Davitt in 1879 to alleviate the plight of tenant farmers; within two months it had spread countrywide to become the Irish National Land League with Charles Stewart Parnell as its president. Its main aim was to put an end to excessive rents and evictions. By coordinating a Land War (1880-82) it put pressure on the British government to enact a series of Land Acts, under which ownership of land was transferred from landlords to former tenant-farmers.

La Tène – site of an Iron Age votive deposit at Lake Neuchatel (Switzerland) which gave its name to a characteristically curvilinear decoration.

Ogham – memorial stones/pillars inscribed in Ogham, an Irish form of script based (like runes) on the Latin alphabet, and composed of a series of strokes above, below, or through a baseline which was usually the vertical edge of the stone.

Pattern – annual ceremonies at a holy well or other sacred place dedicated to a patron saint at which pilgrims perform a prescribed set of prayers and actions in a repeated manner. In earlier times these devotions were accompanied by feasting, games and faction fighting.

Peeler – derogatory term for a policeman; named after Robert Peel who organized the British police force.

Poor Law Union – an administrative division introduced by the Poor Law Act of 1838 in which a workhouse (which provided relief for the unemployed and destitute) was located.

Ribbon lodge – meeting place of the 'Ribbon' society founded in 1832; a secret-society which engaged in agrarian strife against landlords who wanted to clear their land for grazing in order to avail of the high prices for cattle prevailing in the years immediately following the Napoleonic Wars; so-called from the wearing of a white ribbon round the hat for purposes of mutual recognition at night.

Rudge Whitworth – bicycle brand name.

R.M. – Resident Magistrate. A civil officer who presided over courts for minor offences (Petty Sessions) within a particular district.

Shank's mare – one's own legs as a means of conveyance.

Sheela-na-gig – a female exhibitionist figure; a representation of Lust in Romanesque sculpture.

Shebeen – from Anglo-Irish, *síbín*, from *seibe* 'mugful', an unlicensed drinking place.

Sinn Féin – from the Irish 'ourselves alone'; an organization founded in 1905 by Arthur Griffith to establish an independent Ireland. In 1918, its president Éamon de Valera contested the British election and founded Dáil Éireann. The party supported the War of Independence (1919-21) and from this time has been linked with the Irish Republican Army.

Volunteer – member of volunteer movement, the Irish National Volunteers, set up in 1913 as an answer to the *Ulster Volunteer Force* (which opposed Home Rule). By 1914 the movement split into two factions: the majority (who agreed with John Redmond's request to support Britain in the war against Germany) became known as the *National Volunteers*; those who followed Eoin Mac Neill and opposed it became the *Irish Volunteers*.

Introduction

PATRICK LYONS was born into a poor, landless family in Lisronagh, Co. Tipperary in 1861. On reaching his teens he left school and began to work as a farm labourer on a nearby farm. Lyons was extremely fortunate that his employer insisted that he continue his education and tutored him in the evenings after work. Lyons joined the Royal Irish Constabulary in 1886 and remained with the force for 34 years, serving mainly in counties Mayo and Galway. He developed a keen interest in photographing and recording the field-monuments he noticed while patrolling the countryside. Between the years 1897 and 1908 he discovered and brought to notice four ogham stones in the vicinity of Ballyhaunis, Co. Mayo, thus making his name and interest known among antiquarians. Dubbed 'the antiquarian policeman' by Matilda Redington, Lyons admitted in a letter to the son of an R.I.C. colleague, that the finding of an ogham stone in 1897 'diverted my attention from official advancement and made my antiquarian craze irresistible'. Sometime during the years 1897-8 Patrick Lyons first met Hubert Knox, an antiquarian who resided at Cranmore House, in nearby Ballinrobe, with whom he shared his passion for archaeology.

The circumstances of Knox's birth could hardly have been more different than Lyons': born into landed gentry, Knox's mother was Lady Louisa, daughter of the 4th Marquess of Sligo and his father was Colonel Charles Knox, a wealthy landlord. Hubert Knox joined the British colonial service and attained the position of judge in Madras, India, before ill-health forced his resignation. He returned home and devoted himself to the study of archaeology and history, publishing many articles in the *Journal of the Royal Society of Antiquaries of Ireland* and the *Journal of the Galway Archaeological and Historical Society* between the years 1911 and 1918. Lyons played a substantial part in these publications by providing Knox with photographs, measurements, and interpretation of the field-monuments described. Lyons was concerned lest his archaeological pursuits should come to the attention of the R.I.C. authorities and requested not to be acknowledged by name; nevertheless, Knox's papers contain many oblique references to 'my colleague', 'my friend, the Field Antiquary' etc. Lyons' collaboration with Knox lasted for 22 years (through periods in which Knox's health was frequently failing) and it continued right up to Knox's death.

Lyons' association with Knox produced 19 papers which could never have been attempted without Lyons' dedicated work. They are of considerable significance in field-archaeology as they contain detailed descriptions, measurements and photographs of many earthworks that have since been destroyed; the Knox/Lyons interpretation of archaeological complexes, at Rathcroghan and elsewhere, is an important contribution to the archaeology of the west of Ireland in the early decades of the twentieth century.

In 1920 Lyons resigned from the Royal Irish Constabulary in Newport, Co. Mayo and returned to his native Tipperary, where he continued his 'antiquarian craze' in Clonmel for the remainder of his long life. A quiet, unassuming man, he died in 1954 and lies buried in an unmarked grave in Powerstown Cemetery, Clonmel. His major contribution to Irish archaeology deserves to be acknowledged in print.

Chapter 1

Early Life

Among the documents in the Sergeant Lyons Photographic Collection archived in N.U.I. Galway is an intriguing letter in Patrick Lyons' amazingly clear handwriting, addressed to (J.R.W.) Goulden, the son of a former colleague in the Royal Irish Constabulary, who had previously written to inform Lyons of H.R.Goulden's death.* Unfortunately, the letter from Goulden which evoked this reply is not extant and neither are there any references to H.R. Goulden in other documents which might give some detail of their time as colleagues; Lyons' reply to this letter gives a tantalising glimpse into his long and active life:

'Post Office Lane, Clonmel 8.2.53.

Dear Sir,

I thank you heartily for a kind letter. It brings me pleasant memories over the span of 60 years – memories of my comrade the cultured, gentle and virtuous H.R. Goulden. I did not meet him in Mayo but we had been stationed together previously. It is disappointing to me that he did not rise higher in the R.I.C. – but in that service inferior men having "push" and "chuck" took the lead. Save sentimentality the loss was not as much as it seems – for life for a promoted man in the higher ranks was unpleasant.

As for myself, though I passed the "P" I did not ambition beyond N.C. rank. Fate led me in 1897 to find an Ogham (pronounced Ouam) inscription. This led me into a connection with the late Sir John Rhys, Professor of Celtic at Oxford University – which diverted my attention from official advancement and made my antiquarian craze irresistible. I am the only man living who has found 4 Ogham inscriptions and I was made a member of the R[oyal] S[ociety] of] A[ntiquaries of] I[reland] in 1905, a distinction I did not seek. I have been

---

* The letter was discovered in the Goulden papers which were given to John Waddell during research for his paper 'J.R.W. Goulden's excavations on Inishmore, Aran, 1953-1955' (1987-8) which he later archived with the Lyons' photographs (*pers. comm.*).

a correspondent of H.T. Knox of Ballinrobe for 22 years and with Dr. Goddard Orpen – author of "Ireland under the Normans" – for 30 years. These periods overlapped. As the RIC authority disapproved of antiquarian activities I did not come out into the open as an antiquarian until I had left the Service. After retiring the suspicions of the gunmen compelled me to relinquish research and virtually terminated my antiquarian career.

I have not married. All my near relatives in this country are dead and I live entirely alone. I am 91 7/12 years of age.

I have been disappointed that H.R. Goulden never wrote to me. In Mayo I was 16 years in Ballyhaunis – a difficult station – and my duties – with my antiquarian craze – left me little time to spare. I did not seek advancement to Honorary rank in RSAI – but when it came I accepted it.

I am boring you with uninteresting personal details. For the departure of the gentle and kindly H.R. Goulden it is some consolation to receive a letter from his son.
Sincerely yours,
P.Lyons.'

Such is Lyons' modest *curriculum vitae* but, in fact, he did much of the spade-work – both literally and figuratively – for H.T. Knox in the latter's extensive articles on field-archaeology published in the *Journal of the Royal Society of Antiquaries of Ireland* and the *Journal of the Galway Archaeological and Historical Society* between the years 1911 and 1918; oblique references by Knox to 'my colleague', 'my friend, the Field Antiquary' etc. abound but Lyons was not acknowledged by name (at his own request). Praise for Lyons and his work in archaeology was, however, acknowledged by other scholars of the time: Robert Cochrane, Sir John Rhys, Goddard Orpen, R.A.S. Macalister, T.J. Westropp, Edmund Curtis; more recently, 'his contribution in the early decades of this century to the archaeology of the west of Ireland deserves to be remembered [...] his contribution to Knox's several papers on the archaeological remains at Rathcroghan, for instance, was clearly substantial'. In recognition of 'long and outstanding services in the cause of Irish archaeology' Lyons was elected as an Honorary Life Fellow of the Royal Society of Antiquaries of Ireland in 1953.[1]

Lyons' description of his 'antiquarian craze' as 'irresistible' is well-reflected in the photographic collection which was bequeathed by Knox to the Galway Archaeological and Historical Society and is now archived in the Hardiman Library, N.U.I.Galway. Its wide-ranging nature is further evidenced in the photographs, notebooks, letters and papers in the Knox/Lyons Collection in the library of the Royal Society of Antiquaries of Ireland. The notebooks, which had been compiled from the letters filled with detailed antiquarian work sent by Lyons to

Knox during the years 1905-18, were given to Lyons shortly before Knox's death. Written in diary form, the notebooks flit from topic to topic, some obviously answering earlier questions posed by Knox in his letters to Lyons, none of which, sadly, has come to light. In 1929 Lyons requested that the Royal Society of Antiquaries of Ireland take the Knox notebooks for safe-keeping, 'as at my death they are likely to fall into Philistine hands'. Archived in the Tipperary South County Museum in Clonmel are photographs, negatives and letters which relate to Lyons' retirement in Clonmel.[2]

Lyons went on to live for another twenty-five years in retirement in Clonmel and, contrary to his claim of relinquishing research, he published much work on local history in the journals of the *Clonmel Historical and Archaeological Society* and in the local newspaper, the *Clonmel Nationalist*. His interest in archaeology, local history, folk-life and lore continued to the end of his life; in 1950, a few years before his death, he shared his local knowledge with the 13th Infantry Battalion of the Irish Army, in the tercentenary celebrations of the Siege of Clonmel.[3] He is remembered as a quiet, unassuming gentleman-scholar, dressed in homespun tweeds and cap, who spent much time walking around Clonmel and its environs (Plate1). Because he deliberately spent his life away from the glare of the public eye, we are limited to his obituaries as the only published works from which to try and piece together his very long and varied life.

Patrick Lyons was born in Lisronagh, Clonmel, Co. Tipperary on 20 June 1861. His people had been evicted from their land, on which the family had worked for generations; at the time of Patrick's birth they were living in a house nearby, in Tailor Flynn's boreen (Fig. 1) – the local name given to the road running east from Lisronagh Cross to Baptist Grange.[4] A search of *Griffith's Valuation* revealed no landowner named Lyons in the Parish of Lisronagh.

South Tipperary at that time was a place of seething unrest. Memories of the unsuccessful rebellion of 1848 were still very raw. At Ballingarry, some 12 miles from Lisronagh, the confrontation (which was dismissed by a 'most damning phrase thought up by the English newspaper *The Times* of London [as] the skirmish in the Widow McCormack's cabbage patch') was not seen locally as merely an uprising of poets and dreamers; the leaders never expected it would come to actual battle but believed that a mass uprising, as had happened in France, would force the government to abdicate with little loss of life. In the first months of 1848, the distressful state of the country, the plight of the people and their growing frustration made the authorities suspect that a rising was imminent and there were calls for police and troops from many quarters. This

The life, times and work in archaeology of Patrick Lyons R.I.C. (1861-1954)

Plate 1.
Patrick Lyons, aged 85, at Tooracurra, Co. Waterford in 1946.

Reproduced courtesy of the Tipperary South County Museum, Clonmel.

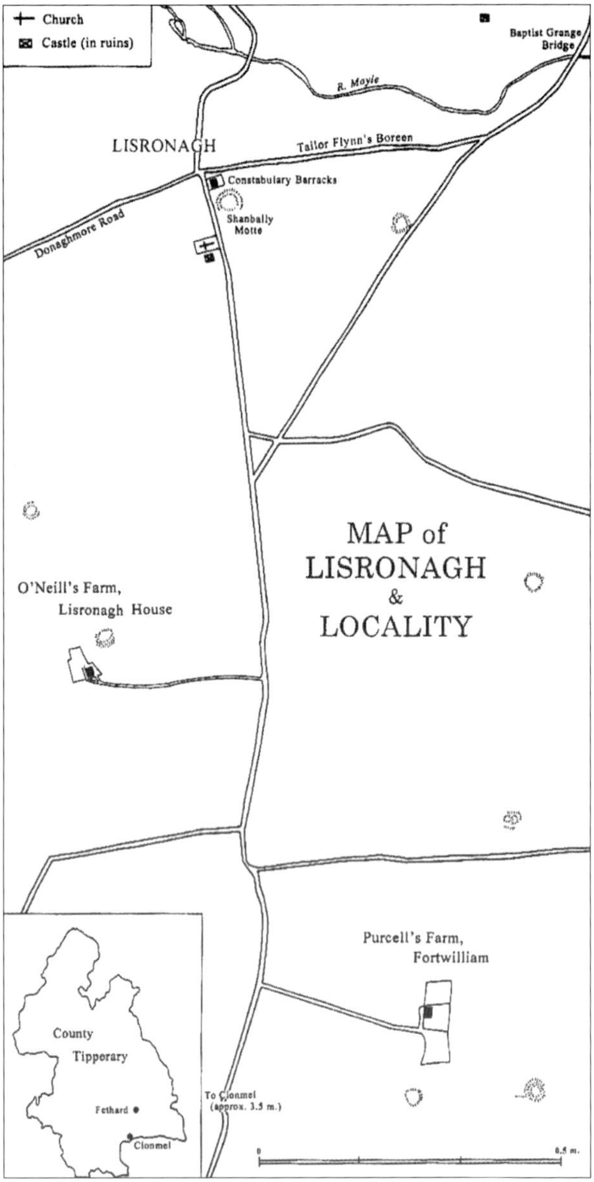

Fig. 1.
Lisronagh and locality where Lyons lived and worked before he became a policeman. Based on information from Col. Eoghan Ó Néill, author of *The Golden Vale of Ivowen*, who was born in Lisronagh House which dates from c.1670.

Map: Sinéad Armstrong-Anthony.

nervousness communicated itself to the unsettled population and "Disloyal" posters and placards began to appear in various places, including Lisronagh. Towards the end of March rumours abounded that the Lord Lieutenant had to leave Dublin for fear of his life and celebratory bonfires were reported all over the Comeragh mountains; on 27 July there was great excitement in Clonmel when fires were lit in the streets and thousands came out in riotous assembly. Despite this intense activity and enthusiasm for rebellion, when the actual insurrection was forced on the people by the sudden suspension of *habeas corpus*, the enthusiasm seems suddenly to have waned; many were anxious to hold back for a couple of weeks in order to harvest the corn that was urgently needed because of the devastation caused by the famine of the previous year and the re-appearance of potato blight. However, on 29 July at Ballingarry, the rebellion escalated when the insurrectionists – under William Smith O'Brien – were confronted by armed police. O'Brien, though showing enormous gallantry and personal courage, was not familiar with the stratagems of a successful revolutionary leader, and so the encounter collapsed and the leaders were arrested.

Although rebellion did not occur in as many places as expected, August and September saw the countryside in turmoil. In September, under cover of a smokescreen made by lighting straw carried on pitchforks, Felix O'Neill (a Fenian leader who lived in Lisronagh House) led an attack on the police barracks at Glenbower near Carrick-on-Suir. O'Neill was shot in the hip and evacuated to the care of his mother and sisters at Lisronagh. Later that month a man-of-war was sent to Waterford; gunboats on the Suir fired blank cartridges during the raid on Portlaw; Dungarvan refused to supply cars for the conveyance of troops to hunt for the insurgents in the Comeragh mountains. In October 'suspicious characters' were seen in the district and there were further rumours of an expected attack on Clonmel. In November things began to quieten down and by Christmas life had returned to normal.

Even though the Young Ireland movement had been broken up and the leaders sent into exile, the Rising of 1848 had a very important effect on subsequent history: ten years later the Fenian organization was launched in America and Ireland. It became particularly strong in rural districts of South Tipperary, drawing its membership largely from the farming community. The Fenians in Clonmel town were kept under continuing surveillance, but in the countryside this restriction was easier to evade and Felix O'Neill set about training young men from around Lisronagh in Fenian tactics. An insurrection was planned to take place on 5 March 1867 – the authorities were probably better informed about the exact date than the Fenian foot-soldiers, because the organization included many spies within its ranks. Unfortunately for the Fenian leaders, one of the greatest

Plate 2.
Kilsheelan motte, Co. Tipperary c.1910. Lyons measured its diameter at base as 46 yards and at top 6 yards and notes that 'no enclosures or outworks' are traceable. The motte at Kilsheelan was erected c.1189 when King John granted the surrounding area to William de Burgh.[6]
Photo: Lyons Collection, N.U.I.Galway.

snow blizzards in living memory occurred on 4 March and Lisronagh was cut off for several days with no possibility of organizing a striking force until the storm was over. The expected general rising did not take place except for isolated incidents. Captain Larry O'Brien and many young men from Tipperary and Bansha were captured at Ballyhurst and brought to Clonmel prison. O'Brien, using acid and file and working for some weeks, managed to cut the bars of his cell window. Outside, Margaret O'Neill (sister of Felix) waited in a covered cart and brought the prisoner to Lisronagh where a dug-out room had been excavated and prepared on the O'Neill farm in which he was immediately hidden. Within two hours military with bayonets arrived to search the hay barns but to no avail. Search parties returned throughout the week but O'Brien remained undiscovered. He stayed in Lisronagh until his injured ankle healed and the hue and cry had died down. Margaret and Felix O'Neill then brought him by covered car to Waterford but realized *en route* that the bridge was under surveillance. A friendly boatman agreed to row the party across the river and they made the rest of the journey on

Early Life

foot. O'Brien boarded a fishing boat and eventually made his way to America.[5]

Patrick Lyons began his long and fruitful life against the backdrop of these troubled times and stirring tales of local heroes must have fired his boyhood imagination. At the age of ten he left the National School and went to work as a labouring boy with the Purcell family of Fortwilliam. Fortunately for Lyons, the Purcells – who were close relatives of the patriot, poet and novelist Charles J. Kickham – had a deep respect for education. After his day's work as a farm-labourer, Lyons spent the evenings being schooled by Purcell, to whom passing on his knowledge in history and literature to such a receptive young mind seems to have brought much pleasure. In his teenage years Lyons may have thought it a hard life, but he later praised his former mentor for planting and nurturing in him a love for the subjects that came to play such an important part in his life.[7]

On reaching adulthood, it seems that the routines of farm-labouring became stifling and Lyons decided that he needed a more stimulating occupation, but, for someone without money, land or formal education there were not many choices. At that time the best option seemed to be the Royal Irish Constabulary which provided continuous pensionable employment; perhaps this choice was in some way influenced by Lyons' childhood memories of his first job, scaring crows off the corn-field beside the Royal Irish Constabulary barracks at Lisronagh (Plate 3)

Plate 3.
Site of the Royal Irish Constabulary barracks at Lisronagh, Clonmel in 2005. Patrick Lyons worked at his first job, scaring crows away from the adjacent corn-field in 1871.

Photo: M. Lohan.

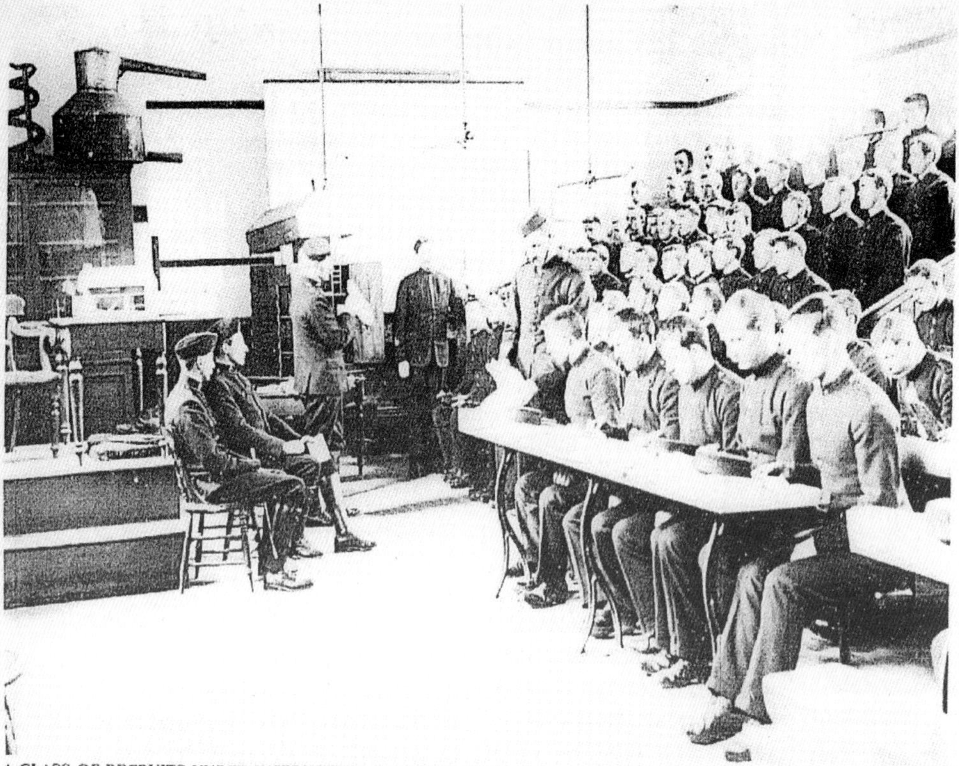

A CLASS OF RECRUITS UNDER INSTRUCTION AT DEPOT c 1899   Plate 25

The class is studying the investigation of serious crime. The instructor (a District Inspector in undress) holds a plaster cast of a footprint. In the background, at top left, may be seen a worm and pot still used in illicit distillation. To the left and behind the instructor are scale models of buildings used as evidence in criminal trials. The gas lighting is of an early type without mantles or globes. The seated officers are in 'fatigue' dress and the Head Constable in the background appears in undress.

Fig. 2.
Class of recruits. Published in *Arresting Memories: captured moments in constabulary life*.
Reproduced courtesy of the Garda Archive/Museum.

where he met, and learned from, policemen stationed there.[8] Lyons continued his education at night classes and as a result was successful in his application to join the police force. Regulations for service required that applicants be aged between nineteen and twenty-seven years (Lyons was twenty-five); at least 5' 8" in height (Lyons was 5'10"); capable of reading, without hesitation, any printed or written document; able to write a legible hand; be of good character for honesty, sobriety, fidelity, and activity; and a single man, or a widower without a family.[9] Lyons fulfilled these conditions admirably.

Chapter 2:
Career in the Royal Irish Constabulary

LYONS WAS APPOINTED to the Royal Irish Constabulary on 21 June 1886. He joined the other recruits, mainly the sons of tenant farmers or rural labourers, in the Royal Irish Constabulary Depot, Phoenix Park, Dublin for six month's training (although it appears from Lyons' service record that he spent less than four months there before getting his first posting). Training was exacting and tough with much emphasis on physical drill and special attention was given to the best methods of arresting a violent person. Along with the usual police duties of prevention, detection and investigation of crime (Fig. 2) and the giving and taking of descriptions of stolen property, the recruit also received instruction in fire drill; many country towns were without fire brigades or water supplies and, in emergencies, were solely dependent on the constabulary. The highlight of the recruits' training was the commandant's parade each Tuesday morning, when all forces paraded and the officers wore full dress uniform, including cocked hats.

The Royal Irish Constabulary was an armed force which was trained, organized and disciplined on military lines with its men widely distributed in 1,500 barracks, strategically located in likely trouble-spots throughout the country. No man was permitted to serve in his home county and all recruits were required to take an oath of loyalty to the Crown. It was inevitable that the predominantly Catholic rank-and-file might be torn between attachment to their country and allegiance to the Crown; to counter-balance, it was considered necessary to have an officer corps, some 200 Sub-Inspectors and 35 County Inspectors, whose social status and education provided them with sufficient authority to control a large body of armed men often faced with irksome duties. Officers were mainly Protestant Irishmen who owed their allegiance firmly to the British government, often university graduates having links with landed gentry in their backgrounds or sons of Protestant clergymen and professionals who could not afford army commissions. The rigid class barrier between officers and men did little to foster a community of feeling between them.[1]

As Lyons was a non-commissioned officer, his service record, as extracted from the Royal Irish Constabulary Register (Fig. 3), merely records the counties to which he was allocated and dates of service therein, not the particular barracks, details of which are not currently available.[2] After 1897 when Lyons' 'antiquarian craze' had become 'irresistible' and he was corresponding with Knox and other eminent antiquarians, his exact whereabouts can be noted: Cochrane (1898) and Rhys (1907) mention that Lyons is stationed in Ballyhaunis, Co. Mayo; Macalister (1915-7) places him in Athenry, Co. Galway (although, according to Lyons' service record, he had been transferred from Galway to Mayo in 1913). To fill in the details of Lyons' career in the Royal Irish Constabulary (1886-1920) local newspapers need to be consulted, particularly reports of Petty Sessions where the names of prosecuting constables and the barracks in which they were stationed were often mentioned. The quality of reporting, however, varies significantly between newspapers: whereas the *Western People*, proudly noting in each issue that it was the 'largest local newspaper in the country', usually reported court cases in great detail, other papers were less diligent, e.g. 'a number of uninteresting cases were disposed by the Court'; 'the business to be transacted was of very little importance, the one case worthy of note being one in which a respectable young man was charged with the larceny of two gun cartridges. He was allowed out on his own recognisances'.[3]

LONGFORD

Lyons was posted to Co. Longford on 8 October 1886. The local newspaper, the *Longford Independent*, regularly reported prosecutions at the Petty Sessions in Longford and Granard and occasionally in Keenagh, Drumlish, Newtownforbes and Edgeworthstown; prosecuting constables were often named but Lyons' name is not recorded. However, many cases were not reported in detail: 'eight or ten jolly young fellows were each fined 1 shilling and costs for drunkenness'; 'the greater number of the cases for hearing were for over-indulgence [...] the constabulary had a few cases against owners of goats found wandering'. In October 1889 at a constabulary inquiry in Longford No.1 barracks where charges were preferred against a constable for insubordinate conduct, Lyons, who was barrack-orderly at the time, was 'sworn and examined'. No other reference to Constable Lyons appears in the newspaper during the remainder of his time in Co. Longford, where (with the exception of a fortnight in December 1890, when he returned to the Depot, in Phoenix Park, Dublin, presumably for further training) he remained until February 1892.

Whether Lyons was stationed at Longford No.1 barracks for the duration of his time, or was transferred elsewhere within the county, it is likely that his duties

Plate 4.
Photograph archived in the Tipperary South County Museum, Clonmel and there described as 'a young man dressed in R.I.C. "undress" or walking out uniform. It is possibly Mr. Paddy Lyons or a colleague'.

Reproduced courtesy of the Tipperary South County Museum.

Fig. 3.
Lyons' Service Record – extracted from the Royal Irish Constabulary Register.

Reproduced courtesy of the Garda Archive/Museum.

as a constable were not onerous. Much of his time was probably spent in keeping records and aiding a largely illiterate population with the compilation of necessary documents. A frequent form of crime is indicated by the frustrated remark of a judge following the conviction of a woman for 'stealing a piece of beef value eight shillings' (for which she was sentenced to seven days imprisonment with hard labour): 'it is very much to be regretted that the traders of

Longford, without exception, indirectly encourage petty thefts of this nature by reason of exposing and piling up their goods outside their houses, thus offering at least an opportunity to the weak and the tempted ones to pick up one thing or other as they pass by'.[4] If Lyons had not yet begun to develop his interest in archaeology and photography, whiling away his off-duty hours may have been a problem as, within the constabulary, recreational opportunities were very limited. Handball, throwing weights, cycling, card-playing, small dances in private houses, playing the violin or melodeon were the chief pastimes.[5]

Lyons began his career as a policeman at a time and in a place of great upheaval. From having been one of the most loyal and peaceful counties in the

Plate 5.
Undated photograph of "The Stone Man" in Foxhall Church near Legan, Co. Longford. Lyons describes it as 'a monument of a Hussey who died about 1645. Forehead is marked obliquely with a rude cross which was done as a protest when the Fox family (Shiminagh) conformed to the Church of Ireland'.
Photo: Lyons Collection, N.U.I.Galway.

country in the 1860s (which was borne out by the low ratio of police to population compared to adjoining counties), Co. Longford in the 1870s had become, together with Connacht, the area where the greatest strides for Fenianism had occurred; local leaders, advocating the abolition of landlordism, helped in the assimilation of the Ribbon lodges (which had their origins as far back as the 1830s when agrarian crime was rampant in the county). The political power of the local landlords was eroded by the Land League's successful support of Parnell in the 1880 election and their prestige was further diminished as tenants began to win power in the Poor Law Boards of Guardians.[6]

Undoubtedly, the Royal Irish Constabulary was unpopular in many areas due to its use in enforcing evictions (Fig. 4); its semi-military role was thrust upon it

Fig. 4.
Eviction duty. Published in *Arresting Memories: captured moments in constabulary life*.
Reproduced courtesy of the Garda Archive/Museum.

by the discontented state of the country throughout most of the nineteenth and the early part of the twentieth century. It is likely that Lyons attended at some of the many evictions that were reported in the local press: '300 men of the Royal Irish Constabulary arrived in this town [Longford] for the purpose of protecting Mr. Gill, the Sub-Sherriff, in carrying out eleven evictions on the properties of Lord Annaly [...] the roads were patrolled by police on Monday night to prevent obstructions being placed on them, as on the first day of the attempted evictions, when the sheriff and police were obliged to return before a very large crowd [...] a large popular [sic.] tree had been cut down and placed across the road. When they reached the scene of the eviction about two thousand people were present who attacked the police and sheriff in a most determined manner and pelted them with stones, mud and every other available missile at hand. Several of the police were struck and badly hurt. One of them had a front tooth broken'; in Granard over 200 police assisted in 40 ejectments.[7]

In October 1887 a great Nationalist Demonstration was held in Longford town at which T.M. Healy M.P. impassionately advocated joining the National League, 'contingents came from long distances with bands and banners and all the adjoining counties were represented. The meeting was held in the main street. The platform was not strong enough and immediately on the people coming on it broke down, but fortunately no one sustained any serious injury [...] a constabulary short-hand writer was afforded a position on the platform'. A year later another large demonstration at Longford 'proved that Mr. Balfour had not knocked the life out of the National League'. In 1889 four Longford Nationalists received prison sentences for 'holding up to the public contempt Wm. Jones in becoming tenant of the farm previously occupied by Mr. Armstrong'. As these men held the positions of chairman of Longford Town Commissioners, chairman of Longford Board of Guardians, and secretaries of Longford and Edgeworthstown National League branches their departure to the railway station to catch the train for Sligo jail was closely guarded: 'the large escort was followed by four mounted constables [... who] proceeded to clear the platform and some lively incidents took place'; on their release a large demonstration was held at which they pledged their willingness to 'make the same sacrifice tomorrow should the occasion demand [...] an attempt was made by a few policemen to gain a footing on the platform but they were ejected and for a time matters looked serious but quickly quieted down'. These events, seemingly, unnerved the local police who requested and were sent reinforcements; but by the following February the *Dublin Gazette* contained a proclamation that Longford 'has ceased to be in a state of disturbance, and that therefore the additional police force appointed will be discontinued after a month has elapsed'. However, at a

Plate 6.
Lyons paid a short visit to Westmeath in September 1907 where he was very impressed by Castletown-Geoghegan motte and bailey: 'It is nearly 100 yds. long, 60 wide. It is like a boot with a high bailey forming the toe and the circular mote – at least 40 ft. high. It is barely a mile from the Castletown [Railway] Station and is well worth breaking a journey to visit'. The motte and bailey was erected by Meyler Fitzhenry c.1190 but was repeatedly attacked by the MacGeoghegans who continued to rule the territory until Cromwellian times having learned to tolerate Norman families in their midst.[10]

Photo: Lyons Collection, N.U.I.Galway.

---

large Parnellite demonstation in Longford (after the split with Healy over the Kitty O'Shea affair) extra police reinforcements were again necessary: 'by the platform a large force of police were stationed [...] a force was held in reserve on the footpath close to the Bank of Ireland [...] notes of the speeches were taken by two constables surrounded by some of the force'.[8]

Aside from the necessity for ensuring that evictions and other emotive gatherings did not escalate into violence, the humdrum daily keeping of law and order was not particularly taxing. George McKee, a constable stationed in Ballina, Co. Mayo in 1892, noted in his diary: 'in July of this year we had a general election of members of Parliament which of course gave the R.I. Constabulary something to do'.[9] Presumably a policeman's lot in Co. Longford at that time was much the same; that it remained so throughout Lyons' career becomes apparent when considering the amount of time he managed to devote to his antiquarian activities.

WESTMEATH

Lyons was transferred to Co. Westmeath on 1 February 1892. Neither his departure from Longford nor his arrival in Westmeath is noted in the local newspapers so it is not possible to establish to which barracks he was posted. Two years later, however, his presence is noted at the barracks in Streamstown, a small village on the Athlone-Mullingar road in which there was a railway station: 'Constable Patrick Lyons of Streamstown, is promoted to the rank of Acting Sergeant. Acting-Sergeant Lyons obtained sixteenth place at the last competitive examinations'. The system by which promotion was achieved was the cause of serious grievances within constabulary ranks. Two lists were compiled from which Constables were promoted to Acting Sergeants: a general list of constables eligible for promotion on the basis of seniority, usually those having served from twelve to twenty-five years and a special list of men who sat a competitive exam, open to all constables with five years service, in which men qualified by obtaining two-thirds of the marks which were for educational subjects (regardless of how they fared concerning police duties). The first sixty places were awarded to the men with the highest marks who were promoted each year to fill vacancies all over the country. Men who passed this examination were known as "P" men and were not required to undergo further literary tests for any higher rank. This seems not to have been of importance to Lyons, as, in his letter to Goulden, he comments that 'although I passed the "P" I did not ambition beyond N.C. rank'.

Lyons' transfer due to his promotion took place in April 1894: 'Acting Sergeant Lyons of Streamstown has joined the police force at the Moate station'[11] Lyons remained there for some 6 months and no details of his work made newspaper headlines.

BALLYHAUNIS

Lyons was transferred to Ballyhaunis on 1 November 1894 where, according to his Service Record he was stationed for the next 18 years (not 16 years as stated in his letter to Goulden). The woeful condition of Ballyhaunis when Lyons began his work there is graphically illustrated in a letter to the editor of the local paper: 'Since the arrival of the rainy season the streets of this town have been sadly neglected (Plate 7). Playful attempts have, from week to week, been made to

Plate 7.
Described by Lyons as 'Wren Boys in action, Ballyhaunis, 26 December 1906'. The condition of the street here is possibly at its best for Christmas.

Photo: Lyons Collection, N.U.I.Galway.

sweep off the mud, or rather to sweep it into small heaps which have lain on, or close to, the channels until added to in successive weeks. Then at intervals of from three to four weeks the remains of these mud-mounds have been carted away [...] the town is reeking with filth, the streets are impassable, the lanes are in a similar way and the yards – indescribable. Pass the entrance to one of the latter (of course there are some exceptions) and you may have a liberal education in 'how to neglect sanitation'. Why allow manure pits at the very back doors of inhabited houses?'[12]

The Mayo countryside, too, was in a very distressful state at this time, as was the country at large. The National Land League of Mayo, founded in Castlebar in August 1879 under the leadership of Michael Davitt in a struggle to reform the land-system, had spread countrywide within two months to become the Irish National Land League with Parnell as its President. Mayo played a prominent role in the struggle and 'agrarian outrages' (maiming of cattle, destruction of property, wounding and even killing of land agents, landlords, and those who were considered 'land grabbers') were commonplace in the 1880s, the violence being fuelled by the fact that two-thirds of Mayo tenants were not eligible for rent-reductions under the 1881 Land Act. Gradually the struggle eased as various land acts, culminating in that brought in by Chief Secretary Wyndham in 1903, increased the pace and scope of the transfer of ownership from landlord to tenant.[13]

During Lyons' early years in Ballyhaunis, the necessity for a police presence at three local evictions made newspaper headlines, and, though Lyons is not mentioned by name, it is quite probable that he was present: 'immense crowds of people had assembled on the scene and their attitude certainly seemed to be one of determined hostility'; 'when an entrance had been effected it was found that some of those who had barricaded the doors and windows had obtained access to the roof through the chimney. One of the persons on the roof had a military horn upon which he blew repeated calls which had the result of collecting up the few stragglers who were still absent from the scene of operations'; 'a horseman was noticed careering over the farm. The sheriff mounted a horse and endevoured to capture him. A most exciting and amusing race ensued, and the attempts of the bailiff to secure the horseman created considerable merriment, the chase continuing for a considerable time, but notwithstanding the assistance given by the police, the bailiff came off a bad second'.

Lyons was promoted to Sergeant on 1 July 1896. One of the regular duties of a sergeant was attendance at court, principally to bring charges for law-breaking, but also sometimes to give corroborating evidence for the defence. The Ballyhaunis Petty Sessions were regularly reported in the *Western People* and Lyons' presence is first mentioned on 21 August 1897, where he is entitled Inspector of Weights and Measures and prosecuted Patrick Waldron for having in his possession a 1lb weight which was 1 ounce and 9½ drachms light. Lyons next appeared in the following July when he brought a prosecution for drunk and disorderly behaviour and the use of foul language (which he was requested to show in writing to the judge). During the next fifteen years or so, Lyons is reported to have been in attendance at 138 cases: lesser crimes range from obstructing the sidewalk, allowing animals to wander on the public road, selling sheep without a certificate that they had been dipped (in a prosecution Lyons stated that 'there were close on 450 defaulters in the district'), adulteration of whiskey, breaches of the Licensing Act; more serous crimes include robbery and larceny, cruelty to animals and children, assault (often while drunk) on civilians and police and four cases of murder, including one infanticide.

As one reads through these reports, an image of a consistently fair-minded,

Plate 8.
Photograph c.1906 of 'a typical Co. Mayo cottage'. It may have originally been a smaller cottage; note the enclosing wall that joins the house in line with the chimney. In the western regional vernacular style the room beyond the hearth originated as an extension to the house associated with the introduction in the 19th century of chimney flues above the open fire which traditionally had lain on the floor at some distance from the gable wall.[16]

Photo: Lyons Collection, N.U.I.Galway.

---

sincere man emerges; favourable comments by magistrates regarding his character-witness of the protagonists abound: 'It is on account of the good character the sergeant gave of you [...] that you are getting off so lightly'; 'Will you look at Sergeant Lyons and swear that you are not the greatest blackguard coming into town?'; 'It was well for the defendant that Sergeant Lyons was there [...] he was the best friend you had in Ballyhaunis that day'. Lyons' compassion is also evident in prosecutions he brought to protect vulnerable persons: 'Sergeant Lyons explained that the assaults were not of a serious nature. His sole grounds for bringing the charge being to have the defendant committed to the asylum as he was insane'; 'Sergeant Lyons said that the verminous state which the children were in was a shame and disgrace. They were so dirty he had to clean them himself. Dr. Maguire said that the sergeant should be very highly commended for the care and interest he took in neglected children'; 'Sergeant Lyons said the defendant was partly an imbecile and was practically destitute and the parties who should be charged were those who supplied him with drink. Mr. Curran told the sergeant to keep an eye on the publicans who supplied men of that class with drink as it was a shame for them'; [Sergeant Lyons]: 'she has a very large family, your worship, and if she is sent to jail it is the poor children that will suffer'.[14]

Lyons' obituary notes that 'as a policeman he worked hard and conscientiously to preserve order amongst his fellow countrymen and to lead them to the ways of thrift and sobriety at a time when intemperance was widespread in many places'.[15] Intemperance was certainly a feature of life in Ballyhaunis while Lyons was stationed there. Over 56% of his court attendances dealt with drink-related cases: 56 charges for drunken and disorderly behaviour often leading to assault (including 4 cases of assault on himself) and 22 cases of breaches of the Licensing Act; a frustrated magistrate commented 'I do not know how this wholesale drunkenness can take place in a little village like Ballyhaunis* without the publicans detecting it in some instances'.

The enforcement of the Licensing Act of 1872 (and its later amendments), with its complicated provisions regarding 6-day licences, which in 1902 were held by 57 premises in Ballyhaunis, 7-day licences *i.e.* premises which could also open on Sunday, and regulations regarding *bona fide* travelers *i.e.* persons who had traveled at least 3 miles and were entitled to extra drinking time, needed constant surveillance; as reported in the *Western People* the prosecutions read like a game of cat-and-mouse in which magistrates and meticulous policemen battle with clever lawyers, whose clients produce the most ingenuous excuses for opening their premises, or being present therein, outside legal drinking hours. Excuses for the illegal opening of premises include: the claim of a publican's daughter that 'she had only opened them that instant to get a bottle of soda water for a child of hers who was unwell'; on being found open at 6.50 pm 'the defendant believed it to be 7 o'clock having got the time from the Post Office the night before. Sergeant Lyons said that he proceeded to the Post Office and found the clock there, according to his watch was 2 minutes slow'; 'the sergeant's presence frightened the publican so much he was unable to give an explanation (laughter) [...] the sergeant appears to have some suspicion in his mind, but were

---

* According to the *Census of Ireland* 1901, there were 599 inhabited houses and 1,513 out-offices and farmsteadings in Ballyhaunis with a population of 3,056 of whom 1,490 were males; in the 1911 census the population had risen to 8,052 of whom 4,103 were males.

the public to be at the mercy of suspicion it would go hard with them (laughter)'. Excuses tendered by customers for their illegal presence include: 'he went in for a postage stamp. Sergeant Lyons asked Grogan for the stamp and he said he put it on a letter which he had posted (a laugh)'; 'I went in for some biscuits'; 'he came in to light his pipe'.

A major problem with the enforcement of the Licensing Act was the fact that public houses were situated in buildings in which other businesses were conducted *e.g.* groceries, hardware-shops. The publican, who often also provided accommodation for lodgers, usually lived in the same house as his business and there was easy access between the domestic and the business areas. The report of a prosecution in 1902 graphically illustrates the problem of securing a conviction: 'Mr. Patrick Tarpey was prosecuted for a breach of the Licensing Act, being a holder of a 6-day licence. A man named Patrick Killeen, a local shoe-maker was also summoned for being drunk on the licensed premises in question. Sergeant Lyons [...] entered the premises about 10.20 pm [on Sunday] through the hall door which was open and went into the kitchen, the door leading thereto being also open. There were three lodgers there as well as members of Tarpey's family. In a little room between the bar and the kitchen he found Patrick Killeen, as it were, coming from the bar which was open. He was under the influence of drink and talking very loudly. Witness went into the shop and found a young fellow there talking to Miss Tarpey. There were glasses on the counter with traces of drink on them, but whether the traces were fresh or not witness could not say. He did not ask any questions about the state of the bar but inquired why Killeen was there and he said he came in with a pair of boots which he (witness) saw and seemed to be only after repair [...]
[Sergeant Lyons continued] 'what attracted my attention to his premises first, was a cart I saw outside the door. Mr. Tarpey told me he was only after returning with his cart, and that he was taking his horse through the hall door into the yard. Chairman: Is that the way they take in their horses in Ballyhaunis? Mr. Leetch said unfortunately it was. The landlords here did not take any interest in the way of providing a circular road by means of which easy access could be had to the back premises [...] he [Mr. Tarpey] had four lodgers in his house that night. One of them kept his bicycle in the shop and had gone in there simply for the purpose of leaving it up. Cross-examined by Mr. Carbery: I do not doubt the sergeant's evidence. He did not find a drunken man coming from the bar. Mr. Leetch: He only said "as" coming from the bar [... Chairman]: it is for you to prove he was coming from the bar [...] the Chairman said there was no evidence to sustain a conviction and the case would be dismissed [...] if he wants to give drinks to his lodgers he should do so in a private room.

Plate 9.
Photograph c.1910 of Tulsk Fort, Co. Roscommon in which Lyons uses his colleagues to give a sense of perspective; he notes that this earthwork 'can make a very strong claim to Norman origin'. As Knox gives no details of its location it is not possible to identify this earthwork .

Photo: Lyons Collection, N.U.I.Galway.

'The charge against Killeen for being drunk on the licensed premises was then taken up. Sergeant Lyons deposed that when Killeen came into Mr. Tarpey's premises with the boots, he was drunk and staggering around the kitchen. The defendant said he might be half-drunk but according to the Act of Parliament he could not be considered drunk (laughter). The bench held the offence proved, but as he had business in Mr. Tarpey's premises they would only fine him 2s 6d and costs'.

Another aspect of the Licensing Act which warranted extra vigilance was the provision regarding *bona fide* travelers. The ease with which attempts were made to flout this provision can be seen in a 1905 prosecution: 'Sergeant Lyons deposed to finding the defendant in Mr. Conry's bar. In reply to certain questions, he stated that he lived two Irish miles from the town which he thought were equivalent to three English miles [... The publican] informed me that the defendant presented himself as a *bona fide* traveler, which was sufficient indemnification for the publican. In reply to further questions the sergeant said he had measured the distance to the defendant's house and found it was only 2 miles 834 yards. A fine of 3s 6d and costs was imposed'.

There was also the problem of 'shebeens', best illustrated in a 1904 case: 'Mary Muldoon was summoned for keeping on her premises intoxicating liquor for sale, she being a person not duly licensed. Her husband is at present in Castlebar jail doing a month for shebeening [...] the defendant's daughter said there was one pint of whiskey in the house which was got for men cutting turf in the bog. [Sergeant Lyons]: I took possession of it and another pint bottle of rum. The defendant was in town at the time [...] I met defendant with a cart of goods [...] but could find no trace of liquor in it. The defendant said she had some drink in for the men in the bog and subsequently she herself stated that she had the whiskey for a child of hers who had the chin-cough, and she had been advised to give it some whiskey by a man who had passed the way on a grey horse. In reply to Dr. Crean the sergeant said he had searched the cart but he believed they had disposed of the drink which was in it before he got an opportunity of making a search. "I believe while I was searching the house a messenger was dispatched to inform her". Mr. Curran said that he was instructed to say that the defendant got the pint of whiskey for a man who was fixing her cart, which had got broken on the road to Ballyhaunis. Chairman: [...] I've never heard such a tale in all my life [...] at this stage Sergeant Lyons asked their worships if they would have any objection hearing Fr. Fallon's views on the matter [... Fr. Fallon]: this woman has caused a considerable amount of trouble in the parish. She promised me several times that she would not keep intoxicating drink in her house [...] She has given drink to a boy who is only 13 years of age [...] I would be very glad if you would punish her as far as the law will permit you'.

A non-drinker himself, Lyons continued his efforts to bring abusers of alcohol, makers, sellers and buyers, before the courts and 'when in due time he won promotion to Head Constable, his district had the reputation of being free of the practice of poteen-making'.[17]

During Lyons' time in Ballyhaunis indignation by local tenant farmers against provisions of the Land Acts continually simmered beneath the surface. It erupted on a number of occasions, particularly when a farm was 'grabbed' i.e. the practice by which landlords sold their land to outsiders rather than to the Congested Districts Board for division among local tenants. Throughout 1901 and 1902 the campaign against the grabbing of Island Farm, situated two miles from Ballyhaunis, was reported in the *Western People*. Mass meetings were organized to

Plate 10.
Photograph, dated July 1907, of St. Patrick's Stone, Carrowkeel [East], Ballyhaunis. Lyons considers that it may have been an altar stone 'that is the top flag of a rude primitive altar and the hollow at its base is just in the position to hold a musical stand'. John Carney with his slean (turf-cutting implement) stands beside it, perhaps to give it perspective. In the *Sites and Monuments Record* this monument is classified as a holy stone (O.S. 103).

Photo: Lyons Collection, N.U.I.Galway.

---

protest against 'the Corick inn-keeper, Francis O'Boyle [who] grabbed this valuable tract of land comprising some 430 acres, for the purpose of converting it into a huge grazing ranch to the detriment of the poor tenantry of the immediate neighbourhood who have to eke out a miserable existence on two and three acres of cutaway bog'. As these meetings were illegal, hoodwinking the police was necessary and was reported gleefully: 'at 4 o'clock the largest and most enthusiastic meeting of the day was held in the village of Island despite the vigilant efforts of mounted policemen on bicycles, who scouted the country armed with telescopes [... the organizers] left Knock hastily pursued by a member of the "belted fraternity" mounted on a "Rudge Whitworth" and in order to keep the "wicked Leaguer" in view he brought the much-talked-of stratagem of "scorcher" into operation. In this manner, every muscle straining, he reached a place called Greenwood, mid-way between Knock and the El Dorado of his dreams, when bang went his machine, whether from a fit of indignation at being used for so low a trick or not, your correspondent has not yet been informed; but, however, ere this dutiful member of the force could arrive on "shanks mare" to apprise his waiting colleagues of the Leaguers sudden descent on the place, a very successful meeting was held'.

Hostility against the police, that 'belted fraternity', sometimes took active form. Sergeant Lyons charged Thomas Donnellon with furiously driving a horse, thereby endangering the lives of the public: 'Three constables were with me on the public road and the defendant drove his horse and car most furiously down a steep hill, and when coming near us he swerved the horse towards us, so that we had to run up on the wall to avoid being run over. They were coming in from Island Farm and as I wanted to identify the persons on the car I shouted to him to pull up but he would not [...] there was a political meeting to be attended that was suppressed'. Even in this case, where the attack was directed at his own person, Lyons' innate compassion is evident; when leniency was requested Lyons said 'I have nothing to say against Donnellon, who is a good young chap and I would like to see him get out of this as lightly as he possibly can. Mr. Curran-Tyrell: It is just what I would expect from you, Sergeant'.

O'Boyle, the new owner of Island Farm, had to be given police protection as he and his family were subjected to hostility whenever they appeared on the farm. Two youths were convicted of intimidation and, on the same day 'in anticipation of a political meeting, a contingent of police from Claremorris was sent to Ballyhaunis'. A few weeks later it was reported that 'a large and representative meeting [...] dwelt on the invading force of haymakers from North Mayo to do the needful for the Erris hotel proprietor. Mr. O'Boyle would very soon find out that it was an expensive luxury to be importing labour from Bangor-Erris to save the hay on Island farm [...] On every occasion last year that the members of the Ballyhaunis and Knock branches attended to help in the good work of bringing home the turf, one hundred policemen were drafted into Island and District Inspectors and County Inspectors were there lounging by the ditches'.

Lyons' last reported duty as sergeant in Ballyhaunis was on 5 April 1913 when he attended an inquest into the death of an itinerant painter, which took place in the barracks some time after his arrest for drunkenness. The jury found in accordance with the medical testimony that death was due to congestion of the lungs and heart failure, having listened to a forcible appeal by the coroner: 'what a great nuisance tramps are to the public. They come into houses to beg, they use abusive language if they are refused, and their constitutions are so debilitated from drink, hunger, and hardship that if a man removes a tramp forcibly from his premises he may fall dead at the door-step or die shortly after, and the man who lays hands on him may be charged with anything from assault to manslaughter.

Now if shopkeepers would only have a little more spirit and back-bone in them and stolidly and resolutely refuse coppers or assistance of any kind to those tramps and itinerant musicians we would soon be rid of the pest, because tramps cannot exist except for the money they collect from shopkeepers'.

In May of that year, the *Western People* records that Sergeant Lyons of Ballyhaunis had been notified to attend the next examination for the rank of Head Constable, to which rank he was promoted on 1 June 1913. A week later he was posted to Athenry, Co. Galway as Head-Constable (and was replaced in Ballyhaunis by Sergeant Edward Carroll who was transferred there from Belmullet, Co. Mayo).[18]

ATHENRY

Life as a Head Constable must have tested Lyons' skills and talents in new ways. Malcolm notes that District Inspectors often sought the aid of Head Constables in the preparation of estimates, accounts, returns and reports. Samuel Waters, an officer in the Royal Irish Constabulary whose years of service were, in the main, contemporaneous with Lyons', recalls that junior officers were not particularly well-trained in police duties and relied heavily upon their Head Constables to conduct the day-to-day administration of their districts. Although the Head-Constable in Waters' barracks had but 'hazy perception of the technical regulations of the Force', this did not prevent him from keeping order in the sub-district, which allowed Waters to pursue a wide range of sporting activities and to socialize with the local gentry, which was 'vital if a Constabulary officer was to retain the confidence of the landed class and the magistracy'. Lyons' obituary notes: 'to the sergeants and constables he [Lyons] gave all the credit for the work done in the R.I.C. in the old days. The Commissioned men, he held, were not real policemen at all' and when Lyons was offered a District Inspectorship he declined.[19] Lyons, whose correspondence tells us little of his 'day-job', remarks in his letter to Goulden 'in that service inferior men having "push" and "chuck" took the lead. Save sentimentality the loss was not as much as it seems – for life for a promoted man in the higher ranks was unpleasant'.

Conditions in Athenry at the time of Lyons' transfer were primitive. Construction had just started on a sewerage and waterworks and there was a chronic housing shortage. The division of the Lambert Estate in 1907 had caused continuing local agitation and the Town Tenants' League was established to ensure that town tenancies be included, as was possible under the Wyndham Act: 'The townsmen began wall-knocking and cattle-driving. The town tenants marched in strength through the Lambert lands and led by a Band, they defied the Peelers'. By the end of 1915 they had secured the sale of the town and 300 acres of land had been divided among the tenants.[20]

Plate 11.
Photograph, dated January 1916, of 'portion of Boreenard leading from the Swan Gate of Athenry to SW'. Lyons notes that this 'little raised road', which was probably paved, is traceable for about 2 miles and was probably the old Galway road; 'it was about 4' high and 8' wide and had a trench about 9' wide on E side, as if a sunken road'.

Photo: Lyons Collection, N.U.I.Galway.

Lyons took up his position as Head-Constable in Athenry at a time when conditions within the force itself were also causing agitation: the Royal Irish Constabulary More Pay Movement held a meeting in Loughrea which was 'well attended from all the outlying stations, all ranks being represented'. This discontent resulted in a pamphlet being sent to police stations throughout Co. Galway asking for representatives to be appointed to give evidence at an enquiry into pay and conditions; 'in Co. Galway, especially, the lot of the policemen is far from a happy one, and a very general discontent prevails. Recently there have been resignations and not a few promising young policemen have been put on the sick list – a fact which is attributed directly to the hardships the men are compelled to undergo. "We are not even decent herds" said an indignant constable, "for herds can stay in their beds at night, while we are compelled to remain out in the cold and wet, looking after bullocks, and finding shelter where we can". The inquiry is regarded simply as an attempt to mark time pending political developments'. The early twentieth century was a demoralizing period for the Royal Irish Constabulary. A succession of weak political administrations undermined the police's authority in the eyes of both Nationalists and Unionists, starved the police force of funds and curtailed its intelligence operations.[21]

The rapid growth of the Volunteer movement nationally, precipitated by the Curragh incident and the Carsonite gun-runnings at Larne and Bangor, was mirrored at Athenry, where it must have caused considerable policing problems. The first Volunteer meeting was held in the Town Hall in February 1914 enrolling 50 members. In June, a muster of over 2,000 volunteers from all over Co. Galway was held in Athenry. 'The different detachments arrived by special and ordinary trains, while several companies marched from outlying parishes into Athenry, distances of eight, twelve and fifteen miles'; 'It was one of the most historic and impressive events that has taken place in Connacht for the last fifty years [...] fully 5,000 people were present [...] the town bore a very congested appearance but splendid order was maintained [...] the interest taken in the review by Galway citizens and merchants may be judged from the fact that many big stores and warehouses were closed down for the day while three steamers in the dock were

Plate 12.
'Blocks near Derrydonnell castle', Athenry c.1913. In this photograph Lyons' diligence in photographing monuments for identification is apparent, as he is unsure whether it is 'a dolmen or perched blocks'. In the *Sites and Monuments Record* a tower house is listed in O.S. 95 in Derrydonnell Beg townland; no megalith is listed in this or adjacent townlands of Derrydonnell More or Derrydonnell North.
Photo: Lyons Collection, N.U.I.Galway.

allowed to remain idle'. By December there were 54 branches of the Volunteers in Co.Galway with a membership which exceeded 5,000. [22]

Presumably, some of the same problems policing a small town and surrounding countryside that Lyons had encountered in Ballyhaunis and elsewhere also occurred in Athenry; however, these were not often reported in local newspapers, international and national events now filling more columns. But in November 1914 a horrific local event galvanized Athenry; 'a shocking tragedy was perpetrated [...] when a 35 year old farmer hacked the throat of his young wife with an ordinary Barber penknife and then, it is supposed, committed suicide [...] Father McGoff C.C. and Head-Constable Lyons were quickly on the scene'.

During the years 1914-8 many reports appeared in the *Western People*, *Connaught Tribune*, *Tuam Herald* and *Mayo News* detailing events of the World War in Europe; there were many accounts of brave men, including some from the Royal Irish Constabulary, who went to fight for what they believed was the defence of liberty.

Plate 13.
Dunmore Castle, Co. Galway from east c.1914. Lyons had visited the castle a number of times in previous years. In September 1906 he notes that 'it is hard to say whether the hill on which the castle is built is artificial or natural. It may be a combination of both [...] the huge outer ramparts which encircled the castle hill lie about in enormous fragments like the debris of a mountain shattered by an earthquake'. Originally built by de Bermingham c.1225 and burnt several times. The present castle, a rectangular tower situated on a motte with the remains of a fortifying wall around it, was probably built in the 14th century with the addition of an extra floor in the late 16th or early 17th century. [26]
Photo: Lyons Collection, N.U.I.Galway.

However, anti-British feeling, which was simmering beneath the surface, was liable to erupt at any time and necessitated constant police vigilance. In July 1915 a man was sentenced to one month's imprisonment under the Defence of the Realm Regulations for hissing and booing at images of King George and Lord Kitchener at a 'cinematograph entertainment' at Athenry Town Hall; 'the authorities took a very serious view of any act that would interfere with recruiting [...] if the defendants lived in Germany and had done the same thing they would be taken out against the wall, and at fifteen paces shot dead'.[23]

The split which occurred within the ranks of the Volunteers in September 1914 concerning Redmond's offer to 'guard the shores of Ireland with the Volunteers of Ireland' resulted in about a twelfth of the whole Volunteer movement coming under Irish Republican Brotherhood control, but it was not until their appearance at the funeral of O'Donovan Rossa in August 1915 that they made any obvious impression. In November of that year a meeting was held in Athenry which maintained that the bungling administration of the country had largely itself to blame, 'but the opposition to conscription is common ground [...] as is the desire to have, at the conclusion of the war, a force of Volunteers who will see to it that there is to be no tampering with the Home Rule Act'; a week later a meeting at Loughrea declared that the Athenry meeting consisted mainly of 'a miscellaneous group of political free-thinkers and cranks who offered disrespect to the great Leader [...] when the Sinn-Fein-cum-Pro-German meeting was published it aroused the strongest indignation and 300 True Men paraded as Loughrea's prompt answer to the Athenry meeting [...] some people thought because the Volunteers were not exercising and going through their drill of late, that the movement was dead and buried, but the answer tonight shows the National Volunteers are always ready and willing to prove their consistency and devotion to Ireland (loud cheers)'.[24]

The arrival of Liam Mellowes (Fig. 5) in Athenry in December 1915 must have caused great consternation to the constabulary there. Mellowes was a shy Wicklow man who had worked with Tom Clarke on the republican newspaper *Irish Freedom* and then became one of the first to train and instruct the Irish Volunteers. In November of that year, Mellowes had been deported but had managed to make his way back to Ireland in disguise. Though his original mission had been to spend a week in Athenry organizing and training the 'Sinn Fein' Volunteers there, Mellowes, decided to make Athenry his base of operations; he carried out an intensive training course, free of charge, in the Town Hall, set up a rifle-range in the yard and cycled between ten and fifteen miles each day recruiting members. Mellowes was deeply religious and his quiet perseverance won him the respect of the clergy which greatly enhanced his popularity in the community.

Fig. 5.
Sketch of Liam Mellowes as published in 'The Rising in Galway' in *The Capuchin Annual* 1966. Neilan notes that Mellowes 'went "on the run" after the surrender in Galway. He continued the fight and became a member of Headquarters Staff during the War of Independence. He was elected to the Dáil for North Meath in 1918, voted against the treaty and was shot as a reprisal on 8 December 1922'.

He was 'a delicate little chap and hardened countrymen in particular found it difficult to credit that they had anything to learn from him [...] they were quickly disillusioned'.[25]

On 15 February 1916, some two months after Mellowes' arrival in Athenry, Lyons was transferred to the Royal Irish Constabulary barracks in Newport, Co. Mayo; neither his departure from Athenry nor his arrival in Newport is recorded in local newspapers.

NEWPORT

Lyons was probably extremely relieved to leave the hot-bed of rebellion in Athenry for the relative peace of Newport where the recently re-organised corps of the Westport Irish Volunteers were neither as enthusiastic nor as active as their leaders desired; 'at Mr. Reilly's meadow for drill on Sunday after last Mass, there was a fairly large attendance considering the very inclement weather but if Westport intends to have a real business-like corps, the present attendance must be at least doubled'. What Lyons' thoughts must have been, when he read that Athenry was the only place in the west of Ireland that answered the call to arms for the Rising on Easter Monday, 24 April 1916, can only be imagined. More than 1,000 Volunteers had mobilized from companies all around Co. Galway. Mellowes' plan was to capture arms and ammunition by taking over police barracks. At Oranmore, the Volunteers captured six policemen before the arrival of a large force of Royal Irish Constabulary forced them to retreat to Athenry; here, they took over the Agricultural College from where the constabulary were unable to drive them, remaining until Thursday, when they moved to new headquarters at Moyode Castle, some ten miles to the south-east. Next day, on learning the devastating news that the remainder of the country had not participated in the Rising and that Dublin was unlikely to hold out much longer, the order to disband was given, the captured constabulary were released and the leaders went "on the run"; subsequently some hundred or so of the Galway Volunteers were arrested and court-martialled.[27]

An editorial in the *Mayo News* on 13 May 1916 encapsulated the situation in Newport: 'we believe that to nobody in Ireland did the news of a rising in Dublin come with greater surprise and consternation than to the Irish Volunteers in Mayo. None of them, we believe, had the least idea that the organization to which they belonged was, in the remotest possibility ever to be used for such purpose'. However on the same day, another article in this newspaper notes that all was not quiet on the western front: 'on Monday, [8 May] Mr. Joseph MacBride, Streamstown, Westport was arrested and conveyed to Castlebar Jail under armed escort of the RIC. Further arrests were effected in the early hours of Tuesday morning, when the following were taken into custody [18 names]. A troop of cavalry numbering about 120 men fully armed, arrived in town about 8 o clock, a.m. and were posted at the several entrances to the town while the arrests were made'.

More mundane local policing was also reported: Lyons' first appearance at the Newport Petty Sessions was to prove his summonses against a number of parties for 'no lights'. During his time as Head-Constable in Newport the Petty Sessions were not often reported, and, when they were, cases consisted mainly of breaches of the Licensing Laws or riding without lights on bicycles. Indeed, the lack of cases brought before the court was noted in the local press: 'the court lasted about ten minutes. What eloquent testimony this is of the good sense of the people of Newport district. Louisburgh, Castlebar and other places might note the fact with much profit'; 'well done, Newport. There was one case, that of simple drunkenness, for trial at Newport Petty Sessions on Tuesday. This is a splendid month's record for Newport district. Long may it remain so'; 'the only cases at these Petty Sessions were one adjourned case of drunkenness since November last and two local cases of trespass. These are the only cases which have arisen in the Newport district, which is one of the largest in the county, for the past three months'.

Plate 14.
Pillar stones at Rosgallive, Mallaranny, Co. Mayo c.1917. Strangely, there is no other reference to this monument in Knox's notebooks. In *Antiquities of West Mayo* Corlett notes that the stones stand one metre apart and are aligned north-east/south-west; there is a tradition that pins and rags were left at these stones, a custom normally reserved for seeking cures at holy wells.[30]

Photo: Lyons Collection, N.U.I.Galway.

Within his own barracks, however, it seems that Lyons was not very popular and was having difficulties enforcing his rule as Head-Constable; in June 1916, at a Police Inquiry a charge of drunkenness was preferred by Lyons against Constable Patrick McCarthy. 'County Inspector Steadman said that this was purely a disciplinary matter and the Press could not be admitted but the result would be communicated to the Press. We understand that the Head Constable was the only witness examined in support of the charge. 10 witnesses were examined for the defence and proved that the constable, who has 27 years service, was sober on the occasion'.

In September 1917 another charge taken by Lyons against one of his sergeants demonstrates his doggedness and also, perhaps, an over-zealousness: 'an R.I.C. Court of Inquiry was held at Newport Police Barracks on Tuesday to inquire into a charge against Sgt. Deignan, Newport of having been guilty of tippling at the barracks [...] Head Constable Lyons stated that the sergeant's gait was inclined to be unsteady as he walked along the corridor but when questioned in the office said there was nothing wrong with him. His voice was changed and there was a smell of drink in the room [...] Mr. Verdon: You have not been very friendly disposed towards the sergeant? Witness: I have no enmity against him [...] Mr. Verdon: How many policemen in your time did you report? – Couple of dozen or so – And out of the couple of dozen or so how many were censured, if one? – I believe there were three men punished, fines in two cases I think – Let us know, because I suggest that it was malice on your part. How many inquiries were held at this station arising out of reports made by you? – This is the fourth I think – Not a bad record, what happened the other times? – Qualified acquittals – Anyhow, Head, you are out for scalps somewhere, like the Mohawks? – No – Is this not a little fad of yours? – No [...] Constable McCarthy gave evidence that the sergeant was perfectly sober and gave no signs whatever of recent tippling [...] He said that on various occasions he heard the Head-Constable abuse the sergeant in the presence of the men. Mr.Verdon: Did he allude to the Germans? – He did. We were going through firing exercises and he said to the whole party "I hope to God the Germans may come and bomb ye" – Did he say anything about married men? – He did. He said that married men are a nuisance, "if I had my way I would not promote married men; they are too much under the control of their Biddys and Marys". President: What has this got to do with the case? – Mr. Verdon: Well, I believe Head-Constable Lyons is a crank [...] President (to witness): Has there been any unpleasantness between you and the Head-Constable? – Yes, he charged me with drunkenness in May 1916. It was investigated by the present County Inspector and I was acquitted of the charge – Has there been any other unpleasantness? – Yes; in March last the Head-Constable on one occasion in his own kitchen where he was parading me for duty, said to me "I believe you are acting unsteady; you are drinking". I asked him how he arrived at that conclusion and to point out anything I had done unsteady or when he saw me drinking. He said "I will not; I reported the matter verbally to my officer". I was a teetotaler at the time for months before and since. Mr. Verdon: That shows the man's hallucinations. Witness – A few nights after that, if my memory serves me right, between 3 and 4 o'clock in the morning, I heard him, shouting "Barrack orderly, barrack orderly". I was barrack orderly. I was in bed at the time. I went to where I heard the shouts, and the Head-Constable was at the foot of his own staircase in his night-shirt. He was knocking with his hand against the side of the staircase. I had to open two doors to get as far as the Head-Constable and to light a candle. He said: "Why do you lock me in my own quarters?" I said: "I did not lock you in; the doors were not locked". He said: "They were" and I pointed out that there were no keys in the doors. He then said: "I'll smash your face; you're a blackguard and too smart for me" He then went out to the front door of the barrack and I went with him. He said: "You are after letting men out this door" and I said "I did not; there are seven men and two sergeants sleeping in the barracks; there are four men in one room and two in the other and two sergeants sleeping in the sergeant's office, and come upstairs now and I'll satisfy you that they are still there". He declined to do so. I went up subsequently and saw that the sergeants and all the men were there. I reported all this verbally to my officer the following morning. I did not wish to have any further reports about it as I intend to retire on pension as soon as I can. Mr. Verdon: This shows the friction between the Head-Constable and the men. His action on that occasion was not the action of a sane man [...] Mr Verdon: Have you applied for a transfer? – Yes – Because of the Head-Constable's tyranny? – Yes, and for my own personal safety and quietness – And so have the other constables? – Yes – Were you stationed at Ballyhaunis with the Head-Constable? – Yes, and I had a few rows with him there too. Witness further stated that he was charged at Ballyhaunis by the Head-Constable who was then a Sergeant, with tippling, and he (witness) was admonished and transferred to Newport at the public expense [...]

'The Head was re-called by the court [...] he had a general denial to give so far as the evidence alleged disciplinary offences against himself. As regards the locked doors he thought he heard someone tampering with the front door of the barrack, and when he proceeded to investigate he found himself locked in – a prisoner in his own apartment. He knocked loudly at the door and called for the barrack orderly at the top of his voice. The barrack orderly opened the door after some delay. After unlocking the door the barrack orderly said it was not locked at all. He (witness) certainly said the orderly was too clever for him but he did not call the orderly any names or threaten to assault him. He (witness) came down to the front door of the barracks afterwards but could not see anything wrong. The barrack orderly invited him upstairs to see whether or not the men were in bed, but he did not go as he believed the men were in. He mentioned the matter to Mr. Adderley the following day but Mr. Adderley did not think he had a good disciplinary case. It was not true that he abused Sergeant Deignan on parade or that he was continually abusing the men. The faintest of criticism of drill was termed abuse. He said many complimentary things on parade that were suppressed. "All my sins" added the Head-Constable, "are remembered, but all my virtues are forgotten".

When the Court of Inquiry concluded its investigations, Lyons was vindicated and Sergeant Deignan was found guilty, reduced in rank to Constable and transferred to Ballina.'[28]

Throughout 1917 the constabulary authorities were becoming increasingly

Plate 15.
Megalith in Drumgollagh, Ballycroy, Co. Mayo c.1916 described by Lyons as a 'wonderful dolmen which is divided into two compartments. The S is entered by a narrow doorway between two jambs. On these jambs the great recumbent stone to the left of the doorway must have rested. There was a small extension in from the doorway, evidently a sort of porch.' In the *Sites and Monuments Record* this monument is classified as a court-tomb (O.S. 56).

Photo: Lyons Collection, N.U.I.Galway.

nervous about Volunteer activity in Mayo which culminated in November with a Sinn Féin demonstration in Westport, 'of immense proportions [it] was most enthusiastic and orderly throughout [...] Mr. Ginnell called on all the hearers who had not done so already to come into the Sinn Fein movement'. In the following March, a bomb thrown by a passer-by through the door of Westport police barracks must have caused much trepidation in nearby Newport; 'a number of panes of glass shattered, [causing] a shock to a few policemen who were in the day room at the time'. In the following week four Newport men were arrested and conveyed to Westport where at a special court they were charged with unlawful assembly.

A week later tensions between the police and people in Westport spilled over onto the streets; 'following the unprovoked baton charge on Thursday the town was in a state of great excitement and the streets were crowded. About 9 o'clock the attitude of the police became unbearable and the people were for the most part making the best of their position, when a baton charge was ordered from Shop Street. The police charged the crowd and many people were severely batoned. It is alleged the police, taking advantage of the darkness, indulged in stone-throwing. A number of plate-glass windows in the town were broken [...] the Sinn Fein's Hall windows were completely wrecked, and it is stated the police were solely responsible for nearly all the breakages. The town was peaceable on Friday night, but about 9.30 on Saturday night the police assumed their aggressiveness and a baton charge was ordered. The police charged the people down Bridge Street and on the way a number of windows were broken [...] a young man named Joyce who was leaving Golden's with a pair of boots, was set upon by the police and was knocked down and treated in a brutal manner. On his way home Joyce collapsed and was treated by Dr. Moran; he was afterwards removed to hospital in a precarious condition. Mr. James Gavin, father of one of the prisoners, was in his own house when a policeman rushed in and struck him with a baton and inflicted a nasty wound over his eye [... necessitating] seven stitches [...]

'On Saturday morning 5 men [names] were arrested by armed police at their homes and brought to the barracks where they were charged later in the day with unlawful assembly and drilling [...] the first prisoner brought before the court in the uniform of the Irish Volunteers immediately turned his back on the court and did not remove his hat [... the others] were then brought before the court [...] a rather lively scene followed in an effort by the police to try and get the young men to face the court. The effort was not successful as during the greater part of the hearing the men did not face the court and ridiculed the proceedings [...] the prisoners were marched under a strong escort of police and military to the 2 o'clock mail train where they were entrained for Sligo jail [...]

'The "new regime" had its innings in Castlebar on Wednesday when the 5 young Westport men who were arrested on Saturday morning and conveyed to Sligo jail on remand were taken back again for "trial" before two Removables [...] on arrival at the railway station they were met by a company of the Essex Yeomanry with rifles and fixed bayonets and about 100 police [...] cowardly brutality [was shown] by the RIC after the proceedings had concluded. A number of children were assembled in the Green quite close to the Courthouse and chalked on their backs were such devices as "Up the rebels", "Up Westport" and an RM who was emerging from the court smiled sarcastically or otherwise at them and they shouted "Oh, oh". Then the police were ordered to clear the Mall and the infuriated imported police mob were [sic.] let loose on the defenceless youngsters and girls. Small groups of people [...] were set upon and batoned while a dead set was made upon Sinn Feiners and those suspected of being such

[...] in their infuriated charge the police upset a perambulator throwing the child (an infant) out on the pathway of the Mall. Two further baton charges took place in quick succession and some of those who ran from the police were followed across the fields for over a quarter of a mile out of the town. The greatest excitement continued for some time but towards dark, quiet prevailed. About 11 o'clock a party of youngsters were singing Sinn Fein songs near the Bridge when a baton charge was ordered by a subordinate official and the streets were cleared and after this all became peaceful'.[29]

Over the next two years Volunteer activity escalated in Mayo and frequent raids on police barracks, ambushes and guerilla attacks became commonplace. Because of the extent of its territory Mayo Volunteers formed four brigades, of which Westport was the headquarters of the West Mayo Brigade under Tomas Ó Deirg; the East Mayo Brigade, based at Swinford was led by Tom Carney who had resigned from the Royal Irish Constabulary to join the Volunteers. Nationally, the campaign against the police was beginning to show results that were even more important than the number of dead and maimed; many members of the constabulary had begun to prefer discretion to valour and to resign from the force. With them went an indeterminable number of others who felt a conflict of Irish loyalties. To fill the gap the authorities began recruiting in England as well as Ireland. The Black and Tans were first seen in Dublin on 25 March 1920 and the Auxiliaries at the end of the following July. Whereas the Royal Irish Constabulary had for a long time been a police force doing a soldier's job, the new auxiliaries were ex-soldiers expected to do a policeman's job and were given free rein to destroy the Irish Republican Army. The brutality with which the Auxiliaries and the Black and Tans set about their task created unrest within the Royal Irish Constabulary, many of whose members refused to be associated with their actions. In Mayo this resulted in many policemen resigning in protest and 'of those who remained it must be admitted that they usually gave warning to the Volunteers of impending raids'.[31]

One particular event in 1920 must have disturbed Lyons in a very personal way: in what must have seemed like a strange twist of fate the man who replaced him in Ballyhaunis had been shot. 'Sensation prevailed in Ballyhaunis early Sunday morning, when a number of shots rang out in Bridge St. and it was later found that Sgt. Ed Carroll and Const. Ryan, when returning from duty in an outside district had been fired on, receiving injuries to the legs from shotguns. It appears the injured men who were accompanied by Const. McDaid surprised a party of men who were carrying out a raid on the excise offices, opposite the post office. The police were three times called upon to halt and not complying with the order were fired upon. It is said that shots were then exchanged, and a bullet was yesterday found embedded in the hall door of the Railway Hotel. The raiding party decamped immediately [...] the Sergeant was removed to Dublin for treatment by the 1.45 pm train. The constable's wounds were slight'.[32]

Lyons gives no clue in his writings as to the reason for his own resignation. In his letter to Goulden he merely remarks that 'after retiring the suspicions of the gunmen compelled me to relinquish research and virtually terminated my antiquarian career'. We know from his Service Record that he was pensioned off on 13 August 1920, aged 59, having served as a member of the Royal Irish Constabulary for 34 years.

That Lyons competently fulfilled his duties is evident from his Royal Irish Constabulary service record on which there are no blemishes; that he was well-respected by magistrates for his fair-mindedness in cases brought before the courts can be gleaned through reading reports of Petty Sessions in relevant local newspapers. However, surviving evidence in the form of Knox's notes transcribed from Lyons' letters portrays another aspect of Lyons' personality: during the time he spent patrolling his appointed area and monitoring all that occurred, Lyons was also finding time to take detailed notes, measurements, drawings and photographs of field monuments, observing folk-life and recording folk-lore. These interests seem to have become all-encompassing and the sheer volume of notes and photographs that remain makes one wonder how he had time for his 'day job' during some of the most troubled times in Irish history.

In the Lyons Collection in N.U.I.Galway, there is one very evocative photograph in which both Lyons' interest in folk-life and his work as a member of the Royal Irish Constabulary combine (Plate 16). Though the photograph is dated August 1910, the date cannot be reconciled with a particular event in Lisduff at that time relating to the land struggle. Unfortunately, there is no reference to this photograph in the lists of photographs (with descriptions) which occur intermittently in the Knox's notebooks. During the years 1905-18 when Knox was transcribing Lyons' letters, 'land grabbing' and associated resistance against landlordism were regularly reported in local newspapers. A confrontation at Lisduff made headlines in the *Mayo News* in April-May 1920 with 'The Lisduff Assembly': 'Huge crowds swarmed into Ballyhaunis on Monday when 8 farmers were charged at the suit of the Crown with unlawful assembly on 27th March when they entered the said farm [Lisduff] and dug up three roods of same [...] there were parties of armed military and police in the vicinity of the Courthouse during the day'. The defendants were tenants with con-acre on the Lisduff farm; they claimed that unknown to them, con-acre had previously been leased to a man who was not a tenant and they wanted 'to put him out of it'. Before the case reached the courts, a settlement between the landlord and tenants, had been arrived at and an order adjourning the case for 3 months was made. The lands were to be surrendered to the tenants on 11 May but as this did not happen, further action was taken; 'stock and property consisting of many horses, cattle and sheep were driven off the farm at Lisduff on Tuesday evening by the tenants claiming the surrender of the farm to them, the drive passing in broad daylight through Ballyhaunis'. A fortnight later it was reported that 'following the recent daylight "drive" of stock off the Lisduff Farm [...] the tenants have now taken

Plate 16.
Photograph, dated August 1910, described by Lyons as a 'threatening notice posted on a wall in Lisduff near Ballyhaunis' – TO BEWARE TAKE NO MEADOWS IN LISDUFF. During Lyons time in the R.I.C. barracks in Ballyhaunis, indignation by tenant farmers against the provisions of the Land Acts continually simmered beneath the surface, erupting into outright confrontation with the police on several occasions. The date of this photograph, however, cannot be reconciled with any particular event at Lisduff relating to the land struggle.

Photo: Lyons Collection, N.U.I.Galway.

over possession and have taken in grazing stock from outside. The proceeding is said to be on the basis of an agreement between the landlord and the tenants'.[33]

Perhaps Knox erred in his recording of the date of the photograph; it is also possible that on some occasion, in or around 1910, the threat of land-grabbing at Lisduff was foreseen but no further action that would merit newspaper headlines was undertaken.

Chapter 3
The 'antiquarian craze'

IN HIS TYPICALLY MODEST WAY, Lyons succinctly describes his passion for antiquities in his letter to Goulden: 'Fate led me in 1897 to find an Ogham (pronounced Ouam) inscription. This led me into a connection with the late Sir John Rhys, Professor of Celtic at Oxford University – which diverted my attention from official advancement and made my antiquarian craze irresistible'. In the letter Lyons explains that because 'the RIC authority disapproved of antiquarian activities I did not come out into the open as an antiquarian until I had left the Service'. Accordingly, Lyons' covert career as a field-archaeologist must be pieced together from two main sources: the notebooks in which Knox recorded Lyons' field-work and speculations and the collections of Lyons' photographs.[1]

Knox's notebooks (hereafter referred to as K.N.1, 2, 3, 4) are a record of the wide-ranging topics in which both he and Lyons shared a deep interest: descriptions and measurements of field monuments together with speculations about their builders; meanings of words and derivations of placenames; folk-life and lore; ethnography; photography (field monuments, artefacts and folklife studies). Extracted from the letters he received from Lyons, often, seemingly, in answer to questions previously posed, Knox's record is sometimes just a sentence or two, sometimes long paragraphs. Reading the notebooks is somewhat akin to listening to one side of a rambling telephone conversation: one can get a general, hazy idea of the subject but, as some essential details are missing, correct interpretation may not be possible. Unfortunately, Knox's letters to Lyons have not been located and efforts to establish if Knox's descendants had retained his papers, including Lyons' actual 'antiquarian communications', have proved unsuccessful: prior to his republication in 1982 of Knox's *History of Mayo to 1608*, Éamonn de Burca attempted to trace the family and discovered that Knox had died unmarried and that surviving family members had emigrated to South Africa to an estate which they named Ballinrobe.[2]

The extant notebooks begin on 21 June 1905;* the first page is indicative of

---

* Among the Knox/Lyons papers in the library of the Royal Society of Antiquaries of Ireland is a letter from Lyons (dated 6.11.1929) with which he forwards 'five notebooks [...] compiled from antiquarian communications sent to me by Mr. Knox during the years when I was a member of the Royal Irish Constabulary.' Four notebooks only are archived and no reference to a fifth notebook could be found – as the latest notebook (K.N.4) ends inconclusively in the year before Knox's death, it is likely that the missing notebook is the first of the series.

the fragmentary nature of Knox's quotations from Lyons' letters:

> 21 June: 'Linnabaustia in Brackloon Td. Bekan Parish. In midst of large rath a somewhat triangular assemblage of children's graves about 30 ft. long E to W. The enclosure is a shallow earthen rampart.
> 27 July: The 18th century custom of seating in Aughamore Church. At proper season rushes were cut and bound in sheaves, and these were spread on the floor during Mass. After Mass they were ranged against the walls. During the ceremony the worshippers sat or knelt on them.
> 14 Aug: At site of St. Cronan's well, L[ough] Mannin are cubical stones about 12" x 4"x 4" with segmental depressions in one face.
> 5 Sept: Near Tullaghan Ogham is a fort with a children's burying ground called Laghty.
> 15 Sept: Souterrains generally have cornices to support roof stones, but one in smaller cashel in Carrownedin has sides, sloping inwards'.

Several souterrains are described on the next two pages. On 14 October the subject again changes: 'The Waldrons are a strong clan about Ballyhaunis. Waldron is a recent form. They are rustically called "Waldor". Thor. Philip Waldron of Drumbaun, an intelligent man has told me that Bhaldraithe is the traditional name', followed by '15 October: Ph. 186.187 On top of Slieve Dart, 2 ½ m. SE from Cloonfad in Flaskagh Td. close to Co. Roscommon mearing [border] is a chamber grave. Mearing runs on top of hill. There is what appears to be an ancient pass over the hill about 400 yds. E.', followed by '6 Nov: Ruined cashel 29 yds. diameter in Thos. Maguire's land in Kiltaboe Td. 3 m. E of Ballyhaunis, 400 yds. S of Ballinlough road. Another said to be in Scrigg Td. ½ m. S. Kiltabo cashel is divided N & S by a wall which joins the S by a v-shaped arrangement. The north junction is destroyed. It is called Cashelgal.' On 18 November the subject returns to a description of a souterrain: 'in the farm of Miss Sheridan of Dunmore in the Townland of Ballaghdorragher'. It is not until 1 December that there is another reference to the first entry in the Notebook: 'Lisheen in Tully Td. Co. Roscommon. ½ m. NNW from Lisnabaushtea in Brackloon in Bekan. See ph. 1' and not until 15 December is there a further reference to the last quotation on page 1: 'In S part of Carrownedin has found a nearly rectangular rath and an earth and stone rath with what may have been a clochan near its western extremity'.[3]

This diary-like record of Lyons' correspondence continues throughout the four notebooks which span the period 1905-18. Transcriptions from Lyons' letters appear to have been written up sporadically by Knox, sometimes with a lapse of days, sometimes weeks; particularly in the later years, when Knox was often ill (as evidence from his correspondence with other antiquarians suggests), the time-lapse often runs into several months. Notebook 3 covers the period from 14 September 1909 to 7 December 1915 and overlaps to a great extent with notebook 4 covering the period from July (no day recorded) 1913 to 29 October 1918. Whereas notebooks 1 and 2 are filled with many short descriptions which flit from topic to topic, notebooks 3 and 4 contain many lengthy paragraphs in which Lyons' speculations and theories regarding the possible origin of the builders of earthworks, such as the Rathcroghan complex, are recorded.

CORRESPONDENCE WITH ANTIQUARIANS

The notebooks provide a tantalizing glimpse into the acquisition and sharing of local knowledge by antiquarians in the first two decades of the 20th century. Lyons' diligence is well exemplified in Knox's quotation from his letter of 30 April 1908:

> 'Perhaps you could be able to obtain for me, from some gentleman interested in antiquities, the loan of a collapsible boat. There are a good many crannogs in this locality which I wish to visit and I can not do so with an ordinary boat as the lakes are inaccessible by carts. Besides, the inconvenience of carting a boat is prohibitive. I can probably convey a collapsible boat on an ass's back. If so it will be a very great convenience. A collapsible to be serviceable must be able to float 16 stone weight'.

Unfortunately for Lyons, his appeal does not appear to have been answered as there are no further references to travel in a collapsible boat, or by any other form of transport, to visit crannógs. Lyons' interest in crannógs is first recorded on page 7 of the earliest notebook (dated 1 December 1905) when Knox records '[Lyons] sends a collection of objects found in the crannog in L[ough] Caheer by James Flatley, a young fellow of Ballyhaunis' to forward to the National Museum; later that year, on 6 September, Knox quotes from Lyons' letter: 'the rectangular rath in Carrowneden is about 250 yds directly N of what seems to be a shore crannoge. This rath, this (alleged) crannoge and the two genuine crannógs are in a direct line and seem to have some relationship. Island Castle is a little W of this line. I have learned that the name of the alleged crannoge is Illaun-nan-Yach, perhaps the island of the steed or steeds'.* Knox records several attempts made

---

*   In the Lyons Collection in N.U.I.Galway there are two photographs of crannógs: these are described by Lyons as 'Principal lake dwelling. Island lake. From N. About 25x15 yds. At present unsubmerged' and 'Crannoge in L[ough] Caheer. Water 32 to 40 ft deep here. W shore of L. Caheer. Looking NW'. Neither photograph depicts identifiable crannóg details.

Plate 17.
'Laght-a-Wohoo', Feamore, near Ballyhaunis c.1916 described by Lyons as 'an outside row of stones forming an oblong with a smaller interior oblong which supported the huge horizontal stone', Marked 'MacMahon's Monument' on O.S.112, it is classified in the *Sites and Monuments Record* as a wedge-tomb.

Photo: Lyons Collection, N.U.I.Galway.

---

by Lyons to investigate 'dry crannógs'. In only one instance does Knox record an actual visit by Lyons to a crannóg: '8 July 1907 Mr. O[rpen] was on a "real live" crannoge for perhaps the first time as we visited the island in Lough O'Flynn'.[4]

The depth of Lyons' interest in the archaeological puzzles of the time and his concern that his discoveries be given to the most appropriate person are evident in Knox's quotations from his letters:

> '15 February 1907: perhaps you could get Mr. Falkiner to visit and deal with a small stone circle which is close to the N side of the railway line about 2 miles E of Castletown-Geoghegan, Co. Westmeath';
> '5 December 1907: Accept the enclosed rubbings of part of the doorway of Donoughmore Church near Clonmel. The one marked A is a vertical jamb rubbing of the outer door. B is a rubbing of the underside of the arch of the same doorway. This is St. Faraunan's church figured on pp.119, 120 of Miss Stoke's book. In the picture of the outer doorway there is, I think, a serious error as the toothing is shown to point downwards. In the rubbing you see it points horizontally';

'16 April 1908: I am returning Miss Stokes' book. You have anticipated my theory on p.168 of "Note". I must have had a sub-consciousness of the matter when I formed the theory [...] Miss Stokes missed this point, though she went very near it. See pp. 37. 43. 46. 47. She did not draw inference from the chancel not being bonded to the nave';

'30 May 1909: Leacht-a-Wohoo (Plate 17) interests Mr. Orpen very much. He says that according to the Dinnsenchus one of the monuments at Brugh na Boinne was Lect in Matae – Petrie translates this name as "monument of the monster" (matae)';

'6 Sept 1910: I went to Meelick yesterday. I was unable to find the stone figured by Mr. Crawford, but it is in existence.* It seems to have got covered up with moss and grass and so I was unable to find it at the time at my disposal. It was seen about 2 years ago, when it was stripped of its vegetable coating';

Lyons' concern with the conservation of field-monuments is evident in his letters; his requests that they receive proper care are recorded by Knox:

'18 February 1906: Two large round white stones – evidently bullauns – were removed out of Kiltullagh Graveyard about 20 or 30 years ago and brought to some place near Ballinlough. This I suppose was done by the clergy to check superstition. You ought to get the B[oar]d of Works to do something to Kiltullagh doorway which has lost a jamb, endangering it';

'20 September 1909: The old church [at Baptist Grange] was as ornate as Donoughmore, judging by two detached flowered capitals which are in the W end [...] I trust you will get Dr. Cochrane to stir in the matter of the remaining chancel-arch so that it may be prevented from collapsing'.[5]

---

* Lyons is describing his attempt to find a particular cross-slab featured in a descriptive list of early cross-slabs and pillars in Connacht catalogued by H.S. Crawford in the *Journal of the Royal Society of Antiquaries of Ireland*: 'Meelick – in the graveyard of the Round Tower 3 m. W of Swineford [sic.]. A slab 4 ft. 7 in. long by 2 ft. wide, on which is carved a Latin cross in a rectangular frame, both cross and frame being covered with interlacing. The extremities and centre are marked by small Greek crosses, and the inscription "or do grigou" [...] occupies the sinister quarters and reads downwards'. Knox's transcription of Lyons' letter continues: 'I found another stone with an antique cross of interlaced work in relief covering a grave 20 yds. in a direct line between the E jamb of the tower doorway and the SE angle of the graveyard, that is 20 yds from the Tower. The stone has a border of interlaced work. The work is very indistinct owing to the low relief and black lichen. It requires to be buried for a while. It is a very artistic and interesting stone'. There is no further mention by Knox in his notebooks that Lyons found the cross described by Crawford; however, a photograph in the collection in N.U.I.Galway, (Plate 18) seemingly refers to the cross-slab found by Lyons on this occasion.

Plate 18.
Photograph, dated September 1910, of gravestone with inscribed cross (with base of the round tower in the background) at Meelick, near Swinford, Co. Mayo. Lyons noticed this gravestone when he was searching for another cross-slab described by Crawford in the *Journal of the Royal Society of Antiquaries of Ireland*.

Photo: Lyons Collection, N.U.I.Galway.

LOCAL SOURCES

It is evident in Knox's quotations from Lyons' letters that Lyons sought local information from as many sources as possible:

> '6 July 1906: Just to S of a hill, which is S and similar to the hill out of which Lisnadhine is made, is a water hole which is called Pullnagunnade – Poll-na-Gunnaide, "Hole of the Guns". Brian Kerins says the people of the Lis at one time threw all their arms into it. Brian and myself are to poke the hole to see if the arms are yet in it. He says there was a sunken road from the lis along the top of the S hill to the hole';
>
> '20 January 1907: An old man walked three miles today for the purpose of meeting me to show me a dolmen. I met him and we went to the place – in the hilly country about half a mile E of Cashelmore. It is one of the finest low

dolmens in Ireland and very like Finn's table on Slievenamon';
'8 Sept 1910: I went to Balla to-day but I have failed to find the mote of Attavalley, though I believe it exists [...] I could get no one to guide me to the spot'.

Lyons frequently named his sources and gave his opinion of their credibility. However, the novelty of a uniformed policeman asking questions about field-monuments begs the question of the responses it might evoke: some might take delight in Lyons being hood-winked with some tall tale, while others might enjoy the feeling of power such requests seemingly bestowed. It seems that Lyons had some appreciation of the need for sensitivity:

'a man told me, in Kilvine, that a man in old times went with his gun and hound and wearing his "uniform" into Leacht-a-Vahoo and that he never came out again and that he was the greatest soldier in Mayo. It is easy to translate this and I think in finding it I sailed pretty close to the wind'.[6]

However, it seems that Lyons' passion for knowledge was sometimes used against him: Bernie Freyne, writing in *Annagh* (the Ballyhaunis parish magazine) remarks that 'the only way a few of the lads who held a grudge against him could get under his skin was to blow up one or two of those (Ogham) stones'. Unfortunately, Freyne does not elucidate further; possibly he is referring to the ogham stone at Tullaghane, discovered by Lyons in 1900, which, according to Macalister, 'had been badly injured some time before by boys, who lit a fire against the stone'. Lyons was aware of one such attempt at the destruction of a standing stone, but the reason, as quoted by Knox from his letter, appears to be quite different:

'2 May 1909: Sends rough drawing of Aghataharn boulder. It was contemplated to split this boulder, but I think I have checked this vandalism. Where it is was an old demesne, probably the Abbey lands. It was held by a Mr. Nolan about 100 years ago. He had a mansion here. He made a drain from Lough Roe to Urlaur Lough, but no one would tap L. Roe when the drain was finished. At last a man from Cappagh was got to do it for 5/-, but a white woman rose out of the Lough and set his house on fire & it was burned when he went home'.[7]

Local folklore regarding the practice of destroying field-monuments is also mentioned in 1995 by McCormick in connection with his excavations (together with Cribbin, Robinson and Shimwell) at Kiltullagh hill, which straddles the borders of counties Mayo and Roscommon. On the Roscommon side of this hill is a low mound surmounted by a standing stone on which holes had been drilled along one side of the stone. Scattered human bones had been discovered during nearby quarrying (which partially destroyed the barrow surrounding the mound). These were dated to the Late Iron Age, around the time when Christianity was beginning to replace paganism in burial practices. 'Local folklore had it that the holes were cut in order to accommodate dynamite for the blowing up of the stone during the War of Independence. The context of this unusual explanation concerns a sergeant in the Royal Irish Constabulary by the name of Lyons. He was an antiquarian whose political outlook led him into ideological conflict with a certain element of the local population. These persons were, however, unprepared to cause actual bodily harm to the RIC officer but instead decided to offend his antiquarian sensibilities by destroying ancient monuments in the area. Folklore held that they had already destroyed the alleged standing stone on the Mayo summit and then turned their endeavours to the Roscommon stone. Holes had been chiseled for explosives before the plan was abandoned. Alas, this intriguing tale has not survived the rigours of archaeological scrutiny. Excavation at the base of the stone revealed a fourth hole, identical to the others, well below ground level. It can be assumed that this hole, and presumably the remaining three were carved before the stone was erected. This feature appears to be

Plate 19.
Photograph, dated 1908, described by Lyons as: 'Pillar stones at Ballyglass, Kiltullagh, Co. Roscommon, From S. The holed one in the distance. The two near stones are in Mayo. The other one is in Roscommon'.

Photo: Lyons Collection, N.U.I.Galway.

presently unique on Irish standing stones and its function is a mystery'.[8] It could be added that this tale would also not survive the rigours of historical scrutiny: Lyons was transferred from the R.I.C. barracks in Ballyhaunis to Athenry in 1913 and so had long departed from the area before the War of Independence.

A photograph in the Lyons' Collection at N.U.I. Galway (Plate 19) may help to solve some confusion regarding the standing stone(s) at Kiltullagh (or perhaps deepen the mystery). McCormick notes: 'Knox's reference [in his paper 'Ruins of Cruachain Ai'] to the two recently destroyed broken stones is interesting [...]

Fig. 6.
Location map and description of the pillar stones at Kiltullagh/Ballyglass transcribed by Knox from Lyons' letter of 27 March 1908.

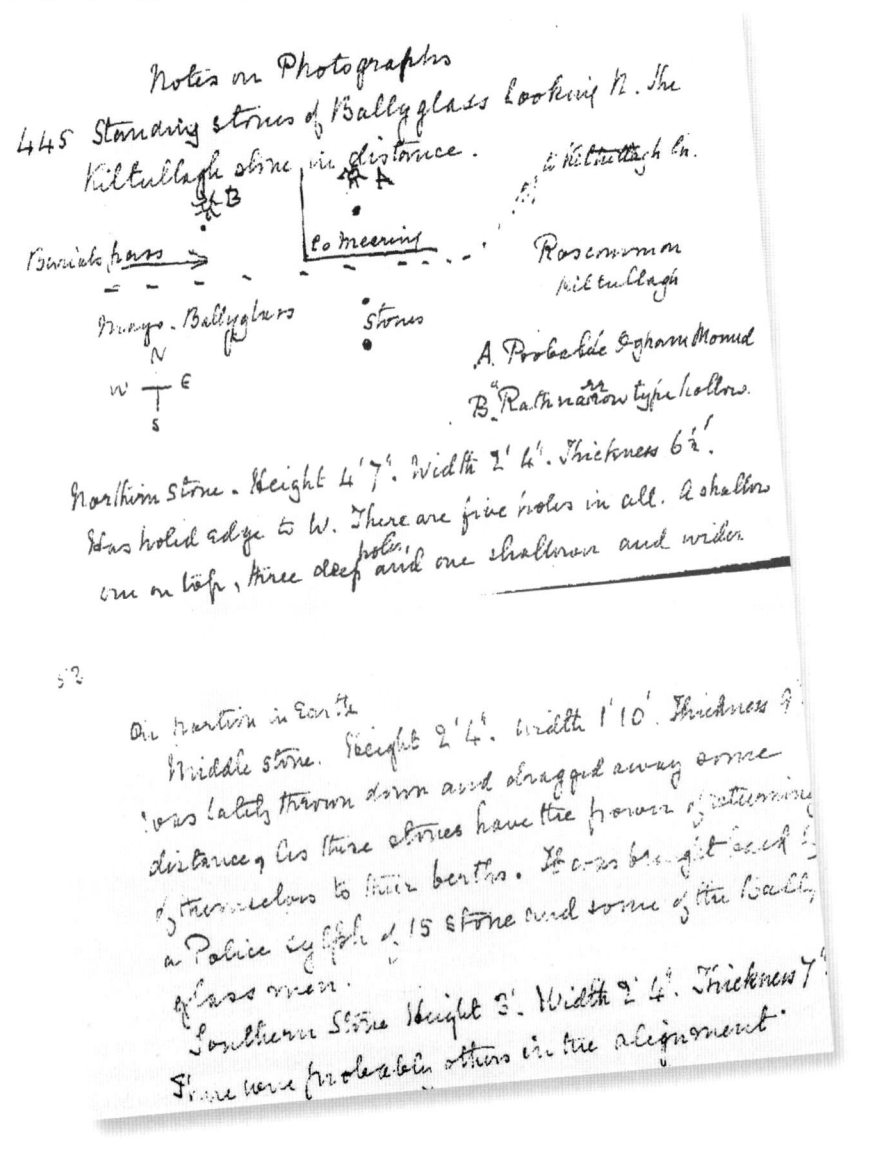

Plate 20.
Photograph of holed pillar stone on Kiltullagh hill in 2005. As the hill is now divided into fields surrounded by stone walls which obscure the view, it is not possible to take a photograph from the standpoint used by Lyons (Plate 19).

Photo: M. Lohan

---

these may be the remains of the standing stones described by the present authors in *Emania* 12 who, at the time of writing, were unaware of the Knox description. These two rectangular slabs of stone were reported to have been the remains of a single pillar stone that had originally stood on the site of the disturbed Iron Age burials discovered during quarrying, and which folklore described as having been destroyed at the beginning of this [20th] century. Geochemical analysis, however, has shown the fragments to be of two different stones, a finding which correlates with the observations of Knox'.

On 27 Mar 1908 Knox transcribes from Lyons' letter, which includes a location map (Fig. 6):

> 'Standing stones of Ballyglass looking N. The Kiltullagh stone in distance [...] Northern stone. Height 4' 7". Width 2' 4". Thickness 6½'. Has holed edge to W. There are five holes in all. A shallow one on top. Three deep holes and one shallower and wider on portion in earth. Middle stone. Height 2' 4". Width 1' 10". Thickness 9". Was lately thrown down and dragged away some distance, as these stones have the power of returning of themselves to their

berths. It was brought back by a police sylph of 15 stone and some of the Ballyglass men. Southern stone. Height 3'. Width 2' 4". Thickness 7".

This quotation seems to imply that the middle stone was re-erected on that day under Lyons' direction. Lyons is obviously aware of the lowest hole in the northern Kiltullagh pillar-stone (which when excavated in 1994-5 was beneath ground level). The possibility that this stone, too, had been re-erected at some earlier time (which may be inferred from Lyons' remark that 'these stones have the power of returning of themselves to their berths') is discussed by McCormick: 'the fact that it is possible for one person to move the stone from side to side when the fourth and bottom hole was exposed, implies that the holes were carved before the stone was erected'.[9]

LOCALITIES OF FIELD-MONUMENTS

Lyons traveled as extensively as possible (usually by bicycle) in his investigation of field-monuments. To some extent the constabulary barracks at which he was stationed dictated his movements: when he was transferred from Ballyhaunis to Athenry in 1913 his focus of interest changed from the Mayo/Roscommon border to east-Galway and on his transfer to Newport in 1916, to north-west Mayo. However, it seems that he also made use of every available opportunity, whether at work or on holiday, to gather information and forward his observations: although the addresses from which Lyons sent his letters to Knox are not often recorded, locations such as Ballina, Clonmel, Craughwell, Dublin, Lisronagh and Portarlington are noted. Knox's quotations from Lyons' letters include:

'6 May 1907: Since I last wrote I have been on cycle detachment in North Roscommon. I had no camera but managed to see some things of interest and to hear of others. Although the country is very fertile, raths are few and small – but I saw a few double-ringed ones';
'1 October 1907: When returning off leave I broke my journey to visit a dolmen at Meehaunbwee, 3 miles W of Athlone. This antiquity has an uplifted stone 12 x 12½ x 2½ ft, perhaps the largest in Ireland';
'31 July 1908: 'I utilized the delay (at Portarlington) to visit Lea Castle on the Barrow 1½ miles E. It is a tremendous ruin';
'26 July 1909: I was at Rathbrit near Fethard the other day, and I found there a rectangular earthen fort in fair preservation. There is a forgotten Norman town at the castle of Kilconnell closeby';
'31 Dec 1913: Lisronagh – The ditches of the de Burgh mote must have been

closed up at the S or they would not have held water. The roads at Kiltinan are practically the same as those at Rathcroghan N Section';

'10 March 1917: Ballina – The dolmen of the Maels is a fine affair. Only the northern part exists. I believe it was originally 24' long, 10' to 12' wide. One end stone remains'.[10]

ASSISTANCE BY COLLEAGUES

Lyons' concern that his 'antiquarian craze' should go unnoticed by his superiors is reflected in his letter to Goulden: 'as the RIC authority disapproved of antiquarian activities I did not come out into the open as an antiquarian until I had left the Service.' However, this anxiety did not prevent him from making use of his colleagues to assist him with his field work, as already noted in connection with the re-erection of the pillar-stone at Ballyglass/Kiltullagh, and is quoted from his letters in Knox's notebooks *e.g.*:

> '17 Oct 1915: I had not with me sufficient force to lift the flag [at the Rath of Feerwore]'.

In some photographs uniformed constables appear to have been used to give a sense of scale (Plate 21).

Lyons' keen interest in field-archaeology and folklife was apparently appreciated by some of his colleagues who sent him their own observations which are transcribed by Knox from Lyons' letters:

> '1 Dec 1906: Encloses Sergt. Mc Evoy's account of Laurencetown mote in Co. Galway';
> '8 May 1913: I forward a 6 in. map of the Inishkea Islands and some rubbings which were taken for me by a comrade who spent last winter on these Islands [...] all these stones occur on North Island. I am told there are none on the South Island. All but the E stone occur on the shell mound near the SE coast of the N Island. It is not long since a scribed stone was destroyed [...] the islanders show names belonging to all three western provinces. They speak Gaelic with a corrupt pronunciation – probably owing to old Scandinavian influence. For instance they make de (properly "dyay") jay; and dia (properly "dyeea") jee-a. They say they can get a favourable wind whenever they want one. Their method is to put up on the strand a small trilithon of stones and blow through it in the direction from which they wish the wind, muttering an incantation the while. I have not been able to get the words of the incantation. A good many islanders emigrate to America and they congregate in the [United] States at Holyoke (I

Plate 21.
Photograph, dated 1915, of uniformed R.I.C. constables standing on an earthwork at Ballybride Co. Roscommon; here Lyons is using his colleagues to give a sense of scale. In the *Sites and Monuments Record* the earthwork is classified as a ringfort (O.S. 39).

Photo: Lyons Collection, N.U.I.Galway.

---

think Mass.) [...] If you have no great use for the map and rubbings perhaps you would be pleased to pass them on to someone who would make use of them'.[11]

BEGINNINGS OF THE 'ANTIQUARIAN CRAZE'

'Fate led me in 1897 to find an Ogham (pronounced Ouam) inscription. This led me into a connection with the late Sir John Rhys, Professor of Celtic at Oxford University – which diverted my attention from official advancement and made my antiquarian craze irresistible. I am the only man living who has found four Ogham inscriptions.' These few unembellished words by Lyons, written in 1953 to the son of his constabulary colleague H.R. Goulden, give the only surviving clue as to when he became interested in field archaeology, but even they imply that his 'antiquarian craze' had begun some time earlier. It is fascinating to speculate on the origin of this craze: perhaps 'the seeds of that interest which was later to blossom into such erudite devotion' were originally planted by Purcell, his mentor, during his employment as a farm-labourer at Fortwilliam, near Clonmel, Co. Tipperary. Lyons was born in Lisronagh which is situated in an area (described by Ó Néill in *The Golden Vale of Ivowen*) where 'one has only to observe the ruined castles and fortifications – and the sites of former castles and earlier earthen forts – to recognize how important it was all through the Middle Ages – Ardfinnan, Cahir, Lisronagh, Fethard, Kiltinan, Clonmel, Tickincor, Derrinlaur, Kilsheelan, Ballyglasheen, Ballyboe, Poulakerry, Ballydine, Ardcolum, Kilcash, Ballyneill, Carrick, Tibroughney, Oldcourt and Ballycaslane.' As these castles are situated within walking distance of Lisronagh, the young Patrick Lyons may have spent many hours wandering around the ruins and reliving their stories. Lisronagh Castle (Plate 22) was occupied by Ireton in 1650 during the Siege of Clonmel and his troops camped nearby in land owned by the O'Neill family; 'Johnny O'Sullivan, a fine local historian and contemporary and friend of Mr. Patrick Lyons, FRSAI said that about the year 1880 or so, when he was around 18, he was digging a pond for cattle in the Big Paddock within the area of the campsite and they dug up thousands of sea shells – oysters he called them, but from the description they were probably mussels. If they were part of the provisions Cromwell's troops had brought from winter quarters in Youghal or even came up along the supply route later on, it's no wonder that they had little stomach for the fight at Clonmel'.[12] Lyons, then also around 18 years of age, if not actually present, must surely have heard of this 'archaeological dig' and grasped how archaeology can combine with history to paint a more comprehensive picture. Perhaps it was here that Lyons' passion for archaeology began.

ASSOCIATION WITH HUBERT T. KNOX

In his letter to Goulden Lyons records that he 'had been a correspondent of H.T. Knox of Ballinrobe for 22 years'. Knox, who had joined the British Civil Service in Madras, India in 1868 and attained the position of judge there, had been forced by ill-health to resign his post. He returned to Ireland to devote himself to the study of archaeology. Knox's family home was Cranmore House, Ballinrobe where his father was 'a wealthy landlord and owned a large part of the town'. Unfortunately, it has not been possible to establish when Knox returned to Ireland or for how long he remained here or whether he traveled frequently between Ballinrobe and his English residence. Knox had been elected a Fellow of the Royal Society of Antiquaries of Ireland in 1896 (and was its Vice-President from 1907-10 and again in 1918-9); his postal address, as recorded in the periodic listing of Members and Fellows in their *Journal*, places him at Beechen, Lyndhurst, Hants. in 1896; Westover House, Bitton, Bristol from 1899–1912; and

Plate 22.
Photograph of Lisronagh Castle as published in *The Golden Vale of Ivowen* (2001). A 16th century tower house, it was occupied by Ireton in 1650 during the Siege of Clonmel.

at Rivershill, St. George's Road, Cheltenham in 1914. Archived with other Knox/Lyons material in the library of the Royal Society of Antiquaries of Ireland are several letters from Knox (at his Bristol address) to Cochrane and Westropp, at dates from 1901-1911, in which he acknowledges Lyons photographic and field-work. The extent of the work which Lyons undertook on Knox's behalf is, however, probably best exemplified by the telling remark in Knox's obituary: 'in spite of increasing suffering he worked indefatigably, and his papers on Galway History and Topography are the more remarkable when one reflects that these were written several hundred miles away from the places they describe'.

So it would seem that Lyons' association with Knox commenced around 1897 or 1898; unfortunately, it has not been possible to establish whether their first meeting preceded or post-dated Lyons' discovery of the Ogham stone at Island, Ballyhaunis in 1897 which he reported to Rhys and Cochrane. If Lyons had accidentally discovered the Ogham it seems likely that he would have looked to the nearest well-known antiquarian for advice about its significance; as the Knox residence at Cranmore is some 20 miles distant from Ballyhaunis, Knox would seem an obvious choice. However, it is tempting to speculate that Lyons had previously met Knox and mentioned his interest in archaeology and that Knox may have suggested that Lyons' occupation as a constable patrolling the countryside would put him in an ideal position to discover new Ogham stones. It seems evident from articles in the *Journal of the Royal Society of Antiquaries of Ireland* in 1895 and 1896, for instance, that the identification of Ogham stones was exercising many minds. Knox revealed his own interest in 1898 when he published 'Note in reference to the Breastagh Ogham' in which he gave details regarding possible identifications of the ancestors of Cairbre (to whom the stone was inscribed) which he extracted from O'Donovan's *Hy Fiachrach*. In the previous year Macalister had published *Studies in Irish Epigraphy* in which he included the Breastagh ogham declaring that 'this magnificent monument is remarkable as being the only known Ogham inscription in West Connacht';[13] perhaps this was the spur for Lyons' quest.

LYONS' OGHAM DISCOVERIES

As references to ogham stones commence on the first page of the earliest surviving notebook in which Knox quotes from Lyons' letter of 5 September 1905: 'Near Tullaghan Ogham is a fort with a children's burying ground called Laghty', it seems possible that the (presumed) earlier notebook may have

Plate 23.
Ogham stone discovered by Lyons in June 1906 in the foundation of Kilmannin church. The photograph was taken when he had raised the ogham stone and placed it about 20 ft. north of the church.

Photo: Lyons Collection, N.U.I.Galway.

contained details of the discovery of the Island Ogham (1897) and also the Tullaghane Ogham (1900). Details of the Lyons' third ogham discovery are first quoted on 8 June 1906:

> 'I have found, today, in the foundation of Kilmannin church, a stone bearing an ogham inscription. The stone is about 4½ ft. long and it is lying on its side in middle of the foundations of the side wall of the church nearest the North. It is about midway in the foundation from E to W and I believe you will be able to make it out in the photo print of the site. The stone is about 8 in. thick and there is only about a foot of it above the ground so that it is possible some of the inscription is covered. I have wired Professor Rhys. I made only a hurried examination of the stone'.

Further details relating to the ogham (Plate 23) are recorded by Knox from Lyons' letters during the next six months:

> '17 June: Mr. Henry of Ballyhaunis is owner of land and will put fence around Kilmannin Ogham Stone which has been raised and placed standing about 20 ft. N of the church';
> '29 June: Encloses Professor Rhys's card and reading of Ogham';
> '24 November: Kilmannin Ogham given to Museum';
> '1 December: Professor Rhys now reads the Kilmannin Ogham as "Lugaddon Mongai Lugedee" and "Ddisi Maqui Se la/bo". With reference to the last word of the second inscription I beg to say that in Munster the old people used to speak of putting a child to bed as "putting him (or her) to Sheebo".* This parental name, like the one on the Island Ogham seems feminine in one of the readings, like modern Sheela'.[14]

Lyons' continuing search for Oghams is documented by Knox in notebooks 1 and 2:

> '6 Jan 1907: I hear a rumour that another Ogham has been got at Scaurdhaun (waterfall) near Claremorris';
> '17 May 1907: There was a castle at Annagh [...] my visit to this place led me

---

* Many years later Lyons wrote a paper entitled 'Shee-Boo' which was published in *Béaloideas*, the journal of the Folklore of Ireland Society in 1943, in which he notes that this expression seems to be a corruption and shortening of Sidhe Bobh Dhearg, the Land of the Celtic God of Sleep . "Even yet, women lulling children to sleep may be heard chanting impromptu melodies based on continuous repetitions of the syllables "ha-boo" (evidently a variant of "shee-boo"), substituting the reputed residence of the God of Sleep for the god himself'.[15]

Plate 24.
Standing stone at Coolnaha, Ballyhaunis c.1907 described by Lyons as an 'Ex-Ogham' stone ie. the scores had been chipped off. He notes that 'the people say that these were exactly the same as the scores on the Island ogham stone with is in full view two miles SSW'.

Photo: Lyons Collection, N.U.I.Galway.

Fig. 7.
Page from Knox's notebook in which he transcribes Lyons' description of the finding of the Ogham stone at Rusheen West and his drawing of the inscription.

Plate 25.
Photograph taken in June 1908 after Lyons had re-erected the Kilmovee Ogham stone on the 'little stone-faced mound beside the decaying sacred bush' which he considers may have been its original location.

Photo: Lyons Collection, N.U.I.Galway.

to examine again the small pillar stone in an earthen ring [in Coolnaha] on the height over the castle site. It is an "Ex-Ogham" stone (Plate 24), that is, the scores have been chipped off it. A series of four strokes remained on it till about 8 or 10 years ago. The people say that these were exactly the same as the scores on the Island stone which is in full view two miles SSW';

7 June 1908 "I beg to report my fourth, perhaps my fifth, Ogham (Fig.7). I found it today in the townland of Rusheen West about 300 yds N of Kilmovee old church at Thubber-na-Bachaille, the well of the (bishop's) staff. There is a Dhouach built around the well and the stone is laid on the top as coping at the W side. I did not stir the stone & more scores may exist beneath; the stone is about 6 ft. long 15 in. wide and about the same thickness'

'16 June 1908: I got it [the Kilmovee ogham] up on the little stone-faced mound beside the decaying sacred bush (Plate 25). This may be its proper location'.[16]

ASSOCIATION WITH SIR JOHN RHYS

In his letter to Goulden Lyons mentions his correspondence with Sir John Rhys, who acknowledges Lyons' field-work in several of his publications on ogham discoveries; it seems likely that it was Knox who introduced them. Rhys was

Professor of Celtic at Jesus College, Oxford from 1897-1915; he was keenly interested in early inscriptions, especially Ogham, in the decipherment of which he was regarded as an authority. It is clearly evident in his publications that Rhys appreciated the accuracy of Lyons' field-work and his well-considered interpretations. He first mentions Lyons in 1898: 'Soon after my return from Ireland this summer an Oxford friend of mine Mr. G.W. Norton, who visits the county of Mayo from time to time, and always keeps a sharp look-out for antiquities, brought me a photograph of the Bracklaghboy Stone [also known as the Island ogham, in which townland it is situated]. It had been taken by Sergeant Lyons of the Royal Irish Constabulary Force and the latter with Mr. Augustine Crean, son of Dr. Crean, Windsor Villa, Ballyhaunis, afterwards visited the stone for me, and I have had a report of it made by the Sergeant'.

Three years later, Lyons is credited with the discovery of an Ogham stone at Tullaghane which Rhys later came to inspect: 'This monument of antiquity was discovered in April 1900 by Sergeant Lyons, of Ballyhaunis, who subsequently took a photograph of it. My host drove me to the spot on Easter Monday. Sergeant Lyons led the way on his bicycle and we were joined by Mr. Austin Crean of Ballyhaunis. These two gentlemen had the stone partly buried in the ground for some time so as to kill the lichen on it but the treatment was only partially successful – probably some lichens are longer lived than others. When we visited the stone it had been set up again, for which I had reason to feel thankful, seeing that no sooner had we reached the spot than we had a heavy shower of the usual kind in April, which made the task of deciphering the writing all the more difficult [...] It is remarkable that there is so little known about the stone and its surroundings: but Sergeant Lyons thinks that the explanation is to be found in a change of population, the earlier inhabitants having been replaced by men from distant localities. He goes so far as to say that a re-settlement of the lands around the place was going on as late as the beginning of the last century, or even later, by men from Ulster and Munster; and as a proof of some such a displacement, he mentions the comparative scarcity of regular Connaught proper names in the neighbourhood. On top of this comes the extinction there of the Irish language, which is nearly complete; however, he has elicited from an old man, John Comber, living closeby, and aged about seventy, that he was the first to till the land in this part of the townland, and that in the days of his youth all the place around where the stone is was moor and bog'.

In 1907 Rhys describes the discovery of the Kilmannin Ogham stone: 'Last Summer, Sergeant Lyons, of Ballyhaunis, wrote to me announcing his discovery of an Ogam-inscribed stone at Kilmannin, near that centre. He sent me rubbings,

Plate 26.
Undated photograph of the Island (Bracklaghboy) Ogham Stone.

Photo: Lyons Collection, N.U.I.Galway.

facsimiles and photographs of the stone and its lettering; but it was evident from the first that it was a very difficult stone to read, and even to comprehend the legend on it. So when I happened to be in Dublin at the beginning of September last, I made a hurried excursion to Ballyhaunis, where I was met by Sergeant Lyons [...] with regard to the description of the stone and the locality I think it best to give it in Sergeant Lyons's own words'.[17]*

ACKNOWLEDGMENT OF OGHAM DISCOVERIES BY OTHER ANTIQUARIANS

It seems most likely that it was Knox who put Lyons in contact with other antiquarians recording ogham finds at the time. Robert Cochrane credits Lyons with the finding of the Island Ogham, (which Cochrane also identifies as the

---

* Attempts to establish if correspondence between Lyons and Rhys is extant have proved unsuccessful: a considerable corpus of Rhys' papers is archived in the National Library of Wales, Aberystwyth, including a substantial group of items concerning early (especially Ogham) inscriptions, together with correspondence with scholars in Britain, Ireland and continental Europe, but unfortunately, this collection has not been catalogued and so is not available for consultation.[18]

Bracklaghboy Stone): 'It was brought to notice by Sergeant Lyons, of the Royal Irish Constabulary now stationed at Ballyhaunis, an unusually intelligent and well-informed man, who in the most praiseworthy manner has, during his limited spare moments, turned his attention to the objects of archaeological interest in his neighbourhood. I am indebted to him for the photograph of the stone from which the accompanying illustration has been prepared'.

Almost a century later the stone at Island is again brought to notice: Peter Harbison suggests that some of the Ogham stones found at sites with no religious connections 'may possibly have been erected by a pilgrim somewhere near his house to commemorate a pilgrimage undertaken to a cult centre some distance away, in the same way that Moslems today in certain parts of the Islamic world indicate on their house-fronts that they have undertaken the pilgrimage to Mecca' and notes that 'the Ogham stone at Island (Bracklaghboy) is located on a hillock where it has a fine view of Croagh Patrick'. (Plate 27).

Plate 27.
Photograph of the Island Ogham in 2005. The pointed summit of Croagh Patrick can be seen on the horizon just above the pillar stone.

Photo: Michael Kelly, Island, Ballyhaunis.

Plate 28.
Photograph (unfortunately, not very clear) taken in June 1908 of the Kilmovee Ogham in which children can be seen sitting on it. On this day Lyons organised the removal of the ogham from its finding place (a low wall surrounding a well dedicated to St. Mobhi) and its re-erection nearby (see Plate 25).

Photo: Lyons Collection, N.U.I.Galway.

In 1917 Macalister acknowledged Lyons' discovery of the ogham stone at 'Rushens, [sic.] Co. Mayo [which] has so far escaped publication, though its existence has been known for several years. It is one of those of which the discovery lies to the credit of Sergeant Lyons of Athenry. I have not yet seen it, but give the following reading from a rubbing and photograph that Sergeant Lyons has kindly put at my disposal'.

In his *Corpus Inscriptionum Insularum Celticarum*, published in 1945, Macalister credits Lyons again with the finding of this ogham stone and comments that Lyons 'also found all the other known inscriptions in this [Costello] Barony'[19].*

---

*   A competitive element in the hunt for new ogham stones is hinted by Lyons many years later in a letter to the Irish Folklore Commission: 'I found my first ogham forty-four years ago. I have found four of these stones and no one else has found as many. Dr. Macalister is a sort of rival, for he has found a whole lot of oghams in one bunch in a cave'; presumably this is a reference to the finding of 6 inscribed lintels in a souterrain in Knockshanawee, Co. Cork in 1911.[20]

Gerry Cribbin, a local historian from Ballyhaunis, notes that when discovered by Lyons the Kilmovee ogham stone (as he refers to the ogham discovered in Rusheen West townland) was built into a low wall surrounding a 'well' dedicated to St Mobhi (Plate 28); 'it appears that McAlister [sic.] deciphered the inscription and later Sgt. Lyons re-erected the stone beside the wall (see Plate 25) with the help of some local men, where it stands to this day'.[21] The value of local knowledge is clearly evident in this instance and points up a problem often encountered in the cataloguing of the Lyons Photographic Collection: inconsistency in nomenclature. Frequently, a popular local name is used in describing a monument instead of the townland name and more than one name is used on different occasions to refer to the same monument.

Lyons' correspondence with antiquarians continued over decades. Knox's papers in the *Journal of the Royal Society of Antiquaries of Ireland* and the *Journal of the Galway Archaeological and Historical Society* contain many veiled references to the extent of field-work done by Lyons. His contribution to archaeology was recognized by the Royal Society of Antiquaries of Ireland who made him a Member in 1905, a Fellow in 1920 and a Life Member in 1953.

LYONS' CONTRIBUTION TO KNOX'S PUBLISHED WORKS

Notes on the Diocese of Tuam, Killala and Achonry (1904) may be the earliest of Knox's publications to include research undertaken by Lyons. Knox begins by stating that 'no history of these dioceses has yet been published, except for Mr. O.J. Burke's *History of the Catholic Archbishops of Tuam*, which is limited in accordance with its title. These notes are intended to show how they assumed their present form and who worked in them in early days and to be of assistance and foundation for whoever may undertake to write their history. In that respect their utility is limited, but as far as they go I hope that they will prove trustworthy. They are published in their present form because they would probably never be published if they were held back to be completely recast and are, even so, better than no history at all. They extend over the three dioceses because the information was collected during the study of the early history of the county of Mayo and not with the object of writing their history'.

The book, which contains no photographs, begins with the life and times of St. Patrick and the early Irish church, then follows the establishment of the diocesan system and details the state of affairs in each diocese up to the 16th century. In the absence of the (presumed) earliest Knox notebook, it can only be

Plate 29.
Cross-inscribed pillar stone at Kildun, Ballycroy, Co. Mayo c.1917. Lyons notes that the stone which is on a low, partly ruined elliptical platform measures about 6'x 1'3" x 9" and that the cross faces ENE; that it is said to have had an Ogham inscription, which 'some gentlemen shooting there had chiseled off about 60 years ago'. In the *Sites and Monuments Record* the monuments listed at this site comprise a mound, a cross-inscribed pillar, an inscribed stone, possible cairn(s), and 2 buildings (O.S. 44).

Photo: Lyons Collection, N.U.I.Galway.

---

speculated that Lyons worked in providing background information for this publication, as the extant notebooks record similar observations by Lyons on ancient roads and ecclesiastical architecture. Regarding ancient roads, Knox notes 'Tochar Phatraic is a very ancient pilgrims' road from the east to Croagh Patrick back to Drum [...] I have not been able to trace the course east of Balla, but feel sure it must have passed by Kiltamagh and Cloonpatrick and Patrick's Well to Balla'; significantly, on page 3 of the earliest notebook, dated 15 October 1905, Knox quotes from Lyons' letter: 'there is what appears to be an ancient pass over the hill about 400 yds. E' [of Slieve Dart, which itself is approx 20 miles east of Balla] followed 13 pages later by 'Sends 2 maps. The Pass over Slieve Dart, summary of information in letters, sent to Archb[ishop of] Tuam on 22 Feb. A probable route is marked in red'. On 26 March 1906, the long convoluted passage (here abbreviated) quoted by Knox from Lyons' letter, records his painstaking efforts to uncover all possible traces of the saint's route:

'After leaving Kilruddhaun St. Patrick must have come on to Aughamore via

Urlaur. He could not have come via Erritt because the country between Kilruddhaun and Erritt was then a morass probably impassable even by kerne [...] for about 6 miles from near Crossbeg to Killunagher bogs and morasses stretched without a break thus barring the way towards Ballyhaunis and the Apostle must have crossed the Lung abor (? H.T.K.) near Cloonroe ('row' as in the word meaning quarrel) and struck the old road northward at the junction now called Bonese's Cross near the W end of Urlaur L. (Loughnanoge). This would bring him by Cartron North a little S of Boleybeg [...] if he had come north by Erritt he would have struck B[ally]haunis region before the Aughamore side. If he did not go S at Bonese's Cross he must either have gone by Kilkelly or by another road a few miles S which is parallel to the Kilkelly road – that is by Cappagh and Raith branching W at Clooncan. It is doubtful if the old road from Raith castle to Aughamore church is of Patrician antiquity. If it is the Apostle may have used it – that is if he came by Kilkelly or Cappagh. If he came by Kilkelly he may have come by a track coinciding with the present road from Kilkelly to Aughamore. A track in ancient times led directly southwards by Carrowneden and it was amplified into a road some years ago. It met the continuation of the main road from Urlaur in by Cartron S. (marked red in the map you have seen) on the shore of Island Lough. In a few days I shall be able to illustrate by maps what I mean'.

There are twenty further quotations in the notebooks which refer to ancient roads, the latest dated 26 August 1909.

Lyons' knowledge of placenames and local family names, often relating to ecclesiastical establishments, is quoted by Knox throughout the notebooks. In April – May 1908 (as usual interspersed with quotations on diverse topics) are what appear to be notes which Knox had previously sent to Lyons for correction and on-going discussion, commencing:

"Notes". List of Rectors and Vicars in Tuam D[iocese]. Kiltullagh. "Vagiwir", the vicar's name, seems to be Maguire. MacGeever is an alternative. I cannot trace any of them around here, but Maguire is a common name. The rector was probably related to the vicar. The name seems to be the same as vicar's.

> BEKAN. There are Kilduffs yet in Bekan Pa[rish] I believe the only place where they occur around here.
> AUGHAMORE. The family name, Henry, is common in Aughamore and scarcely anywhere else. Some of the handsomest young women I have seen belong to a Henry family in B[ally]haunis'.

The last quotation from Lyons' letters relating to these "Notes" records that 'the

Plate 30.
Tubberkevna, Kiltamagh, Co. Mayo c.1910. Lyons notes that the original ancient well, situated nearby, 'having run dry a curate got its sanctity transferred to this, a mere drainage pit'; he draws attention to the modern offerings of pins etc in the niche. 'Tubber Kevna' is named in Lisnamaneeagh townland on O.S. 80. In the *Sites and Monuments Record* ecclesiastical remains, holy well and cross are listed at this site.

Photo: Lyons Collection, N.U.I.Galway.

Plate 31.
Photograph, dated 1916, described by Lyons as 'St. Dominic's well in Cahergal, 2 miles from Newport, Co Mayo. The affair is a mere retaining basin on the top of a hill. It is in what appears to be a ruined rath which seems to have contained 2 caves […] the retentive nature of the soil created a "well" in the sou[terrain]. Then this well got a reputation of holiness by association with a sepulchral cave […] it is called St. Dominic's Well, probably a priestly parrotism for Tobar na Dhabhach, Vat Well'. In the *Sites and Monuments Record* it is classified as a cashel (O.S. 67).

Photo: Lyons Collection, N.U.I.Galway

last syllable of Clooncan is pronounced like the English word "can". Ceann = a head'.

Included in the Knox/Lyons papers in the library of the Royal Society of Antiquaries of Ireland is a set of two notebooks in which Knox describes 176 ecclesiastical sites and castles (with accompanying negative numbers dating from 5 June 1899 to 4 September 1908). The first notebook begins: 'Notes on Archaeological Photographs – As far as my information goes I follow the method of description adopted by Mr. T.J. Westropp in his paper on the Churches of County Clare, Proceedings of R.I. Academy 3rd Series vol. vi. No.1, p.100. Those marked R. have been accepted for the collection of the R.S.A.I. or at least for choice'. The second notebook ends with a catalogue of some 400 negatives, following a sequence of folio numbers (with many gaps in the sequence) which are not in date order but relate to the site descriptions, followed by the note that 'all subjects are in the County Mayo, unless otherwise marked. X means that a print has been sent to the R.S.A.I. collection. But many Bromides were sent up when I thought that Platinomatte prints were considered permanent. Also I sent batches for the keeper to choose such as seemed suitable for the collection. 1 July 1918 H.T. Knox'.[22]

It seems possible, given Knox's opening statement regarding the limited utility of his *Notes on the Diocese of Tuam, Killala and Achonry* but of their being a 'foundation for whoever may undertake to write their history', that in this set of two notebooks Knox had re-arranged some of the information already acquired for *Notes on the Diocese of Tuam, Killala and Achonry*. By including extra information later provided by Lyons, he was preparing for publication a paper on the churches of Co. Mayo and the origin of the ecclesiastical divisions in that county, as Westropp had done for Co. Clare.

※

Knox's next publication was 'Notes on gig-mills and drying kilns near Ballyhaunis, County Mayo' in the 1906-7 edition of *Proceedings of the Royal Irish Academy*, in which Lyons work is evident throughout. Both horizontal and vertical waterpowered grain mills have been in use in Ireland since the 7th century. The excellence of their construction has been noted and some incidents in the lives of the saints imply that their erection was the task of specialized millwrights. The horizontal-wheeled mill consisted of a 2-storey wooden wheelhouse, the lower section of which contained the timber wheel while the millstones were on the upper floor. Water from a fast-flowing stream was directed into a hollowed-out wooden flume or chute. This was splayed internally, ensuring that a water jet of sufficient pressure was directed onto the dished vanes or paddles of the wheel forcing the water-wheel, which was mounted on a cup-shaped pivot stone, to rotate. A timber drive connected the wheel directly to the upper millstone i.e. no gearing was involved. Hence, every turn of the wheel resulted in a corresponding turn of the millstone. In vertically-wheeled mills the driveshaft is set horizontally resulting in indirect power transmission to the millstones i.e. right-angled gearing is needed which gives the advantage of adjusting millstone speeds according to the power of the stream. In the early 17th century vertical-wheeled mills became the dominant type. However, Lyons' discovery of working horizontal mills in the Ballyhaunis region in 1906 and that most of the existing vertical mills were known to have originally been of the horizontal type graphically illustrates the continuation of structural design for almost 1500 years of milling history.[23]

Included in Knox/Lyons material archived in the library of the Royal Society of Antiquaries of Ireland is a letter dated 6.12.1905 from Knox, (then resident in Bristol) to Cochrane, which reflects the extent of Lyons' work for this paper and the regard in which Knox held him: 'the photographs which accompany this are taken from negatives belonging to Sergeant Lyons or were printed by him. I have sent them up though not always very good to show the class of monuments etc. mentioned – when able to do so I will send Platinotype prints of some of these and of others for the Photog[raphic] Collection. Sergeant Lyons is a very keen antiquarian, but has unfortunately not had opportunities of book study or meeting antiquaries. We have been in correspondence this year and he has written to me the descriptions which I have embodied in the typewritten notes etc. I suggested sending you a report of his finds, but he has no time to work them out and asked me to do some from his letters, which I have done and here are the results – which he has seen – Ballyhaunis is a rich region of antiquities. He has discovered also Gig Mills actually at work. Mr. O'Reilly's article in Proc R.I.A. XXIV C, p. 55 treats them as extinct, that is the horizontal water wheel. A photograph which Sergeant Lyons has sent me shows such a wheel as is figured there. As far as books now at hand with me and our volumes show, they seem to have been forgotten or ignored, if still in use elsewhere. He is getting me full descriptions'.

Knox echoes these words at the commencement of this paper: 'Mr. O'Reilly's article on "Ancient Water Mills" in the Proceedings of the Royal Irish Academy, vol. xxiv., Section C., p. 55, treats of the horizontal water-wheel as no longer in use in Ireland [...] as the tendency is to convert them into vertical wheel mills, and as they are likely to be extinct soon, I have here put together information which has been given me from County Mayo' and then describes in detail the mills of William Flatley (Plate 32) and Patrick Gannon (and their associated drying-kilns). In the first pages of Knox's earliest extant notebook are many transcriptions from Lyons' letters about his discoveries of mills and milling artefacts, perhaps implying that the (presumed) earlier notebook also contained details; Knox's notebook contains 24 transcripts from Lyons' letters dating from 22.11.05 to 9.7.06.

Plate 32.
Wheel of Flatley's gig-mill at Cullentra, near Ballyhaunis c.1906. In the *Sites and Monuments Record* a horizontal watermill is listed in Cullentra townland (O.S. 92).

Photo: Lyons Collection, N.U.I.Galway.

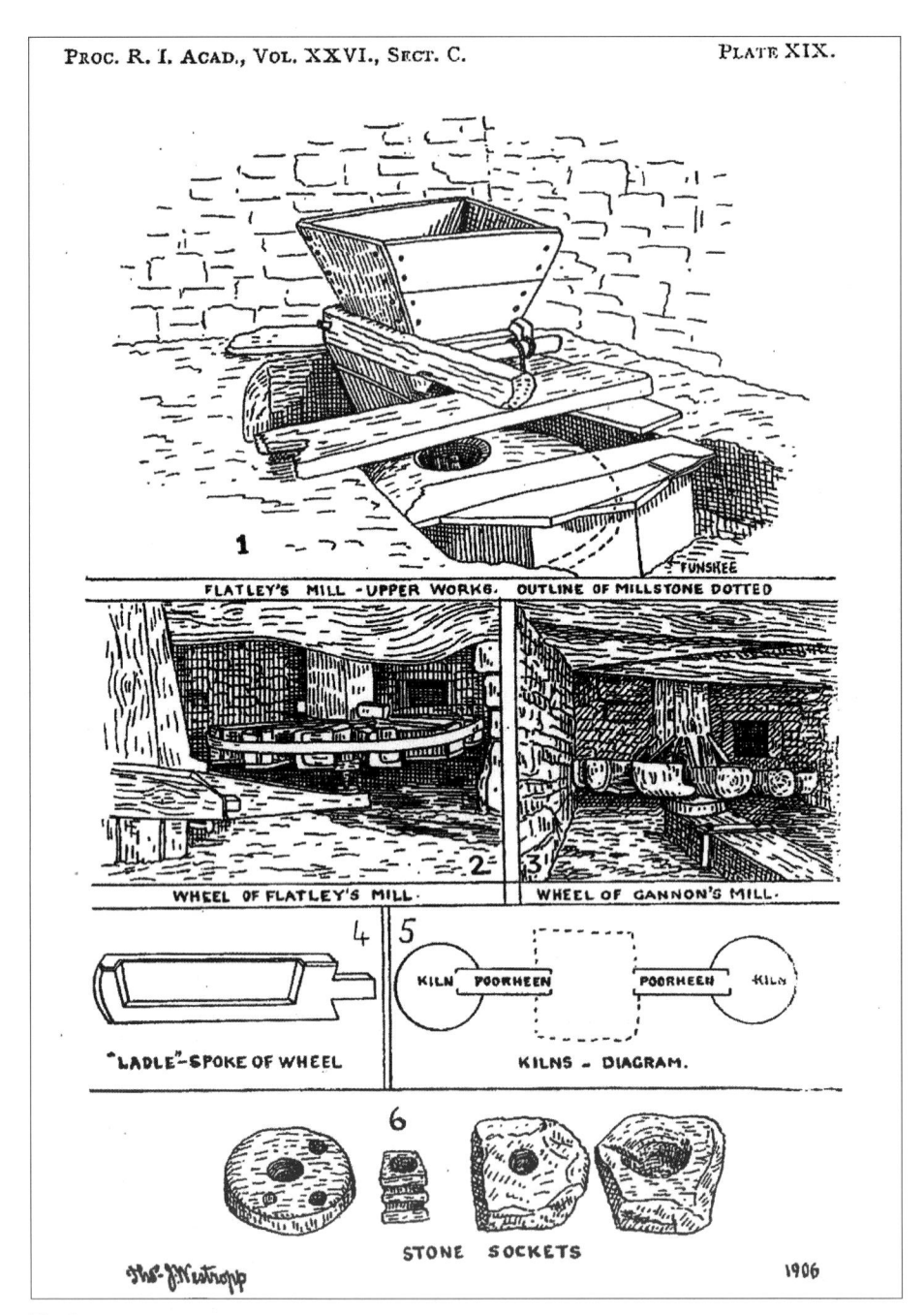

Fig. 8.
Drawing executed by Westropp to illustrate Knox's paper 'Notes on gig-mills and drying kilns near Ballyhaunis, County Mayo' as published in *Proceedings of the Royal Irish Adademy* 1906-7.

Plate 33.
Photograph c.1907 described by Lyons as 'under millstone near site of ancient mill at Kilgrariff Brook, a tributary stream of Flatley's mill'. In the *Sites and Monuments Record* an enclosure and millstone are listed (O.S. 92).

Photo: Lyons Collection, N.U.I.Galway.

Plate 34.
Photograph c.1907 described by Lyons as the back of a millstone in Dhine Brook; he identifies the men as B. Cunnane and B. Kerins.

Photo: Lyons Collection, N.U.I.Galway.

References are made to other mills brought to Knox's attention by Lyons: on 26 Jan 1906 Knox records that:

> '[Lyons] forwards bucket of a gig mill made by Michael Costello of Brickeens, whose mill is on infant river Robe, whereof I have a photo. This is a correct copy of the buckets used formerly in the maker's mill. Unlike the buckets of Gannon's mill the bottom is horizontal. The sloping bottom is only a refinement as the buck[et] runs away – as it were – from the water'.

Other milling artifacts given by Lyons to Knox include:

> 'a stone which is perhaps the socket of a gig mill shaft. I got it – on loan only – from Tom Freely (Pat) of Scregg. It has been in his family for generations but all idea of its use has been lost';
> 'a stone pivot of the spindle of an ordinary breast wheel mill which was in use until about 20 years ago when it was replaced by iron. The stone was in use for about 20 years. The spindle is the vertical rod which is attached to the upper stone in these mills. It receives motion from the crown wheel. The pinion at the base of the spindle in this particular mill is a curious affair'.

Twenty-four photographs taken by Lyons of mills and millstones survive in the Lyons Collection in N.U.I.Galway.

Knox, however, notes Lyons' dissatisfaction with the quality of some of the negatives:

> 'I send you some negatives of millstones. They are badly done but I can "cob it again" [sic.]. There are several more to be taken'.

Regardless of quality, Knox realized that no photograph could adequately illustrate the intricate parts and workings of these mills and kilns. Instead, his article is illustrated by superb line-drawings executed by Westropp (Fig. 8), which include diagrammatic plans of the kilns, drawings of the individual mill apparatus, together with reconstructions of the mill wheels.[24]

The Lyons Collection in N.U.I.Galway contains a fine photograph (Plate 35) described by Lyons as 'an ancient gig mill dug up in a bog near Bagnelstown, Co. Carlow. Right hand spout throws water direct. Left hand one at angle across it to strike wheel at the same place. Left hand one throws parallel with beam. Reconstructed in field. Great beams sawn in two for lifting. Photo by Denis Pack-Beresford, Fenagh Hse, Bagnelstown, shortly before 1909'. This is the only

Plate 35.
Photograph c.1918 taken by Denis Pack-Beresford which Knox describes as 'an ancient gig mill dug up in a bog near Bagnelstown, Co. Carlow. Right hand spout throws water direct. Left hand one at angle across it to strike wheel at the same place. Left hand one throws parallel with beam. Reconstructed in field. Great beams sawn in two for lifting'. This is the only photograph in the collection in N.U.I.Galway that is attributed to someone other than Lyons.

Photo: Lyons Collection, N.U.I.Galway.

---

photograph in the collection in N.U.I.Galway that is attributed to someone other than Lyons.*

The publication of Knox's paper on gig mills appears to have been a cause of concern to Lyons: his anxiety about being 'outed' as a covert archaeologist is

---

* Corlett bases a short article entitled 'Milling around Bagnelstown' around this photograph, a copy of which is in the Lyons/Knox collection in the library of the Royal Society of Antiquaries of Ireland. He notes that 'the photograph accompanied a letter addressed to Lord Walter Fitzgerald at Kilkea Castle, Co. Kildare, dated 23 March 1909. The letter is signed by Denis P. Beresford, who may have been the photographer'.[25]

reflected in Knox's comment in his notebook regarding Lyons' letter of 1 February 1906:

> 'Particularly asks me to omit his name from all I write on antiquities, prefers it should not appear in any way'.

This seems a strange request as Lyons' contributions to archaeology had already been attributed by Cochrane in 1898 and Rhys in 1901. We can only presume that Lyons was concerned, solely, that his name should not appear in publications by Knox because Lyons' work is later acknowledged by Rhys, Orpen, Macalister, and Westropp, seemingly without protest.[26] It is interesting to speculate that Lyons' anxiety may have been related to the fact that in Knox's papers details of his field-work were being published alongside Lyons' opinions and speculations which, though accepted by Knox, differed, sometimes substantially, from currently accepted published theories.

Knox acquiesced, but why would he not? He must have been very grateful to have a colleague to provide him with detailed measurements, descriptions, interpretations and photographs, especially in the failing health of his later years. His collaboration with Lyons continued for the next 13 years, during which time a further 18 papers written by Knox, which acknowledge field-work and photographs by 'my friend the Field Antiquary', 'my indefatigueable colleague' etc., were published: 7 papers in the *Journal of the Royal Society of Antiquaries of Ireland* and 11 papers in the *Journal of the Galway Archaeological and Historical Society*. Their final joint paper 'Notes on the Burgus of Athenry' was published in 1920 in the same edition of the *Journal of the Galway Archaeological and Historical Society* which includes Knox's obituary notice. With the exception of papers describing Tooloobaun castle, the castle and burgus at Kilcolgan, the church ruins at St. Marchan's lough, and the monuments in the medieval town of Athenry, the papers attempt to describe and classify earthworks in the counties of Mayo, Roscommon and Galway, focusing particularly on the Rathcroghan complex.

When reading these papers, in many of which Knox returns again and again to points made in earlier papers, sometimes to elaborate his theories, sometimes to change his opinion, perhaps the *caveats* which he (occasionally) includes should be borne in mind *e.g.* ' these speculations are based on but little evidence, and should be taken as only suggestions of theory which may lead others to find evidence in support or disproof'.[27] It is difficult at this distance in time (and space) from Knox to appreciate his early twentieth century antiquarian delving in the fields of early Irish history and mythology and his (sometimes) far-fetched inclusion of aspects of these with Lyons' archaeological investigations in order to prove his theories. It is easy to get lost in the labyrinthine style of writing in which he heaps up comparisons and allusions in an attempt to prove his point, often without drawing all the strands together into a recognisably cohesive entity. Three mains strands of Knox's opinions (often enmeshed) emerge: the origin of mottes; the sepulchral or ceremonial nature of earthworks; racial theories regarding the builders of field monuments.

KNOX'S THEORY ON THE ORIGIN OF MOTTES

With the publication of his paper, 'The Croghans and some Connaught Raths and Motes' in 1911 Knox joined in the scholarly debate concerning the interpretation of 'motes' (now more usually known as 'mottes' *i.e.* round mounds, flattened on top, on which the Normans built their fortifications), a topic which had been polarising antiquarian opinion in the first decade of the last century. The theory proposed by Armitage, that 'moated hillocks' in England and southwest Scotland were Norman-built and that evidence from Ireland proved the same, had been challenged by Westropp who believed that an attempt to include Ireland in any such theory required local study combined with an ability to consult literary and historical sources; though accepting that some motes may have been built as late as Norman times, his own field-work combined with evidence from annalistic sources had shown that other 'motes were of early and possibly prehistoric date'. The debate was broadened when Orpen, who could range over the native sources with complete familiarity, entered the fray. However, though they studied the same sources, Westropp and Orpen came to different conclusions: Westropp interpreted the word 'mote' as being an Anglo-Norman name for any type of earthwork while Orpen believed that it applied in particular to a new kind of monument introduced by the Anglo-Normans. From his examination of early castle-sites and their records Orpen concluded, as Armitage had done with the British sites, that Irish motes were erected by Norman castle-builders, maintaining that if it was the case that they built on pre-existing 'motes' they would have occupied those parts of Ireland where these earthworks are found.

Knox begins his paper by admitting its 'second-hand' nature: 'the letter L in certain places denotes that I am indebted for the descriptions and the plans, which have been drawn from his field notes and sketches to a friend who, I regret to say, does not allow his name to appear, and who has not had time to prepare for publication the notes which he has kindly been giving me for some years. Acquaintance with many high motes of Leinster and Munster and other earthworks there, led him to the study and understanding of these works, which, though less important, throw light on the history of this country. The frequency with which the letter occurs shows how deeply I am indebted to him. For the opinions I am responsible; but we agree substantially regarding almost everything and the words used regarding the works are often his own, with but trivial alteration'.

Lyons is attributed in 38 descriptions of raths and motes out of a total of 47 and he provided plans for 28 monuments; 7 of the 11 published photographs are included in the Lyons Collection at N.U.I.Galway.

In this long (and sometimes very convoluted) paper, Knox attempts to describe and classify earthworks as either 'croghans' i.e. sites for the inauguration of kings which may be also royal fortresses, 'raths' which he describes as 'earthworks of Pre-Norman dwelling-places, whether defensive or not' or 'motes' which are 'defensive earthworks which may be considered to owe their origin or present shape to the Norman settlers', while at the same time noting the similarities between them and the difficulty of definitive classification.

Knox's theories, based on Lyons' field-work, came in for immediate criticism from Goddard Orpen who claimed that in his paper 'Mr. Knox has animadverted on some views of mine with reference to the Norman theory of motes in Ireland [...] I imagine that anyone not well versed in the literature of the subject on first reading Mr. Knox's paper, would be apt to suppose that he differs profoundly from the views I have advocated, and has adduced some weighty considerations against them. But after reading his paper several times I have come to the conclusion that Mr. Knox, so far as he expresses a positive opinion, has substantially accepted the view which Mr. Round and Mrs. Armitage were the first to put forward somewhat tentatively, as regards motes in Ireland, and which I have since elaborated'. Orpen maintained that he was 'endeavouring to perform one of the primary duties of an antiquary, namely, to classify and distinguish objects which have some features in common, but which belong to very different periods of time and are the outcome of very different states of culture'. While asserting that he welcomed Knox's contribution to the subject Orpen qualified this by saying that 'Mr. Knox nowhere states his own views tersely or in words which I can easily quote, but I do not think I am misrepresenting him by stating it shortly as follows:- Rathcroghan, Emain Macha, Magh Adhair and Clogher are, I understand him to say, fortified mounds, and, though dating from prehistoric times, should be classed (along with Norman motes, from which they are essentially indistinguishable) as the earthworks of private castles'. Orpen concludes that Knox's false deduction that Norman mote-castles were no new military expedient had led him to the 'extraordinary suggestion with which he ends his paper, that the distribution of motes in Ireland, which (in any view) coincides almost precisely with the known area of early Norman domination, is to be explained by the hypothesis that the incoming Gaelic tribes, more than a millennium earlier, had erected these motes precisely where the Normans afterwards wanted them, and used them almost nowhere else'.

Orpen's barbed comment 'Now I think Mr. Knox cannot be familiar with the motes in early Norman districts, and cannot have noted the recurrent characteristics of the best-preserved examples, or he would not class the mound of Rathcroghan with them' throws obvious doubt on the value of second-hand notes: even though Knox's notebooks often refer to Lyons returning to re-check data, his interpretations of monuments were necessarily subjective and Knox seemingly accepted them too readily and without corroborating evidence. That Lyons may have been concerned is reflected in quotations by Knox from his letters *e.g.*:

> '8 Aug 1910: The ramparts on the S and E [of the mound at Killedmond] with the sloping angular platforms are quite clear and definite. As regards the central and northern portion the explanation I give is merely my theory, which I must ask you not to accept without caution, but the features are there and let who will interpret them'.[28]

Knox continued his attempts to categorise earthworks in his paper 'Seven Mayo earthworks' which was published in the 1911-2 edition of the *Journal of the Galway Archaeological and Historical Society*. Again, he refers obliquely to Lyons: 'these plans and descriptions have been prepared from field sketches and measurements and notes supplied me by a friend who has a wide experience of Irish earthworks. He has given the facts – I am responsible for the opinions here expressed'. It would be interesting to know if this article was submitted for publication before Knox's paper 'The Croghans and some Connaught Raths and Motes' was published in the *Journal of the Royal Society of Antiquaries of Ireland* (which also includes the critical reply by Orpen). Knox's unqualified acceptance of responsibility 'for the opinions

Plate 36.
Photograph c.1910 described by Lyons as the 'fortified homestead' at Portaghard; as Knox gives no details of its location it is not possible to identify this earthwork.

Photo: Lyons Collection, N.U.I.Galway.

---

here expressed' differs considerably from his earlier statement, 'for the opinions I am responsible; but we agree substantially regarding almost everything and the words used regarding the works are often his [Lyons] own, with but trivial alteration'; possibly Orpen's criticism of Knox's unfamiliarity with the 'motes in early Norman districts' may have influenced the change in wording.

Knox begins the article: 'Having brought to notice of this Society the "Norman" mote controversy and suggested that we should help in the study of our earthworks by recording their remains [...] I now offer my own contribution [...] The works are all of interest in some way and illustrate the variety of forms'. Knox describes seven very dissimilar monuments and attempts to classify them: Currykilleen mote is 'the type of Norman high mote and bailey castle but with important variations of Gaelic type'; Brees castle stands on 'an oblong hillock carved to shape [...] supported by a wall, of which only the inner skin remains, which was continued vertically by the walls of the platform and barbican. The castle walls may be said to begin at the foot of the mound'; Portaghard 'at south end of a ridge projecting into a lake – less a fort than a fortified homestead' (Plate 36); the moat at Balla ' consists of a slightly-raised garth of 200 ft. by 90 ft. and may be described as a "moated grange"; Raha whose 'general aspect is unlike works of Norman origin and differs essentially in that the mound and the large N enclosure are two separate works joined by a small enclosure of slight defensive value – this work might be classed as a "manor house"; Carrowkeel fort 'was cut out of a slightly elongated esker and consists of an oval-shaped mound which slopes to a ditch and rampart' but no classification of this monument is attempted. For these six earthworks detailed plans and sections have been drawn; there is no plan (or photograph) for the earthwork at Ballyhowley which 'having no apparent interest owing to so much being obliterated, is described because it shows how we may find remains illustrating early history in almost any situation. Here we have the modern house, the castle and the earlier mote, an orderly development'.[29]*

All 6 photographs which illustrate this paper are included in the Lyons Collection in N.U.I.Galway.

In 1914 Knox further elaborated his opinions on the origins of mottes in his paper 'The Ruins of Cruachain Ai', which 'may be taken as a continuation of the article on "The Croghans" etc, in the Journal [*of the Royal Society of Antiquaries of Ireland*] for 1911 [...] My friend had not then closely examined and measured the other works. The results of his subsequent labours are now given, showing that the works surrounding Rathcroghan are far more varied and interesting than any former mention of the region suggests' The paper, which Waddell notes 'even for its time is often less than illuminating', is based on Lyons' fieldwork and speculations in which Lyons tries imaginatively to re-create the landscape of the time.

Seemingly, the number and complexity of field-monuments in Rathcroghan allowed free-rein to a fertile imagination; surrounding the great circular mound

---

* Unfortunately, as Knox does not give exact locations for these monuments (or in some cases the townland name) it has not been possible to identify all of them and check their classification as recorded on the *Sites and Monuments Record* for Co. Mayo: the name 'Currykilleen' does not appear in the Index of Townlands; on O.S. 91 a castle is recorded in Brees townland; Portaghard townland is not listed in Co.Mayo. (Portagh townland is in Mayo O.S. 90/91 but no monument is recorded there in the *Sites and Monuments Record*); on O.S. 90 an enclosusre is listed in Balla townland; there is no Raha townland in Co. Mayo; on O.S. 101 an enclosure is listed in Carrowkeel townland; on OS. 92 an enclosure is recorded in Ballyhowley townland.

are 52 others which include pillar stones, burial mounds, earthworks with banks or platforms, linear earthworks forming avenues, enclosures with souterrains and a megalithic tomb.[30] In this paper Knox's theories regarding the origin of motes and their primary sepulchral or ceremonial usage (see below) become extremely entangled.

Lyons is attributed with 32 plans; 6 of the 38 published photographs are included in the Lyons Collection in N.U.I. Galway.

Knox's descriptions and classifications of the various field-monuments seem to be intended to further bolster up his original premise i.e. that the Normans built residential works on earlier mounds which were either ceremonial or sepulchral in origin. In his youth, Lyons would have seen some of the well-preserved Norman fortifications in Co. Tipperary and, later, when he developed his 'antiquarian craze' and studied available publications about them, apparently tried to see traces of these great structures in the field-monuments he was investigating in the west of Ireland. The topic of the 'Normanisation' of Mayo and Galway continues in quotations from Lyons' letters throughout Knox's notebooks:

> '26 Apr 1908: The enclosure close to N of older castle at Island is a flat mote and a rather fine one. It has two minor enclosures. This enclosure has perplexed me much for many years but my Roscommon and Tipperary experiences have enlightened me. The mote had a port to the lake, which washed its N rampart [...] Here as at Oran and Runnamoat the earthwork was constructed with a view to convenience of water and high ground was rejected. The same may be said to some extent of Barretstown, Co. Tipperary'.
>
> '1 Dec 1909: Can it be supposed that the Danes and Norwegians, the progenitors of the Normans, occupied a good deal of this country for upwards of two centuries without throwing up earthworks? Or can it be supposed they could have held the country without having done so'?
>
> '16 Sept 1910: It seems there is a cordon of Norman works around Balla mote, as at Ballyhaunis. I have particulars of a work probably Norman a mile N of the one near Balla which I described in my last [letter] [...] I believe I have "spotted" another small Norman work 250 yds. E of the Priory work, beyond the brook. This goes far to complete the cordon of minor works on the E but the series seems incomplete or rather wanting on the W of the Clare R[iver]'.

Lyons had been invited to become a member of the Royal Society of Antiquaries of Ireland in 1905, presumably in recognition of his successful discovery of four

Ogham stones. His success in contributing to archaeological knowledge in that field and his enthusiasm for archaeological conundrums perhaps inspired his attempts in the identification and dating of 'motes'. From the extant Knox notebooks we know that Lyons was considering this topic as early as 1907: on 24 March of that year Knox quotes from Lyons' letter:

> 'I visited today at Coolnaha – near the clochan – the ruin of a cashel or cashelesque rath which utilizes a circular hill. It is, in view of the Armitage-Orpen-Westropp discussion, a very illuminative antiquity'.

In later years Westropp was fulsome in his praise of such field-work: 'No local society has done more for field-work than that centred in the city of Galway. It is not in rivalry of its workers but rather to spread the knowledge of the important remains in their purview to antiquaries outside of Ireland (who may too easily overlook what has been done in this district) that I undertake this paper. Mr. Hubert T. Knox, Mr. E. Holt, Mr. Lyons, and Miss Matilda Redington have laid Irish archaeology under a debt of gratitude for what they have done. I had the great advantage of seeing several of the places here described under the guidance of the two latter antiquaries'.[31]

KNOX'S THEORIES ON THE ORIGINAL SEPULCHRAL/ CEREMONIAL NATURE OF EARTHWORKS

Knox's insistence that the Normans recycled monuments built by 'Gaelic tribes' of early or possibly prehistoric date is complicated by another aspect he brings to the argument. In his paper 'The Croghans and some Connaught Raths and Motes' he poses the question: 'Was every high mound made by the Gael originally sepulchral or ceremonial?' It is a topic to which Knox frequently returns in his later papers on earthworks. The quest to find the answer appears to have been behind every investigation Lyons made of each new earthwork he encountered. It seems possible that, before Lyons began forwarding details of his field-work and observations, Knox had impressed on him the importance of attempting to answer this question; whatever validity there may be in this assumption, this topic is recorded in quotations from Lyons' letters (often in obscure detail) throughout the four notebooks:

> '22 Nov 1905: NOTE CROSSBEG. In a former letter he mentioned that there is a true mote, sepulchral because much too small for residence, in this townland';

'8 Oct 1910: About 600 yds N of Rathcroghan are two works very distinctly Norman. I believe the mound called Rathcroghan was originally moulded on the top like Rathbeg and the other mound, and that its sepulchral character was ruined by invaders, probably Norman, who seem to have turned it to military or residential uses, & who were probably fired out later with great vehemence & great pains taken to obliterate their connection with this particular work'.

Lyons' 'labours' subsequent to the publication of 'The Croghans and some Connaught Raths and Motes', as quoted by Knox from Lyons' letters, illustrate the lack of clarity with which he reaches his conclusions *e.g.*:

'15 Nov 1911: I'm inclined to differentiate Rathmore of R[ath]croghan (Plate 37) from all the other works I know as it seems originally to have been a sepulchral mound like Rathveg and to have been later turned into a residential one. I am driven to this conclusion by the likeness between the conicality of its garth with same feature on the apse of Rathveg. Also it is hard to account for the ruined ridges on the slope of Rathmore, under the present rampart, by any other theory. They are very like the ruins of zonal rings on Rathveg [...] There is good reason to think that the rampart of Rathmore is merely an upper

Plate 37.
Rathmore at Rathcroghan c.1910 described by Lyons as showing the 'ancient gangway' (on the right) from NW.

Photo: Lyons Collection, N.U.I.Galway.

Plate 38.
Aerial photograph of Rathmore from north. The sloping entranceway is clearly visible on the left.
Photo: Department of Archaeology, N.U.I.Galway.

> sepulchral zonal trace or band which has been strengthened to afford a defence and that the traces on the sides of the work to S and E are the remains of similar lower bands'.[32]

In his second paper of 1914, 'Dumha Brosna', Knox begins with the throw-away remark that this field-monument 'might be described carelessly as a somewhat injured high mote and bailey rather than a sepulchral monument'. He proceeds to give a detailed description of the mound and conjoined embanked earthwork and lists its 'decided resemblances and differences' with the mound at Rathcroghan. He then compares it to other mounds, including those at Carnfree, Carnabreckna and Masonbrook (about which he later published papers). This leads him to define his classification 'dumha': 'taking all these works together we may now, I think, hold that the boss [mound], the flat band, usually slightly below field-level, and the outer bank are the essential features of this type of monument, and that there is no fixed proportion between the diameter of the boss and the width of the band and bank'. This type of field monument which 'probably exists all over Ireland, but has not been especially noticed' is most frequently found in Co. Roscommon. It seems that Knox retains the Irish word 'dumha' for a burial mound or barrow because this type of field-monument is 'absent from such books relating to English earthworks as I have been able to consult. Not one instance of this type have I found. No doubt it would be treated in England as a Disk Barrow [ie. a central mound occupying a small area of the total enclosure defined by the ditch and external bank – a ring barrow in today's terminology] but the Disk Barrows which are described are not such as these. We cannot suppose that it would have been wholly ignored if it had occurred often among the hundreds of barrows, many of the same very low relief'.

Though Knox gives an unusually clear definition of a 'dumha' in this paper, it is evident from the quotations in his notebooks from Lyons' letters that Lyons is not so certain e.g.:

> '25 Sep 1913: The second mound at Knockadoo, kindred in type, proves the original character of K[nockadoo]-Brosna, also the use of the word dumha. K[nockadoo]-Brosna has scarcely been used residentially. There is no use in theorizing extensively or dogmatically about any type of Irish earthwork. Every day I go out I see something new. We do not know really what other antiquities the country may contain. When the relatively small territory which has been searched with some consistency has contained such surprises, what may not the remainder contain? A large enclosure as at Knockadoo-Brosna would be required for a large family. A polygamous chief would have a lot of offspring and they in turn would polygamously multiply. We are too influenced in considering these matters by our present rate of increase & modern family & sepulchral arrangements'.[33]

Perhaps Lyons' lack of certainty about the classification 'dumha' as a distinct type of earthwork may be the reason that there is not even an oblique reference to him in this paper and the plan of Dumha Brosna was made by Mr. J. McDonagh, C.E.; an editorial note at the end of the paper states: 'the illustrations accompanying this paper have been kindly presented by the Author' [to the Royal Society of Antiquaries of Ireland]; neither is there a copy of the published photograph in the Lyons Collection at N.U.I.Galway.

With the passage of time, perhaps Knox realised he was fighting a losing battle in trying to gain acceptance for his opinions; in 1915, when his next paper, 'Rath

Plate 39.
Photograph, dated 1914, of Carnabreckna, near Tulsk, Co. Roscommon, described by Lyons as 'Dumha from SE'

Photo: Lyons Collection, N.U.I.Galway.

Brenainn', was published, Knox seems to ask the reader to maintain an open mind regarding (the un-named) Lyons' interpretation: 'My colleague has made observations on this work which I now give as nearly as possible in his own words [...] his plans and descriptions and the observations which are quoted above have an especial interest because they are founded on his own study of earthworks during some years and are wholly free of any bias which might have arisen from a study of the legendary and historical references quoted below. And these have a special interest again in their bearing on those views and explanations [...] We may say that in the latter part of the sixth century a residential rath was attached to the sepulchral ring so that they formed but one work, as my colleague has already suggested upon independent grounds'

In this paper Knox describes a conjoined earthwork with attached annexe situated 'on the crest of a high hill 2 miles west of the town of Roscommon, in the townland of Rathbrennan'* (Fig. 9) where, according to *Silva Gadelica*, St. Patrick met the King of Connacht. Noting its comparison with Teach Chormaic (the supposed house of the heroic King Cormac mac Airt) and the Forradh ('royal seat') at Tara, Knox suggests that the King of Connacht 'made the western rath as a residence attached to the sepulchral ring in imitation of the High King's

---

* The *Sites and Monuments Record* for Co. Roscommon lists 7 sites in Rathbrennan townland: 2 ringforts, 2 ringfort sites, 1 annexe site, 1 annexe (disused) and 1 mound. (O.S. 39).

official residence at Tara'.[34] Strangely, no correspondence from Lyons on the subject of Rath Brenainn is recorded in Knox's notebooks. It seems unlikely that references to it may have occurred in the (presumed earlier) missing notebook as this would have been written-up some ten years earlier (prior to June 1905 when the first extant notebook commences). The explanation for the absence of references may lie in the fact that Knox may have quoted directly from Lyons actual letter(s) when preparing this paper. Some confusion in Knox's recording of Lyons' letters is evident in the notebooks around this time: for some two years before 'Rath Brenainn' was published, Knox was recording his letters from Lyons in two notebooks which overlap in date; K.N. 3 covers the period from 14 September 1909 to 7 December 1915 and K.N. 4 the period from July (no day recorded) 1913 to 29 October 1918.

A plea for open-mindedness also appears in Knox's paper 'Carnfree and Carnabreckna' published in the 1915-6 edition of the *Journal of the Galway Archaeological and Historical Society*. Having described the 'group of six sepulchral monuments on Carnabreckna hill' Knox then states that 'during the last few years, my colleague, the Field Antiquary, examined these rings and flattish residential raths closely as well as many other sepulchral works, and in the course of a tour, in May 1914, gradually came to the following conclusion respecting them:- "That over large areas of country the Celts adapted suitable sepulchral works of their predecessors as homes and that many of the low residential raths were originally works of the Rathcroghan type". Knox, having been taken to task by Orpen a few years earlier, must have been aware that this paper could very well come in for further criticism and inserts the *caveat* that Lyons 'recognizes that he raises two very contentious points, the conversion of the rings, and the assignment of the conversion to the Celtic race. He does not hold his conclusions dogmatically, only offers them as tentative suggestions which afford the best explanation of the facts at the present moment, and he acknowledges that serious objections may be raised'.

Knox considers that the complex of monuments on Carnbreckna hill might be described as 'a humble relation' of the Carnfree group of 'seven works, none conspicuous or remarkable in size, even insignificant in general appearance, [which] are, except one, on the plateau of a high hill forming a long ridge [...] the exception is a cashel, including a church site and a pillar stone [... which is] on the lower eastern slope of Carnfree Hill, near the summit [...] Rathcroghan is 5 miles distant to the N.W. in view of Carnfree'. Waddell notes that this complex

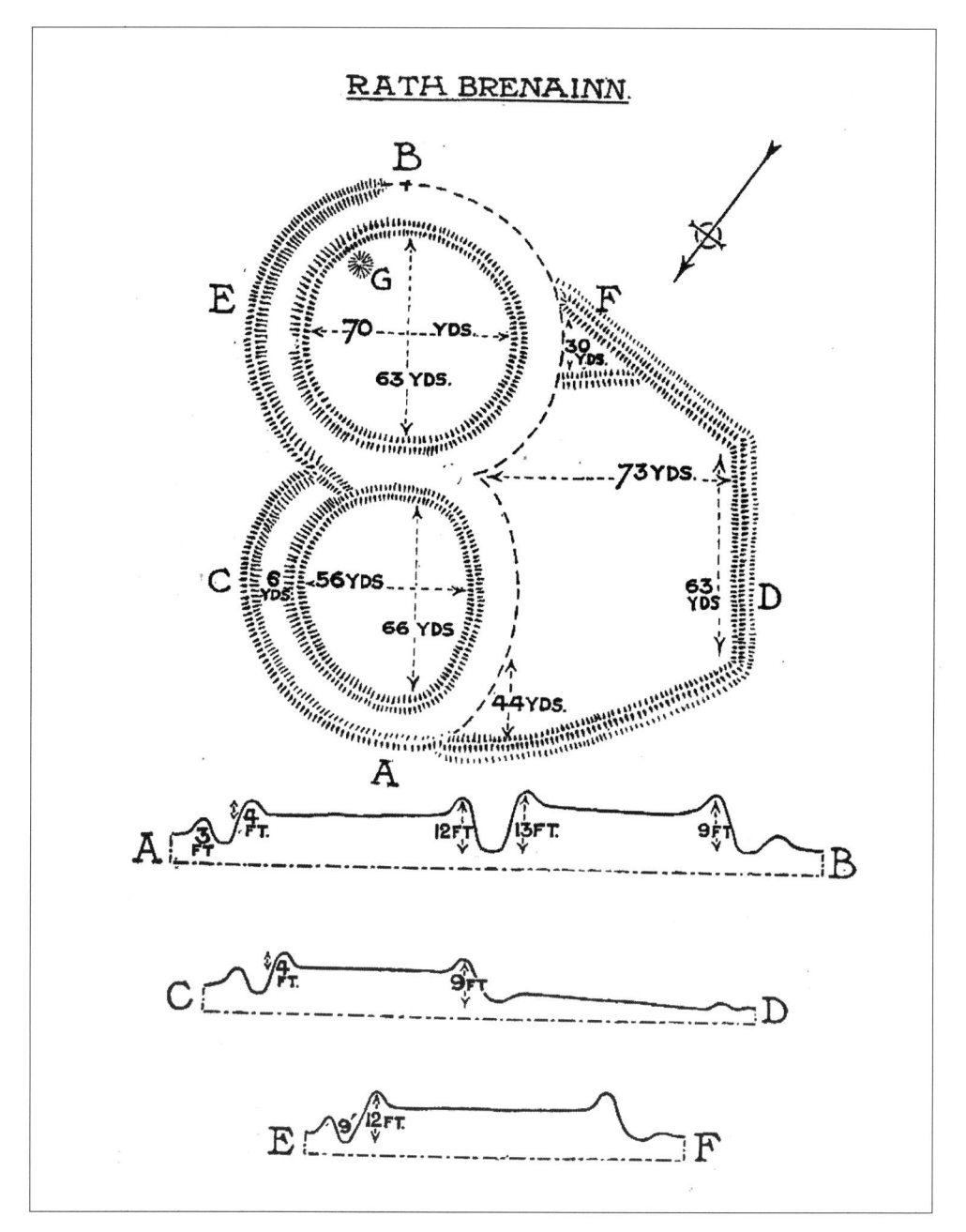

Fig. 9.
Lyons' plan and section of Rath Brenainn, Co. Roscommon. Knox notes that 'these two rings are a very close copy of the King of Ireland's Raths at Tara [...] the bailey [annexe] is a later construction which may be ignored, save as a sign of Norman occupation or of Norman influence'.[34]

Plate 40.
Aerial photograph of the conjoined earthwork at Lismurtagh/Carrowgarve near Tulsk, Co. Roscommon. Knox suggests that this site could possibly be Dumha Selca (the 'mound of the hunt'); Fitzpatrick proposes the enclosed mound (left centre of picture) as Dumha na Selga and the ringfort (to its right) as a residence of the Mac Branain chief of Corca Eachlann and keeper of Ó Conchobhair's hounds.[35]

Photo: Department of Archaeology, N.U.I.Galway.

---

of monuments (with the exception of the cashel) may have 'eventually superseded its celebrated neighbour [Rathcroghan], at least as an inauguration and assembly place'. The complex contains two monuments of the type named 'dumha' by Knox: Dumha Selca (known from literary sources as 'the mound of the hunt') and the 'Altered Dumha'. Lyons' plan and section of the 'Altered Dumha' (Fig. 10) shows a mound (ring barrow) altered by the addition of a ringfort cutting across its northern section. Knox explains his choice of the name 'Altered Dumha': 'as no name is known [for this earthwork] we have given it this descriptive title' and then adds 'but it is possible that the "Altered Dumha" is the Dumha Selca'. This possibility is further developed by Fitzpatrick who (noting that O'Donovan's identification of the mound had never been challenged) proposes that 'Dumha Selga could equally be the mound that constitutes part of the impressive conjoined earthwork [Altered Dumha] that straddles the boundary between the townlands of Lismurtagh and Carrowgarve (Plate 40) [...] geophysical survey of the monument suggests that the northern earthwork is a ringfort (with a possible house site in the interior), which deliberately subsumed part of the mound or barrow of earlier date lying on its south side'[35]. Knox suggests another association for the 'Altered Dumha': he observes that the earthwork is 'a close parallel to Rath Brenainn' (some 10 miles distant to the south) in which he had seen similarities with Teach Chormaic and the Forradh at Tara (as published in his previous paper 'Rath Brenainn').

5 of the 10 photographs published in Knox's paper are included in the Lyons Collection in N.U.I.Galway.

Lyons had been forwarding his observations on field-monuments in the neighbourhood of Carnfree and Carnabreckna to Knox for many years:

> '16.9.1907: On the hill of Carnabreckna (perhaps "Brehon's Cairn") a mile NW of Roscommon Town is a line of three earthworks from N to S. A common *lios* to the S, next a small mound with a *cupan* in the centre and last – to the North – an earthwork like the Falkinerian hollow* but with higher outer fence – 200 yds. E is a good earthen cairn but scooped out in the centre'.[36]

In 1918 Knox turns his attention, once again, to the complex of field-monuments at Rathcroghan that appear to have had held continuing fascination for both Lyons and himself; 'Cruachan Ai Roads and Avenues' concentrates on the series of linear earthworks at Rathcroghan. In this paper, for the first time in their

---

* The expression 'Falkinerian hollow' is derived from Lyons' reading of a paper published in the *Journal of the Royal Society of Antiquaries of Ireland* in which unusual earthworks situated in close proximity to raths and other ancient remains in Rathnarrow, Co. Westmeath are described and illustrated; as the author has 'never seen anything exactly like them', he appeals to members for information on their probable origin and use. This type of earthwork would now be described as a saucer barrow i.e. a very low mound which covers the whole area enclosed by the ditch and external bank. Lyons obviously kept this paper in his mind during his investigations of field-monuments as this expression is applied to many other monuments as recorded by Knox from Lyons' letters e.g.

12.3.1909: 'I have found a good "Falkinerian" monument near Ballyboy cashel. The cashel is really in Cappagh townland where the long series of graves are'.

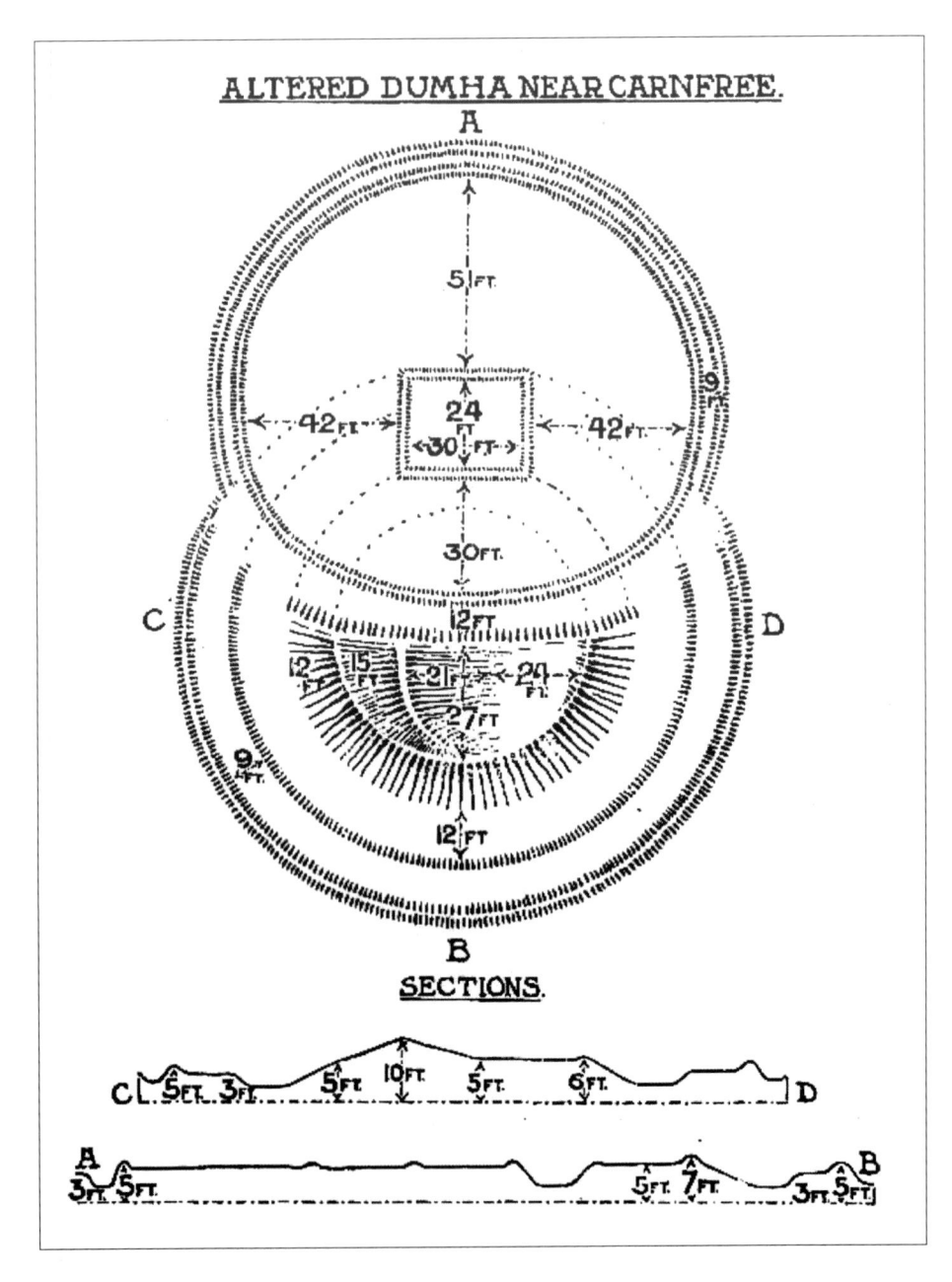

Fig. 10.
Lyons' plan and section of the 'Altered Dumha' at Carnfree, near Tulsk, Co. Roscommon showing the mound altered by the addition of a ringfort cutting across it. Fitzpatrick notes that a geophysical survey of the monument suggests that the ringfort (with a possible house site in the interior) deliberately subsumed part of the ring barrow of earlier date lying on its south side.[35]

collaborative ventures, Knox discusses how his opinion regarding the function of these monuments differs greatly from that of Lyons. Knox states that he had earlier formed the opinion that the earthworks and their blocking arrangements were made for driving cattle to and from their pastures; however, 'since then the Field Antiquary has supplied me with the particulars of other avenues connected with certain works [... which are] undoubtedly sepulchral or ceremonial works and afford evidence to support a view [...] that the Linked Forts are now sepulchral whatever may have been their origin, that the high mote-like mound in Corraun and the wide, low mound on Rathscrigg are sepulchral mounds, and that the peculiar arrangements in connection with them were made for use in funereal and other religious processions'.

Although Knox accepts Lyons' theory regarding these particular monuments, he maintains that his own (imaginative) theory may apply to others. 'It has been objected to my theory of arrangements for access to the Linked Forts that it is much easier to drive cattle along a narrow way than along a very wide one. This is true, but if the road is in constant use by large herds the great width tends to keep it in condition generally, unless the narrow way is paved or given some artificial hard surface. According to my view the cattle were collected in the morning and driven to the pastures beyond the tillage, and brought back to their proper homes in the evening, as is done to this day in some countries. The evidence of other avenues made for other purposes does not affect my theory. All roads and avenues must be classified on their merits, and according to our own individual assessment of weight of evidence. For this reason the following plans and descriptions are submitted for the judgment of our readers'. To elaborate his opinion Knox then describes, accompanied by plans and sections, two very different archaeological complexes: a group of five earthworks in Creeve, some 8 miles south of Rathcroghan and a group of earthworks (including a possible megalith and souterrain) at Knockfarnaght, Co. Mayo.

The photograph of Knockfarnaght which accompanies this paper is included in the Lyons collection in N.U.I.Galway. Lyons' description of this photograph (Plate 42) is transcribed by Knox in his notebook:

> '9 Mar 1917: What looks like a mound in the photo of Knockfarnaght is in virtually the centre of the outer ring of the work. The white stones to the right are the outer small oval to the NE. The dolmen or at least one or two stones of it can also be seen to the right. The shape of the oval ought to be rather clearly visible and the dolmen can be seen beyond it rather noticeably detached'.[37]

Fig. 11.
Aerial photograph of linear earthworks in Rathcroghan complex adjacent to Courtmoyle earthwork (17 March 1982), as published in 'Rathcroghan – a royal site in Connacht', *Journal of Irish Archaeology*, 1, (1983, 40).

Plate 41.
Photograph, dated 1915, described by Lyons as the 'great sunken ring' at Creeve, Co. Roscommon. In the *Sites and Monuments Record* an archaeological complex is listed comprising a ring-barrow, 2 ringforts and 2 enclosures (O.S. 34).

Photo: Lyons Collection, N.U.I.Galway.

Plate 42.
Dated 1916, this photograph is described by Lyons as 'sepulchral rings at Knockfarnaght, near Lahardane crossroads. NE shoulder of Nephin in background'. In the *Sites and Monuments Record* for Mayo an archaeological complex is listed comprising 2 ring-barrows, 2 enclosures, possible megalith, possible souterrain, hut-site (O.S. 47).

Photo: Lyons Collection, N.U.I.Galway.

KNOX'S RACIAL THEORY CONCERNING THE BUILDERS OF FIELD-MONUMENTS

In his 1917-8 paper 'Ballygurraun and Raheen Group of Works in Earth and Stone', Knox, having described a 'cemetery' just outside Athenry comprising 29 monuments and so-called 'because the sepulchral works seem to predominate',* then proffers his theory regarding the builders of field-monuments in earth and stone. Based on Lyons' speculations, it delves into the realms of ethnology and is a reflection of the racial speculations that were such a feature of 19th and early 20th century antiquarian papers. His quotations from correspondence with Lyons illustrate that discussion on this subject had begun some years earlier:

---

* In the *Sites and Monuments Record* for the townlands of Ballygarraun North, Ballygarraun South, Ballygarraun West and Raheen (O.S 84) field-monuments comprise 5 hilltop enclosures, 1 bi-vallate ringfort, 3 enclosures, 1 unclassified earthwork, 1 souterrain, 1 road, 2 follies, 1 garden feature.

25 Oct 1914 (following a lengthy description of the field-monuments in the neighbourhood of Rathcroghan): 'It is pertinent to ask – what race built these mounds? The time to answer the question has not come, but it is no harm to advance a tentative theory'.

During the next few years there are many lengthy transcriptions from Lyons' letters in which this question is elaborated; perhaps the escalating gravity of the political situation in these years (both nationally and internationally) curtailed Lyons' opportunities for active fieldwork and so prompted this intellectual endeavour. Lyons distinguishes two 'antique races' in Ireland: an obliquely-eye-browed race similar to the Mongols who were a 'lithic people' and who built at least some of the stone cashels; a brown-eyed Gipsy-like race, often called Iberian, but who originated in Central Europe. They were a 'humic race' and lived on scarped hills 'where such were available, elsewhere, they lived in the open, with or without palisading.' The 'lithic' people were forced westwards (which explained the lack of cashels in the central plain) and the 'humic' race 'seems to have clung on to the central plain by fusion with the Celts [...] the Mongols were the most intellectual race of the three, but the Celtic blend improved the strain, and the rich and flexible Celtic tongue became a potent literary weapon. The intellectual superiority of Celto-Mongol in Mayo, or Munster, is very marked when compared with the Celto-Brownie people of Galway'.

On 21 March 1915: Lyons refers Knox to 'an interesting article on Siberian Aborigines in the last number of "Times" Lit[erary] Suppl[emen]t' (to which newspaper Lyons had been subscribing since 1905 and which may have influenced his ethnological speculations) as further explanation of his theory:

'When I speak of Irish Mongols it is these I mean and not the stock pig-tailed product of East Asia. I feel sure that we have in addition an Esquimaux element (round faced and dark haired, low sized and stout) mingling with the earlier "Mongolian" stock'.

Later that year Knox summarises Lyons theory in his notebook:

'19 November 1915: P[atrick] L[yons]'s Theory. Europe seems to have been occupied first by a dark Mongol, or Mongoloid, race, which came either from Asia or America. Then the Brown race from the south cut into them and nearly divided them into two sections, the western of which was entirely conquered by the Brownies. Then came the Celts and close on their heels their cousins the Germans. There can be no doubt but that both Greek and Roman civilization is largely owing to the Celticized mixture. Their assumed ancient position in the Sarmatian Plain gave them facilities for throwing colonies into the southern peninsular. Their irruption into Asia Minor must have been a swarm from the Sarmatian hive and not retrogression from the west'.

In the following years quotations from Lyons' letters show that discussion continued and connections with Egyptian (and other) civilizations were considered:

'10 April 1916: I hope you will tackle the racial question in Ireland. I cannot give concrete instances, but the higher organized Celts, Celto-Mongols and Celto-Brownies (Iberians) do not, apparently through instinctive repugnance, mingle conjugally with the lower aborigines, some of whom are perhaps pre-Mongoloid, perhaps of Boreal (or Esquimaux) origin';

'30 Jan 1917: I propose "Lithic" for the Dolmen Builders as a name, "Humo-Lithic" for the rath makers and "Humic" or "Humistic" for the ring and boss-mound people who are less lapidarian than the others';

'28 Feb 1917: I merely urge that the stone pyramid has an earthen prototype. I think it would be much more correct to say that the Egyptian pyramid arose from a northern type than the reverse. A northern race, probably Celtic, made an irruption into Egypt in prehistoric times, and the earthworks of the people may have been translated into stone by the genius of the native [...] Certainly there does not seem to be much connection between the mastaba, which seems to have been the original Egyptian sepulchral work, and the pyramid [...] The remaining pyramidal works are slight, those not yet reported, the one at Caherroyan and one SW of Dunmore. Those reported are Bohola mote, Cauraun of Kilerr, Creeve, Dunmore Castle mound and Mount Shaw. Of the large works, Bohola (Plate 43) is the most perfect. The remainder are only partially pyramidal'.[38]

EXCAVATION WORK

The wealth of detail painstakingly recorded by Knox in his notebooks bears witness to the many hours that Lyons spent carefully measuring, recording, photographing and interpreting field monuments. Details of two in-depth investigations undertaken by Lyons, both in the neighbourhood of Loughrea, Co. Galway, are also recorded; his 'digs' at Feerwore and Masonbrook.

Knox begins his 1915-6 paper 'The Turoe Stone and Rath of Feerwore' by explaining why the excavation was undertaken: 'Mr. Coffey has assigned the Turoe Stone (Plate 44) to the earlier La Tène period, and mentioned that the

Plate 43.
Photograph c.1907 of earthwork at Bohola, near Kiltamagh, Co. Mayo, which Lyons considers to be an 'earthen prototype of the Egyptian pyramid [...] the humbler stages of improvement of the Egyptian pyramid are probably not in existence in Egypt'. As Knox gives no details of its location, it is not possible to identify this earthwork.

Photo: Lyons Collection, N.U.I.Galway.

---

original site pointed out to him was outside the rath at the foot of the slope of the hill, but did not give distance (Pr. P.R.I.A. vol. 24, C. p. 260). Last November [coincidentally named] Patrick Lyons, who had been employed by Mr. Dolphin for 40 years as a herd, pointed out as the exact site a spot about 10 yards to the west of the rath, which may be said to be at the foot of an upper slope, with another considerable slope below it. We may rely on the correctness of the tradition as transmitted to him [...] On the outer face of the west rampart near where the carved stone stood is a large sloping flagstone, seen in the picture, which was thought likely to cover a cave's mouth. The photographer took the picture standing practically on the site and facing east north east before the excavation, which has not altered the outline as the material was replaced carefully'. The photograph, (Plate 45) which depicts 8 men standing on the rampart behind the stone (and used as reference points in Knox's description of the site) is included in the Lyons Collection in N.U.I.Galway but, strangely, there is no reference in this paper, oblique or otherwise, to field-work by Lyons.

Knox describes the rath as 'trivial' and gives details of an excavation there on 20 November 1915 when a (supposed) cist containing carefully-buried animal bones was discovered in the rampart. 'The contents of the cist indicate cremation, and the animal remains a funeral feast. The finely carved stone suggests that this rath was occupied by some important person in life or in death [...] One hundred and fifty yards north-west of this rath in the townland of Fearta, and near the boundary between Turoe and Knocknadaula townlands, is a small regular dumha, much ruined, [probably the 'small tumulus' excavated by Coffey in 1904], the only one of the usual Roscommon type as yet reported in Galway [...] Fearta, "Graves" is a suggestive name [...] Cnoc na Dala, Hill of the Assembly'.

However, Knox's transcriptions from Lyons' letters show clearly that this paper is based completely on work done by Lyons, including the excavation:

'17 Oct 1915: I visited the "rath" at Turoe from which the Turoe stone was moved to its present site. This rath is a trivial affair, 34 x 30 yds. Ramp[art]s 4' high outside and 3' inside, 6' thick. On the W there are 2 rough conglomerate blocks disposed as if there had been a curved alignment of such stones enclosing a smooth space on the W side of the rath. This space is the traditional ancient site of the Carved Stone. On the outer face of the W ramp[art] near where the stone must have stood is a large sloping flag which seems to cover a "sou" [souterrain]. I had not with me sufficient force to lift the flag [...] If there really is a grave chamber under this stone it may be that the Carved Stone was an identification mark for the grave';

'21 Nov 1915: I went to Turoe yesterday [...] I then dug a pit in the rath rampart close to the stone on the inside, 6' long, 4' wide and 4' deep. In this area I

Plate 44.
The Turoe Stone, Bullaun, near Loughrea, Co. Galway, one of the few examples of Celtic La Tène stone carving in Ireland.

Photo: Department of Archaeology, N.U.I.Galway

found a lot of bones without cohesion, among which was a horse's tooth and one other tooth. On the inner side of the excavation towards the rath garth and in the middle of the rampart I found a small very rude cist 3' long, 1' wide and 1½' deep. This contained a gray greasy clay interspersed with slight fragmentary traces of bone. The cist faced E and W, long axis. I found no metallic or lithic article of antiquity. The cist was at a depth of 2½'. There was a dual burial here, a human burial in the cist and on the outside (to the W) between the cist and the great stone a burial of a "lower" animal, probably a horse [...] The rath seems to have contained two sou[terrain]s in its eastern side and there is probably another close inside the cist site [...] The cist burial is crematorial and probably Celtic. Was the Turoe stone a Celtic emblem? Or was it the indication of former souterrainic burials in the rath'?

'23 Nov 1915: The Turoe stone's original site was about 10 yds. W of the rath according to Patsy Lyons who has been herd to the Dolphins for 40 years and knows well the traditions of the place. It is at the bottom of a slight slope from the height on which the rath stands, but not at the bottom of the main slope'.

However, Raftery casts doubts on Lyons' certainty (as recorded by Knox)

Plate 45.
Photograph, dated November 1915, showing the site of the 'cist' discovered by Lyons at his excavation at the rath of Feerwore, near Loughrea, Co. Galway.

Photo: Lyons Collection, N.U.I.Galway.

regarding the contents of the cist and its dating: 'A local herd informed me that the bank was considerably higher 20 years ago than at the time of excavation, so that the top of Knox's cist would have been about in the middle of the bank; in other words, the cist, with cremation (so described by Knox), was inserted after the erection of the bank'.

Knox and Lyons were probably fascinated by the account published in the *Proceedings of the Royal Irish Academy* in 1904 of the excavation by Coffey of 'a small tumulus' in the townland of Fearta and hoped to emulate his success. In the centre of the tumulus Coffey found a female skeleton; 'on the south side of the body were some remains of red deer and remains of a small horse. Directly below the bodies of the woman and horse a cremated interment was found on the level of the old surface of the ground – an almost plain urn inverted over the burnt bones [...] the impression made to my mind when excavating the tumulus was that the upper interments were contemporary with the cremated burial. We have here, possibly, a case of the burial of a slave or concubine, perhaps as guardian of the grave, with the chief or important person for whom the tumulus was erected.'

Although Lyons' field-work is unacknowledged by Knox in this paper, it was confirmed by Matilda Redington, then Secretary of the Galway Archaeological and Historical Society, in a letter dated 26.6.1916 to the National Museum and there archived: 'Within the last few months [...] my friend the antiquarian policeman (Sgt. P. Lyons, R.I.C.) [...] ascertained that the Turoe Stone is not in its original site and proceeded to identify the latter. As I understand from him, it stood outside but very near an ordinary rath of no size or importance called 'Feerwore'. He thinks he can trace a semi-circle of big stones round the site, and, as it runs into the rampart of the rath, he made a cutting through the latter and came upon a small and rude cist containing a sticky matter. I think he said it was 18 inches square and he believes it to be connected with cremation. If this be so, its discovery may help to date these raths; and yet, perhaps not, for the rath may have been cut through an earlier burial ground'. However, Waddell notes that Lyons may have been mistaken: conflicting local information by the grand-nephew of a man who was present when 'the Dolphin family had the stone moved with horses and slide-car to Turoe House, places its former location in a small, slight hollow about 100 metres west of the site of the ringfort and near the bottom of the low hill of Feerwore'. Although the results of a subsequent magnetometer and phosphate analysis of the area were inconclusive, 'it does now seem likely that in the 1850s the Turoe Stone was moved from this inconspicuous position at the bottom of the hill to Turoe House. Ironically, this low-lying location must raise the possibility that the stone had once been more prominently sited at some unrecorded spot on the higher ground of Feerwore and, at some time, been displaced and rolled downhill'; however, the original location may still have been near the fort.[39]

In 1916 Lyons assisted Macalister in an excavation at Masonbrook; a reading of Knox's 1917-8 paper 'The Masonbrook Ring & Mound' (based on transcripts from Lyons' letters) in conjunction with Macalister's publication of the excavation demonstrates Knox's eagerness to publish even when the evidence is inconclusive. Knox begins his paper: 'The results of exploration of these works in the summer of 1916 have been recorded by Mr. Macalister with opinions regarding their probable uses and dates expressed with the caution due to knowledge and experience. Though he has not found material for a decided opinion, it would be a mistake for us to ignore his views until they become definite; we ought to apply them in a like spirit to our local antiquities, getting things in readiness of the time when we attain full knowledge, though that time is probably far distant. For this purpose the first necessity is a list of such works as may be held to fall within two classes with which he has dealt, with notes showing how his results may bear upon them'.

Knox attempts to list and classify similar monuments and notes that 'these Masonbrook Works fall under two heads. The first is that which I have called the Rathcroghan type of Ringwork, the Boss and flat Band and outer Bank or Ring, all comparatively low in most cases [...] the second is Doon Hill, the great mound in Masonbrook Demesne [...] starting with this foundation, a list will be made of other works which seem to be of these classes'.

6 of the 10 photographs published in this paper are included in the Lyons Collection in N.U.I.Galway.

Correspondence between Knox and Lyons regarding Masonbrook commenced some four years earlier and is quoted by Knox from Lyons' letters:

> '20 July 1913: On a ridge at Masonbrook, 2 miles E of Loughrea, I saw an earthen ring having inserted in its rampart at about equal distances seven rude stone pillars each about 4 ft. high. It is only by chance I saw it as it is in a wood and nearly covered by laurel thicket. The ring is about 15 yds. in diameter and the rampart is about 6 ft. thick and 2 ft. high [...] take it that the pillars are representations of the slaves buried standing as sentinels about the grave of

chiefs indicating perhaps the relinquishment of this cruel practice. Before the rise of the wood the place was conspicuous'.

'29 July 1913: The ring at Masonbrook is sepulchral if it is not a fake. I do not suspect the latter, but stones under cover of trees take on a juvenile aspect'.

Macalister notes that the Masonbrook ring, which had been brought to notice in recent years in papers by Knox, is 'of earth, about 70 feet in external diameter, and about 3 feet high, on which are implanted a series of seven stones four to five feet in height. In the centre is a low mound of earth capped with a pile of stones [...] strongly suggestive of a small burial carn [...] but unmistakable evidence came to light that it was of quite recent formation [...] the Mound is a narrow oval on plan, the top surface measuring 115 feet in length and 20 feet in width [...] there can be no doubt that it has been scarped artificially to its present form [...] I can only guess that it was an assembly or inauguration mound, possibly having some radical connexion with the great ring-fort close by. One difficulty about this explanation is that such an assembly mound seems as a rule to have been associated with some remarkable interment; but I cannot satisfy myself that there was ever any interment in this mound. There is no trace whatever of any building having been erected on the summit'.

Knox's transcription from Lyons' letter of 18 July 1916 describing the excavation differs somewhat from Macalister's published account:

> 'Macalister & I dug out all within the ring stones. Found a loose cairn of stones probably fairly modern, and under it a mound of earth which did not contain a cist; but above the normal virgin earth level floor was a layer of black burnt earth (probably mixed with charcoal) containing the teeth and bones of animals. These Prof[essor] M[acalister] took to Dublin to have examined. He now considers that the monument was a place of worship and of sacrifice; and it is interesting as proving that the men of the Bronze Age (to which he thinks it belongs) met for religious purposes at places *other* than their burial sites. The scarped hilltop at Masonbrook was tested by digging holes in several places, after which he decided that it was an esker scarped to shape (P[atrick] L[yons] had done so before) and that it may have been an assembly mound and place of inauguration'.[40]

LAST YEARS OF LYONS/ KNOX COLLABORATION

The infrequency and brevity of Knox's quotations from Lyons' letters during 1917 suggest that Knox's health was deteriorating; a letter in the Knox/Lyons collection in the library of the Royal Society of Antiquaries of Ireland confirms this. Dated 6 February 1918, it was written by Knox (then resident at Rivershill, St George's Rd, Cheltenham) to Westropp and depicts the failing antiquarian: 'I am sending you a batch of prints for R.S.A.I. [...] I fear I shall never write anything more or do any real study. I have gone down very much in the last 4 months and find even such trivialities as sorting photos rather trying at times. Would you mind telling me whether you keep photos in *slip-in* albums or stick them down? If you stick them down, it is a waste of time and trouble to write more on the back than the No. and the Name in pencil for reference to the list. I have written a good deal on backs hitherto in order that there might be no diffi-

Plate 46.
Photograph, dated 1915, described by Lyons as 'a souterrain near the caher or cashel in Ballygurrane, near Athenry. An opening in the roof.'

Photo: Lyons Collection, N.U.I.Galway.

culty in identifying anything that might be loose. I see I am winding up my time by another period as Vice-President, an honour which pleases me as showing that I have in some measure helped the work of the Society'.

Despite his failing health Knox continued with his antiquarian endeavours, as can be seen from his publications. In the 1917-8 edition of the *Journal of the Galway Archaeological and Historical Society* he published three papers: 'Caher and Rath caves of Galway & Meath'; 'The Masonbrook Ring & Mound'; 'Ballygurraun and Raheen Group of Works in Earth and Stone'; in 1918 he published 'Cruachain Ai Roads & Avenues' in the *Journal of the Royal Society of Antiquaries of Ireland* and in the following year 'St. Marcan's Loch & Ruins'. Evidence for work by Knox in his last years can also be seen in a set of two notebooks archived in the library of the Royal Society of Antiquaries of Ireland; these contain a list and descriptions of 176 ecclesiastical sites and castles accompanied by a catalogue of some 400 negatives, (which, as noted earlier, he may have been preparing for publication) the last page of which is dated 1 July 1918. Archived with the Lyons Photographic Collection in N.U.I.Galway are two documents that bear witness to his work in 1919: a letter dated 11 August 1919 from Knox to Matilda Redington in reply to antiquarian queries previously posed by her; handwritten notes dated 1 July 1919 and entitled 'Millstones' describing ancient millstones found in the Ballyhaunis region which 'may be of use if any one should be inclined to study these very small ancient millstones, which are probably to be found all over Ireland. The very small size of really ancient stones suggests that these little mills are by descent, hand querns worked by water'.

Knox's death is recorded in the 1920 edition of the *Journal of the Galway Archaeological and Historical Society*; in the same volume is 'Notes on the Burgus of Athenry: its First Defences, and its Town Walls', written by 'H.T. Knox and a colleague'. This paper is the only one in which Lyons' authorship is obliquely acknowledged. Lyons' work is evident throughout, commencing on the first page when he compares the settlement at Athenry to that at Kiltinan, Co. Tipperary (though without giving any details). The paper begins: 'There is no evidence of a pre-Norman settlement having existed at Athenry [...] The Anglo-Norman conquest however, gave it importance as a defensive halting place on the main road from Meath, and from the Lord of Connaught's chief castle of Loughrea to his main seaport, Galway'. The extensive town walls which enclose the medieval town of Athenry are described in great detail, as is its castle; then follows 'notes on some early Connaught castles bearing on probable entrances'; the paper

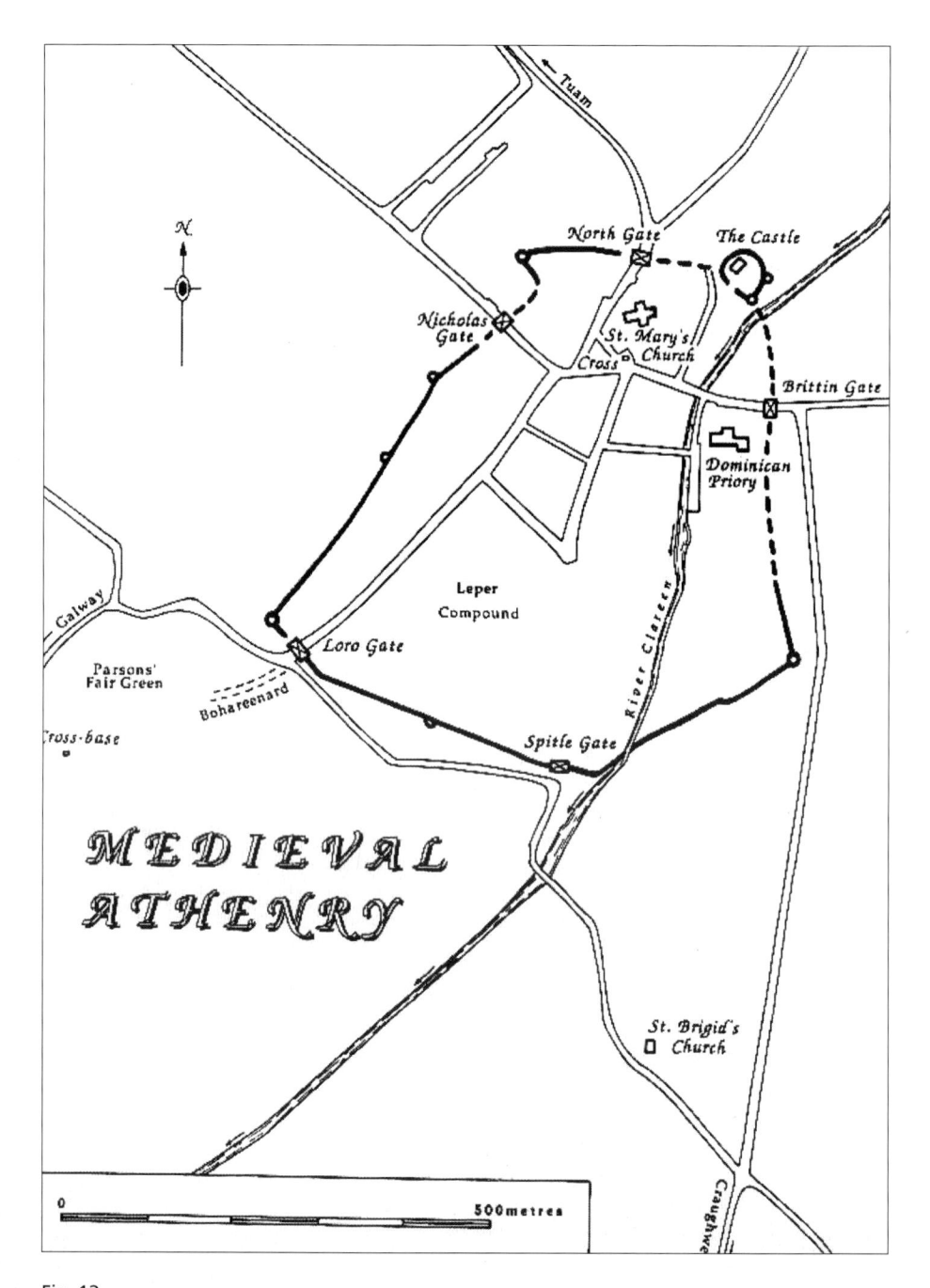

Fig. 12.
Map of medieval Athenry as published by Rynne in A. Simms and J.H. Andrews (eds.) *More Irish country towns*.

Plate 47.
Athenry town wall c.1913 showing tower on eastern wall from SW.

Photo: Lyons Collection, N.U.I.Galway.

Plate 48.
Athenry town wall c.1913 showing the tower at junction of E and SE walls.

Photo: Lyons Collection, N.U.I.Galway.

Plate 49.
Athenry town wall in 2006 showing the tower at junction of E and SE walls.
Photo: David Lohan.

concludes with a detailed map of 'Athenry, ancient town, suburbs and castle'.

Only one of the five published photographs which accompany this paper is included in the Lyons collection in N.U.I.Galway. However, in this collection, photographs of monuments in Athenry greatly outnumber those taken by Lyons in any other place. They comprise: Dominican Priory (12), town walls (11), castle (10), St Mary's Collegiate Church (8), Cross (1); the 6 dated photographs bear dates of 1913. Presumably most, if not all, of the other photographs were taken during the years 1913-6 when Lyons was stationed at the Royal Irish Constabulary barracks in Athenry; they show many features of the medieval town, since destroyed by modern development.

Meiler de Bermingham is generally credited with the foundation of the Anglo-Norman town of Athenry. Having assisted Richard de Burgh in the conquest of Connacht, he was granted lands to the east of Galway city in 1235 and, probably around 1238, he erected a castle overlooking the ford across the River Clareen.

Extending south and westwards from this he laid out the town of Athenry. As part of the general development of the new town, de Bermingham introduced the Dominicans in 1241, allegedly at the express request of St. Dominic. The town was granted a weekly market and annual fair in 1244. A three-year murage grant was obtained in 1310 and it would appear that the town was originally walled around that time. History, however, records that the walling took place after the Battle of Athenry in 1316 which was 'the most sanguinary engagement recorded in our history since the [Norman] invasion [...] in which the native troops were signally defeated. The walls of Athenry are said to have been built from the spoils of the battle; and the power of the O'Conors, which here received its final blow, was totally destroyed'; however, this may merely mean that the original walls, which were probably of wood were rebuilt in stone, or, that the existing walls were fortified by the addition of wall towers.

Athenry continued to be a place of considerable importance in the west of Ireland until the mid 16th century. O'Sullivan notes that the cause of its decay is well-described in a letter of 20 April 1567 from Lord Deputy Sir Henry Sidney to Elizabeth I: 'The toune is large and well walled, and it appereth by matter of record there hath been in it three hundred good howseholders, and since I knew this land, there was twentie, and now I finde but fower, and they poor, and, as I write, readie to leave the place. The Crye and Lamentation of the poor People was greate and pityefull, and nothinge but this. Succor, Succor, Succor. The Erle of Clanricarde could not denye but he helde a hevie Hande over them. For which I ordered him to make them som Recompence, and bounde him not to exacte upon them hereafter'. The 'pityefull' appeal does not appear to have had any effect, however, as Athenry still continued to decay and what was once the bastion of the Anglo-Normans in Connaught became reduced to the state of an insignificant village. The arrival of the Cromwellians in 1652 further added to its miseries. The coming of the railroads in the 19th century, which made Athenry an important junction, revived the town; unfortunately, commercial buildings since the mid 20th century have not always integrated sensitively with the medieval town.

Correspondence between Lyons and Knox regarding the antiquities of Athenry commenced within a few weeks of Lyons' arrival there to take up his duties as Head Constable:

> '27 June 1913: The town walls of Athenry are but slight (Plates 47-8). The towers have three stories, one solid lower story and two upper stories

Plate 50.
East window of Athenry Dominican Priory c.1913 described by Lyons as 'probably one of the best pieces of restoration in existence'. Macalister notes that 'it must have been a very fine specimen of geometrical tracery [...] There were six lights. Nothing remains but the points of attachment of the tracery to the window arch, and even the cusps are hidden by the masonry of the Jacobean window that has been inserted into the opening.'[41]

Photo: Lyons Collection, N.U.I.Galway.

The 'antiquarian craze'

Plate 51.
Photograph c.1913 showing defacement of the west wall of Athenry Dominican Priory, the outside of which then – as now – serving as wall of a handball alley. Cromwellian occupation in the 17th century began the ruination; in the 18th century it was used as a barracks (which was demolished when the Priory tower collapsed). When visited by members of the Royal Society of Antiquaries of Ireland on their excursion in 1895 it is noted that the nave 'has a beautiful W window of 4 lights, decorated Gothic, opened and repaired in recent conservation'; yet, Macalister's sketch in 1913 shows it blocked up and he notes that there were 'three or perhaps two [lancet windows] in the west. There may have been a west door under these'.[41]

Photo: Lyons Collection, N.U.I.Galway.

Plate 52.
Athenry Dominican Priory c.1913 showing the aisle and part of the nave. Lyons draws our attention to the 'original pillar' which can be seen in the masonry in the ruined arcade and notes that there is an original arch at the far end.

Photo: Lyons Collection, N.U.I.Galway.

Plate 53.
Photograph c.1913 of a ruined 'altar tomb' in Athenry Dominican Priory near the altar. Lyons draws our attention to 'a small effigy of Lady and Child on support of arch to right' and notes that this is 'probably a Burke tomb'.

Photo: Lyons Collection, N.U.I.Galway.

connected by a spiral stair case. The towers were mere watch towers, but they were not easily assailable by an unprepared army'.

'23 Aug 1913: The East window of the Dominican abbey here is a unique thing. The window prior to the burning [in 1423] was very large and it seems to have been destroyed in the fire. On restoration the tracery was symmetrically trimmed inward from the outer moulding and masonry inserted with room for a smaller window in the centre having tracery in practically the same style (Plate 50).The result is probably one of the best pieces of restoration in existence';

'Dec 1913: Athenry Castle (Plates 54-9). It is very probable that the first Bermingham took possession of a large Celtic fort on this site. The fort was thoroughly isolated by marsh and inundation. There must originally have been an island, perhaps a crannoge on the site. The barbican was separated from the town wall merely by the town ditch. An underground passage led beneath the fort (castle) ditch and the town ditch and wall to the Franciscan Abbey* (Plate 60), which is only about 70 or 80 yds. from the Castle.

'13 Dec 1913: The castle is quite insulated by a wide marsh – but there was no regular ditch except on W side. There is no trace of a ditch save on NW, W, and SW. The barbican seems to have been on a kind of a low bank rising out of the marsh. The Town Wall has, I believe, disappeared at the point of nearest proximity to the Castle. It is represented by the back walls of a row of cottages (Plate 61)'.

'18 Jan 1914: I have at last realized that the town wall of Athenry has been built on a pre-existing clay rampart. The former ditch was utilized for the purpose of the wall'.

'26 Jan 1914: The town of Athenry also extended along the Galway road. Considerably over a square mile is seamed with its remains, a somewhat loose aggregation of rectangular enclosures [...] I have not been able to get particulars of the site of the battlefield [...] I learn that large quantities of human remains have been found within the "Back Lawn", a space inside the walls on the E of the town'.

'9 Feb 1917: Orpen has told Miss M[atilda] R[edington] that N gate of Athenry (Plate 63) is 14th century, just after Battle of Athenry in 1316 when the town walls were built';**

---

* This building (which is the remains of St. Mary's Collegiate Church, the former parish church of Athenry) has been incorrectly identified by Lyons as a Franciscan Abbey. Rynne notes that this is a common error based on a 17th century mistranslation of the Latin name for Adare, Co. Limerick where a Franciscan Friary had been founded in 1464.

** Rynne considers that it may be a late 16th or early 17th century addition.

'10 Feb 1914: The Market Cross (Plate 64) which is now within the town anciently stood about 300 yds. SW of the Swan Gate, which anciently seems to have been the site of the market. The plinth is still on the site, near the middle of a large rectangle which was enclosed by earthen ramparts';

'22 Feb 1914: I am mistaken as to the Market Cross* having been outside the town. The plinth outside the Swan Gate was for a pillar on which the schedule of tolls was suspended'.[41]

Plate 54.
Athenry Castle from NW c.1913. Lyons draws our attention to the barbican which 'rises over cabin in ditch to which it serves as gable'. This feature can be seen more clearly in Plate 55.

Photo: Lyons Collection, N.U.I.Galway.

* Rynne has identified this monument as the 'last remnants of a fine, late-medieval Gothic cross of the "tabernacle" or "lantern" type'. So-named because of the rectangular shape of its crosshead, it comprises a plain, tapering shaft set into a sculpted socket on the top of a stepped pyramidal base. Dating from the 15th century, the crosses are well-known in Britain and continental Europe; in Ireland, however, the Athenry cross is unique. Although its long shaft is now missing, the Athenry cross may have been up to 5 metres in height; carvings of two opposed jani (mythological quadrupeds with single horns) resemble those on the doorway of the abbey at Clontuskert, Co. Galway which is dated to 1471.

Plate 55.
Barbican of Athenry Castle c.1913 described by Lyons as 'barbican tower from W showing trace of window opening on town ditch, now represented by a lane'.

Photo: Lyons Collection, N.U.I.Galway.

Plate 56.
Photograph c.1913 described by Lyons as 'elevated doorway on E wall' of Athenry Castle.

Photo: Lyons Collection, N.U.I.Galway.

Plate 57.
Photograph c.1913 described by Lyons as 'inside of S window on 1st floor' of Athenry Castle. Rynne notes that the type of carving on the windows in Athenry Castle is more usually seen in ecclesiastical buildings.[41]

Photo: Lyons Collection, N.U.I.Galway

The 'antiquarian craze'

Plate 58.
Athenry Castle c.1913 described by Lyons as 'SE angle of garth or yard'.

Photo: Lyons Collection, N.U.I.Galway.

Plate 59.
Athenry Castle in 2006 showing SE corner of castle wall as restored by the National Monuments Branch of the Office of Public Works.

Photo: David Lohan.

Plate 60.
Photograph, dated 1913, of window in chancel of St. Mary's Collegiate Church, the old parish church of Athenry, incorrectly described by Lyons as Franciscan Abbey.

Photo: Lyons Collection, N.U.I.Galway.

Plate 61.
Photograph c.1913 described by Lyons as 'town ditch close to N of Laragh (or Eastern) Gate site. Back walls of cabins are on line of town wall of which traces exist. Revetting to right shows line of outer rampart, which has virtually disappeared. Arm of stream flowed through this ditch'.

Photo: Lyons Collection, N.U.I.Galway.

Plate 62.
Photograph c.1913 described by Lyons as 'tower and outer ramparts and ditch of Athenry town, looking S from near reputed site of Laragh Gate towards E wall tower. Wall to right is E boundary of Dominican Priory grounds'.

Photo: Lyons Collection, N.U.I.Galway.

Plate 63.
Athenry North gate c.1913.

Photo: Lyons Collection, N.U.I.Galway.

Plate 64.
Athenry Market Cross c.1913. This 15th century cross has been identified by Rynne as the last remnants of a Gothic cross of the 'tabernacle' or 'lantern' type.[41]

Photo: Lyons Collection, N.U.I.Galway.

KNOX'S OBITUARY NOTICES

Knox's obituary in the *Journal of the Galway Archaeological and Historical Society* notes that 'probably no branch of Archaeology appealed to him more strongly than the prehistoric Raths and Caves that abound in the West of Ireland. In spite of increasing suffering he worked indefatigably, and his papers on Galway History and Topography are the more remarkable when one reflects that these were written several hundred miles away from the places they describe [...] Mr. Knox left the Galway Archaeological Society [sic.] a large collection of photographs taken by himself and some notes in MS for the assistance of future scholars'.*

Knox's death is also recorded by the council of the Royal Society of Antiquaries of Ireland of which he was a Fellow. 'In spite of increasing infirmity, he laboured indefatigably, although lately much hampered by having to employ others to examine and measure the monuments he described. He was a conscientious antiquary, most careful in sifting evidence before committing himself to a statement, even in the smallest details. Quiet and very retiring, he laboured at the work in which he put his whole heart, and he has been well described by a friend as an "undemonstrative enthusiast". His article on the ancient "Burgus of Athenry", written between crises of intense suffering, and lately published in the *Journal of the Galway Society* [sic.], was his last contribution to Irish archaeology. His contributions to our Journal, numbering 23, will be found in Vols. XXVII to XXXV'.[42]

Lyons' sense of loss at the death of Knox can only be imagined: the ending of the correspondence in which they shared their antiquarian interests for 22 years must have caused an enormous gap in Lyons' rather solitary life, perhaps even more especially as it occurred about a year or so after the Royal Irish Constabulary Court of Inquiry at which Lyons' unpopularity with his staff was high-lighted (See Chapter 2). Unfortunately, Knox's notebooks record no personal communications from Lyons nor is there any mention of visits. Presumably whenever Knox returned to his family home at Cranmore, Ballinrobe he would have made personal contact with Lyons, during the time when Lyons was stationed at the R.I.C. barracks in Ballyhaunis; after Lyons was transferred to Athenry in 1913 personal meetings would have become increasingly more difficult to arrange and after Lyons' transferral to Newport in 1916 probably completely impossible. That Lyons was aware of Knox's failing health can be inferred from Lyons' letter to the Royal Society of Antiquaries of Ireland dated 6 November 1929 in which he asks the Society to take Knox's notebooks for safe-keeping: 'These Note-Books were sent to me by the late Mr. Knox a short time before his death – when he was no longer able to do antiquarian work'; presumably Lyons received these notebooks some time in 1919 as the latest quotation from Lyons' letters made by Knox in his notebook is dated 29 October 1918.

---

* Strangely, the acquisition of the collection of the Knox/Lyons photographs is not recorded in the Proceedings of the Society as published in its *Journal*.

LYONS' INTEREST IN FOLKLIFE

Lyons' love of folklife and lore is a central part of his 'antiquarian craze' and Knox's four notebooks are interspersed with Lyons' observations; his interest in this field is as wide-ranging as his archaeological investigations and covers such diverse topics as devotional practices and festivals (both pagan and Christian), superstitions, cures, legends, ballads and anecdotes, commencing on the first page of the earliest (extant) notebook:

> '27 July 1905: The 18th century custom of seating in Aughamore Church. At proper season rushes were cut and bound in sheaves, and these were spread on the floor during Mass. After Mass they were ranged against the walls. During the ceremony the worshippers sat or knelt on them';

The last quotation from Lyons regarding local tradition is recorded by Knox on 15 October 1917:

> 'There was apparently a dolmen in Knockinn* and the people seem to have thought that no one could have been tall enough to reach from the "headstone" to the "footstone" but Finn. The burial tradition has lived anyhow'.

'WREN BOYS' AND 'MUMMERS'

A subject of continuing interest was the tradition and customs of visitations by disguised local men; there are dated photographs in the Lyons Collection in N.U.I.Galway of 'Wren Boys' at Ballyhaunis (1906) and at Newport (1916 and 1917) (Plates 66-8). Knox's notebooks contain many long descriptions transcribed from Lyons' letters:

> 26 Jan 1906: 'When the Wran [sic.] Boys first paraded the "fool" had a sheaf of straw affixed as a tail [...] there is something in the costume as if the "fool" was formerly intended to represent our amiable friend the devil. The man dressed in female garb is called the "oonsheech". This word is not in O'Reilly. It is the feminine of fool – a word which seems not to have a feminine in English'.

In mid-Summer 1906, Knox quotes Lyons' observations on the differences between 'bonfire night' (St John's Eve, 23 June) in Tipperary and Mayo and the link he proposes between the mid-Summer and mid-Winter festivities:

---

* The *Sites and Monuments Record* for Co. Mayo records a mound and enclosure at this site; on O.S 88 it is recorded as 'Finn Mac Cool's grave'.

Plate 65.
One of the few posed photographs in the Lyons Collection in N.U.I.Galway, this fine folk-life study of a woman working at a spinning-wheel is simply described by Lyons as 'The Spinner'. It is possibly the oldest photograph in the collection as it is the first photograph in an album of 90 pages in which the only dated photograph bears a date of 1906.

Photo: Lyons Collection, N.U.I.Galway.

The 'antiquarian craze'

Plate 66.
Photograph, dated December 1906, of Wren Boys in Ballyhaunis described by Lyons as the 'senior team in action. Sashes are blue'. Photo: Lyons Collection, N.U.I.Galway.

Plate 67.
Photograph, dated December 1916, of Wren Boys at Newport. Lyons notes that the 'straw armour is the traditional "Wran Hunting" costume' in Newport'.

Photo: Lyons Collection, N.U.I.Galway.

Plate 68.
Photograph, dated December 1917, of Wren Boys at Newport.

Photo: Lyons Collection, N.U.I.Galway.

'28 June: I have not seen them drive cattle through the fire here [in Mayo]. It was done in Tipperary when I was a child [...] here they often get bread in the middle of the night and eat it with fresh milk drawn from the cows. When milk is not available some people make oatmeal "brochan" or porridge to use with the bread. These of course are sacrificial observances. The driving of cattle through the fire seems to be an apology for the sacrifice of one or more beasts, and the immolation of the wren on 26th Dec. seems also sacrificial. The large animal being offered when the sun is strongest and the small one – perhaps the smallest of our warm blooded fauna – when he is weakest';

'6 July: In Castlebar [the] fire dwarfs all I have ever seen in the bonfire way and the populace – old and young – go mad with joyous excitement. A feature of the celebration is the use of unlimited squibs and crackers of rather potent home manufacture. These are generally used in a way dangerous to the public, but if the Police interfered it would lead to a general riot. There is no such exhilaration in connection with any Christian festival – not even Christmas which is a mere whiskey-bibbing [sic] affair'.

In February 1908 Knox quotes Lyons' description of marriage practices in which 'Mummers' play a significant part:

'The marriage usages in vogue here and all over Connaught, also in part of the Midlands, seem to have originated in the capture of the bride and subsequent attempts at her recapture. A considerable number of people on side-cars and horses assemble on the wedding morning at the bride's house. The parties drive to church – the bride and groom sitting demurely side by side. After the wedding the cavalcade drive at a furious rate to the bride's house where refreshments are ready – the groom holding the bride with his arm round her waist. At night a lot of young fellows dressed fantastically with straw come uninvited to the wedding house and practise rough horse-play on the women – the bride included. They are pacified with refreshments after which they generally withdraw. The journey to church seems to symbolize capture and the "drive" after the wedding – at headlong speed – seems to symbolize flight. The visit of the disguised party seems a relic of attempts at recapture. The disguised men are called "cluimaires" (pron. "climeras"). The word means in the singular an untidy person and is not in O'Reilly, and the spelling here given is conjectural. Another name here is "wholpers". This may be "fabhalpaire", pr. "folferra" plural "fabhalpaire" pr. "folperri" from "fabhal" an expedition, a journey (OR). This, if it is correct, is probably the correct ancient name for a recapture gang. The name in S. Tipperary for such a gang is "ban-beggars" perhaps "woman-beggars" from "bean" a woman and bacaighe "beggars";

> '30 Jan 1917: The Straw "armour" is the traditional "Wran Hunting" costume here [Newport]. All mummeries of the kind consist essentially of disguises, for originally the performers personated deities, and to do this thing they had to disguise their natural features. For this reason the Greek dramatic performers wore masks, because their art was in its origin sacerdotal';
>
> '9 Feb 1917: The underlying reason for the Climmeras, that is the religious reason, seems to be that the gods were supposed to visit the wedding feast, partake of the viands, and give their blessing to the nuptials [...] Of course the priests who personated the gods (they are at the game yet) had to disguise themselves in order to heighten the supernatural effect [...] the Climmera visitations are now mere orgies of licensed blackguardism'.

In 1920 Lyons sent to the Royal Society of Antiquaries of Ireland 'two straw head-dresses used at a Wren-Boy celebration at Newport, Co. Mayo, on St Stephen's Day, 1919'; Wren-Boy dress and practices became the subject of the first paper published under Lyons' name. He notes that the ceremony was observed merely as a pretext to 'collect backsheesh' by 'a great many knots of small boys and rude young men, and, though tolerated, is regarded with disfavour'; but that two or three generations earlier it had not entirely lost its 'primeval seriousness' and was a vital part of Christmas celebrations when 'it was a great honour for a parish contingent to capture the "wran" of a rival parish and bear him in triumph with their own'. Lyons interprets the inclusion of a male and a 'sham female' in mock conjugal union exchanging 'grotesque endearments' as a survival of a ceremony of 'fructification', the straw head-dresses representing the colour of the sun. He finds it 'noteworthy, that the rhymes sung by the Wren-Boys are, and have been in English, even in places like Newport where Irish was the prevailing speech amongst the people'.

Lyons' interest in the customs and traditions of the Wren Boys continued throughout his life; in a hand-written letter, dated 24.2.1947, on file in the archives of the Irish Folklore Commission, Lyons mentions: 'I have ascertained from David Condon of Clonmel that the use of the tambourine in Wren Processions has been traditional here'.[43]

PEOPLES OF IRELAND

Another recurring topic is Lyons' fascination with the racial characteristics and customs of the itinerant community (then known as 'Tinkers'); two much 'posed' photographs (unfortunately undated) survive (Plates 69-70). First mentioned by Knox, on 18 April 1906, the quotation from Lyons' letter simply reads: 'see articles 'Cant', 'Shelta' and 'Sheltru' in Chambers' Encyclopedia re Tinkers'; a month later, Lyons sends his own observations:

'19 May 1906: 'The authors say they [tinkers] speak a jargon which is the lost bardic language of Ireland. I heard them speak it myself – when they were in mischief and Robert [presumably Peel, who instituted the Irish constabulary] was advancing at the double. They use Christian slang and oaths but I believe they are not Christians. At least they seem not to marry regularly – though their unions are indissoluble [...] the tinkers have Irish names and characteristics. The old folks are trilingual, Gaelic, Cant, and English. Their prejudices are Catholic – though they have little or unpractical [sic.] religion. But there occurs among them occasionally specimens of a dark-eyed, staring, wild type that can hardly be Celtic [...] note in the "Morning Costume" picture the woman nearest the left. She is of the dark, staring type. See the man on the left. This man's physiognomic affinities are Celtic [...] it is probable that they are foreign or semi-foreign tribes of metal workers who were in Connacht with chiefs and took clan names – as was common – on the break up of the clan system; also independent metal workers who owing to their comparative isolation retained the tribal system after it died out in the country. The Celtic facial and other affinities may have arisen from the practice those people often had of kidnapping suitable children – at least tradition so accuses them';

Plate 69.
One of two photographic studies c.1906 of the 'Tinkers' camp at Spaddagh, Ballyhaunis' (see also Plate 70) which Lyons sent to Knox as visual evidence of his opinion regarding their ethnicity.
Photo: Lyons Collection, N.U.I.Galway.

Plate 70.
Lyons describes this photograph as 'Tinkers' camp at Spaddagh, Ballyhaunis, morning dress'; the woman nearest left is 'the dark-eyed, staring wild type that can hardly be Celtic', while the 'physiognomic affinities' of the man on the left are Celtic.

Photo: Lyons Collection, N.U.I.Galway.

'14 Aug 1906: There are in this locality some specimens of a small, black-haired, brown-eyed, flat-nosed, olive-skinned, people who are probably Iberian – but they are very rare. The main stock is represented by a sallow, gray-eyed type with somewhat retreating forehead and chin. Individuals of this type have generally projecting upper teeth – probably the result of the mastication of raw flesh by their ancestors. Dragging raw meat off bones would produce this formation. The type next in importance is the fair-haired, classic-featured type. The two latter seem to have come via the north. A mixture of the first and third produces what is called the Milesian type. It is very common about Granard in Co. Longford – chiefly persons named Reilly'.

Over the years Lyons describes the differences in facial and other characteristics he observes in the populations of different areas and, though he admits difficulty in finding 'pure specimens', ascribes races of people to particular locations. He became confident in the validity of his own ethnological opinions:

'15 Oct 1914: Irish Annals and legend only confuse Irish ethnology, as they confuse the study of antiquities. I would strongly advise an enquirer to rely on his observation and not to mind this literature [...] of course the inner meaning of, and inferences from the folk-tales are valuable, but not for ethnological research';

'17 Oct 1914: 'All this theory about the Spanish breed being prevalent in Galway City is mere Moore Melody romance. The brown-eyed people of Galway are aboriginal. They do not, as far as I can see, extend to west of the Corrib city'.[44]

Lyons' speculations into the successive races who colonised Ireland, beginning with the Mongols, then followed by the Iberians and Celts, were incorporated into Knox's 1917-8 paper 'Ballygurraun and Raheen Group of Works in Earth and Stone' (earlier described, see pages 97-9).

DEVOTIONAL PRACTICES

The rituals performed by pilgrims at devotional sites and their superstitions regarding them were keenly observed by Lyons and frequently recorded by Knox, particularly in the earliest notebook:

'30 April 1906: I visited the antiquity at Cappagh near Dunmore called 'Altar' by the O.S. genius – 1 inch.* In interest it probably beats Thubbernaneeve. I shall content myself for the present by saying that there is an oblong well 12ft. 10in. by 10ft. 3in. outside. Interior width 7ft. Width of doorway 2ft. [...] It is called Thubber-na-Crush–Neeve. The Well of the Holy Cross';

'23 June 1906: The bullaun stone near the old church at Holywell** is an object of devotion. It is sunk in a bank of earth 5 ft. x 2½ ft. x 2 ft. high [...] There is a channel out of hollow. The diameter of the hollow is 1 ft. 5 in. & depth about 9 in. At the pattern none but "craw thumpers" – that is the ultra pious – perform devotions at the stone. These admirable people say seven "Hail Marys" and seven "Holy Marys" at the stone when they have finished at the wall';

'6 Sept 1906: About 1½ miles S of Kilkelly and between the two roads leading from B[ally]haunis to that place is a well called Thubbercoghlan*** at which "stations" were made on Garlic [sic.] Sunday up to about 30 years ago. It is

---

* It is also marked 'Altar' on sheet 8 of the O.S. 6-inch map and is classified on the *Sites and Monuments Record* for Co. Galway as an altar.

** The *Sites and Monuments Record* for Co. Mayo records ecclesiastical remains, including a church, holy well and a cross at Holywell (O.S. 103).

*** The *Sites and Monuments Record* for Co. Mayo lists a holy well and sacred tree at Tobercoghlan, which is situated in the townland of Cloghvoley (O.S. 81).

Plate 71.
'Pattern at Lady's Well, Baunmore, Athenry' c.1915. Lyons draws attention to the different postures of the pilgrims, 'people may be seen kneeling while saying the initial or concluding prayers'.
Photo: Lyons Collection, N.U.I.Galway.

---

walled in like an ordinary well and has steps leading to the water but it was dry when I visited it. On its wall is a small flat stone with two remarkable holes but not thorough [sic.] – one considerably larger than the other – which must have had a use in connection with stations. Closeby is a lake called Lough Coghlan. About 20 yds. NNE of the well is the rotten stump of the sacred thorn bush of the place. This stump is carefully and regularly fenced round with stones at the base';

'8 Sept 1906: I have not been able to find any clue to the ancient history of Thubbernacrushneeve. It was one of the greatest shrines of the west. The devotions were under the auspices of the clergy down to a comparatively recent period. A Dean Egan was identified with the place, and five Paters and five Aves for the repose of his soul are said at his tree at the conclusion of each station. I have not been able to get accurate particulars of the method of performing the station up to the present – but it begins at the New Altar and ends at the Douach. This Altar was used at Patterns for the celebration of Mass. The old altar was used in the Penal times. The water of the well must not be used save for drinking, but at the outflow there is a place for ablution fenced off with a ruined stone circle. A tree stood near the Dean's tree to which a cross was attached. A man from Dunmore named Petty cut down the tree and the cross flew into the breast of an old barefooted man who was passing by. It afterwards passed into the possession of a priest named Loftus. Part of the ceremony in the Dhouach consists of three turnings sunwise';

'6 Oct 1906: There is an enchanted cat at Thubber Coghlan. He used to be on a bush that is there – but it is withered now. Lights are often seen on Lough Coghlan. A man with a candle in his hand was seen to walk across the lake the other night. I saw the light myself but I did not see the man [...] Now we have the pre-Christian cult of T[hubber] Coghlan. A cat-like demon was worshipped or placated there and the cult has survived Christian observance because offerings are left at the well though the Pattern has long ceased';

'22 Oct 1906: It seems that all these lakes (L. Caldra, L.Coghlan, etc.) are enchanted and there is an enchanted horse in each of them. One of these horses was lately seen and it had a green saddle. Of course no enchanted horse would wear an orange one';

'6 May 1907: Thubber-Mhuira* – half a mile S of Elphin was a famous place of pilgrimage. A few people visit it yet on 8th Sept. Nativity of B[lessed] V[irgin] M[ary]. It used to be the scene – on pattern days – of fierce faction fights between the Beirnes and Carneys. One of the Carneys – who though he has completed his century is yet alive – when marshalling his faction at the well on pattern day heard the Angelus ringing at noon and he exclaimed "Good God! Tis twelve of clock and not a blow struck yet."

On 8 April 1915 Knox records a list of 'Notes regarding photographs by P.L.' in which the description of a photograph (no reference number given) appears to relate to a photograph which is included in the Lyons Collection in N.U.I.Galway (Plate 71):

'Pattern at Lady's Well at Baunmore, 1 m. E of Athenry. To show the postures of the people and different types. A weak perennial spring within the enclosure. Opposite the opening are carved figures in stone of, I think, the Virgin and Child. The "station" consists of – 1st 9 "Our Fathers" and 9 "Hail Marys" – Then 3 circuits of the enclosure on bare knees, or 15 circuits walking barefoot. The devotees genuflect when passing the images on each round. There is no rule regarding the prayers said during each round, but the same prayers are said at the termination as at the beginning. People may be seen kneeling while saying the initial or concluding prayers'.

---

* The *Sites and Monuments Record* for Co.Roscommon lists a holy well at Tobermhuire, which is situated in the townland of Cloonboyoge (O.S. 22).

The O.S. Revision Name Book of 1928 records a local belief that the well had been in use since the 14th century. Pilgrimage to this well may have begun some time after the battle of Athenry in 1249, when (as quoted by Hardiman from the *Annals of Clonmacnoise*), 'the [Irish] nobility of Connaught went to *Athenrie* to prey and spoile that towne, on the day of our Lady the Blessed Virgin Mary, in the middest of harvest. There was a great armye, with Terlaugh mac Hugh. The sheriff of Connaught with many Englishmen were in the said towne before them. The sheriff and Englishmen desired them, in honour of the Blessed Virgin Mary, whose day then was, to forbeare with them that day, which the said Irish nobility refused to give any respect [...] They assaulted the town [...] where the Virgin Mary wrought miraculouslye against the said nobility'.[45]

The pattern is still a very popular devotional practice and takes place every year on 15 August, the feast of the Assumption of the Blessed Virgin Mary.

PRESERVATION OF ARTEFACTS

Lyons' concern for the preservation of artefacts which were brought to his notice is clear from quotations in Knox's notebooks; while stationed at the R.I.C. barracks in Ballyhaunis he frequently forwarded artefacts to Knox:

> '1 Dec 1905: Sends a collection of objects found in the crannoge in L[ough] Caheer by James Flatley, a young man of Ballyhaunis, who wishes to present them to the Nat[ional] Mus[eum]. L[yons] thinks it best to defer doing so lest the find be noised abroad and the place ignorantly ransacked. Wishes Flatley could get something for this but F. is a very decent young man and does not mind giving them up';
>
> '2 February 1907: I beg to enclose a flint arrow or spearhead which I beg you will accept. It was found about a year ago in Lauralea (Knox territory) about ¾ of a mile E of Boleyboy. When it was found a piece of the shaft was attached but through neglect this has crumbled away. The article was found accidentally in tilled land by a young farmer. I think the stone of which it is made is to be found here in small detached pieces, but I think it would be well to have expert opinion lest the head or its material may have come from the arsenals of Antrim. This find helps to confirm my theory that there were pre-Celtic settlements in the neighbourhood of B[ally]haunis. In the place where this article was found there are no actual marks of such settlements, such as those which are presumed to exist closer to B[ally]haunis, but low knolls, the remains of eroded eskers, exist and these may have been the sites of Pre-Celtic forts or habitations';

Plate 72.

Photograph, dated November 1906, of an 'Ancient boat in R.I.C. yard, Ballyhaunis' awaiting dispatch to Dr. Lane Joynt of Dublin. Lyons draws our attention to the stern panel which 'seems to have been to check leakages arising from breaches in the boat material due to the short grain of the wood'.

Photo: Lyons Collection, N.U.I.Galway.

> '21 July 1907: A diminutive trunnioned bronze cannon was found some years ago in Knockbrackboy a few miles E of this place. I am trying to get on its trail. It must have been a wall gun of C[aislean] na Drancaddha';
>
> '2 May 1909: There seems to have been a flint factory on the E shore of Island Lough. I have not been able to find finished flints, but this is not wonderful as the finished ones would have been taken away. A beautiful arrowhead, of the style of the spearhead I sent you, was found some time ago in a bog near Lough Caheer a mile E of Island L[ough]'.

That Lyons was dedicated to the preservation of artifacts, regardless of size, is clearly evident in his treatment of a boat found at Island, as quoted by Knox from Lyons' letters:

> '24 Nov 1906: The Island boat has been purchased by Dr. Lane Joynt of Dublin. I think it is ultimately intended for the Royal College of Surgeons. I have it on a cart in the b[arrac]k yard ready to send it on. It is a very fine affair. It had an

affixed panel at each end but only the stern one remains. The one at the bow end was rectangular and counter sunk into the wood of the boat body. The panel at the rear is shaped irregularly. The use of these panels seems to have been to check leakages arising from breaches in the boat material due to the short grain of the wood at the ends. The stern panel is held on by wooden pegs. There is a small patch below the water line to the left of the stern. The patch is held on by iron nails which look modern';

'1 Dec 1906: The Island canoe – In the underside of its bottom at the centre line are marks of a row of pegs about six feet apart driven upward into the wood as if to hold on an unattached keel';

'13 Dec 1906: I have found the bow panel of the Island Canoe. It is of black oak and quite sound. It has on its area three irregularly placed peg-holes each 1 in. in diam'.

On the last pages of Notebook 1 (perhaps to fill up the available space) Knox records some 'Notes on Photos' in which he includes a description of photograph No. 436 (Plate 72), the Island Boat:

'4 May 1907: No 436. Stern of boat showing patch. See peg holes. The holes in the bottom were drainage holes. The pegs were truncated cones ½ in. in diameter at the base. One extracted showed the knife marks and it had around it some rushes in which it was wrapped to make it tight. There are probably two additional and larger drainage holes at the beginning of the stern rise. This boat has been taken to Dublin by its owner Dr. Lane Joynt FRSAI. Length over all 22' 2". Width at Stern 2' 7". D[itt]o at bow 2' – Length occupied by end slope at bow and stern 1' 9". Depth inside 16" – Thickness of bottom at Stern 3½" – D[itt]o at central drain hole, 2½" – Where natural depressions occurred in the tree they were allowed for inside – that is, the excavator did not go so bare at these points as elsewhere'.

Unfortunately, the events of the finding of this boat are not recorded in the first extant notebook which begins on 21 June 1905; presumably Lyons had been in negotiations with Dr. Lane Joynt for some time and regarded him as a suitable person to conserve the boat. Joynt appears to have been in continuing correspondence with Lyons, as later recorded by Knox:

'3 June 08: Sends bronze axes, two, and a spearhead made by Dr. Lane Joynt of Dublin FRSAI. In imitation of old. Very good. The patina given by vinegar and sal ammoniac'.[46]

RESEARCH IN FOLK-LIFE STUDIES IN RETIREMENT

That Lyons continued his interest in folk-life and lore after his retirement to Clonmel in 1920 can be seen in the list of his publications (Appendix 2). In 1940 Lyons' knowledge became more accessible when the Irish Folklore Commission began to record his memories and observations on country life and customs: 19 pages of typewritten notes are on file in which Lyons answers questions (using the standard format of the Commission questionnaire) about his memories of peasant dress as worn by men, women and boys from 1861-1940; he provides information under various headings *eg.* colour, fabric, decoration, customs etc. He concludes the questionnaire, in his inimitable style, with the comment 'the writer has heard of an instance in which the long-trouser innovation was denounced from a Catholic pulpit. The preacher addressed the people to resign the long trousers to men with flat hooves and crooked ankles'. Lyons does not elucidate further, but presumably the exhortation meant that only men with 'devilish' intentions would wear these trousers; perhaps the 'innovation' that troubled the priest was the change in trouser design to fly-fronts which first appeared in the mid-nineteenth century. [47]

Throughout the 1940s Lyons sent hand-written notes and letters of his memories of folk-life and lore to the Irish Folklore Commission, many of which were later published in *Béaloideas*, the journal of the Folklore of Ireland Society.

ASSOCIATION WITH GODDARD ORPEN

In his letter to Goulden Lyons states: 'I have been a correspondent of H.T. Knox of Ballinrobe for 22 years and with Dr. Goddard Orpen – author of "Ireland under the Normans" – for 30 years. These periods overlapped'. Lyons first met Knox in 1897 or 1898 and it seems likely that he introduced Lyons to Orpen. According to O'Connell 'about 1910, he [Lyons] collaborated with Dr. Goddard Orpen in the exploration of earthworks'; this remark probably refers to the publication of Orpen's paper 'The Mote of Castlelost, County Westmeath' in which Orpen acknowledges Lyons' research (see below). The earliest reference to Orpen, as transcribed by Knox from Lyons' letters, occurs on 30.8.1906:

> 'I think I have found Mr. Orpen's rectangular fort near Tuam. I think I shall be able to show that it is of the same type as a rectangular one in Carrowneden'.

This does not, however, imply actual correspondence between Lyons and Orpen;

The 'antiquarian craze'

Plate 73.
Aerial photograph of the impressively embanked ringfort at Rathra, Castlerea, Co. Roscommon. The mound to left of centre was described by Lyons to Knox in 1907 as having 'a pretty deep fosse at its base, but no dyke' and the low mound to right of centre had 'the base of a slender limestone pillar on its top'.

Photo: Department of Archaeology, N.U.I.Galway.

Plate 74.
Photograph c.1907 described by Lyons as 'Mote in Moate Td., Ballyhaunis. The fosse towards E'. In the *Sites and Monuments Record* this monument is classified as an enclosure (O. S. 103).

Photo: Lyons Collection, N.U.I.Galway.

in the absence of the (presumed) earliest notebook in which there may have been details of correspondence, the earliest date recorded by Knox from Lyons' letters is 29 June 1907:

> 'On Mullaghadooey Hill two miles E of Castlerea is a fine conical mound [...] On the slope of this hill about 400 yds. W from the mound above described is the most remarkable rath I have yet seen. It has four dykes and three fosses. The outer dyke is a mere "bead" on the outer edge of the first fosse as at Barrinagh. The two next dykes are high and stout and the fosses deep. The inner dyke is but a bead on the outer edge of the garth bordering the inner fosse. The garth is divided in two nearly equal parts by a modern earthen fence; near its (the garth's) centre is a mound exactly similar to the one on top of the hill but a little smaller. It has a pretty deep fosse at its base but no dyke. This is to S of the fence dividing the garth. To N of this fence is a low mound with the base of a slender limestone pillar on its top. The diam. of Rath & Fosses etc. "overall" is 126 paced yards. Width of fosses etc., 31 yds. Diam. of garth 64 yds. The rath is in the townland of Rathra. I have written to Mr Orpen regarding these antiquities'.

It seems that Lyons managed to convey his sense of excitement to Orpen about these earthworks, of which there are 7 photographs in the collection at N.U.I.Galway (all, unfortunately, in a poor state of preservation); a week later Lyons showed other 'finds' to Orpen, as Knox records from Lyons' letter:

> '8.7.1907: Mr. Orpen visited Moate (Annagh mote) (Plate 74) and Barrinagh (Sheeaunbeg). He seems to agree with me as to the site of Ballyveel Castle. He was very much struck with Barrinagh mote – as he well may be – it is the most perfect antiquity of its kind, I believe, in existence. The whole thing save the wood of the stockades is as the Normans left it. Mr. O[rpen] agrees with me that the rectangular hollow on the inside of the fosse on the N side near the site of the passage on to the low external esker was the stable for the horses of the knights and squires. Mr. O[rpen] was on a "real life" crannoge for perhaps the first time as we visited the island on Lough O'Flynn'

Lyons' correspondence with Orpen is noted by Knox throughout the next 7 years:

> '3.9.1907: I was through mid-Roscommon a few days last week. I found a magnificent Norman mote at Runnamoat (Fig. 13), 6 miles W of Roscommon town at the mansion of Major Chichester Constable [...] I have informed Mr. Orpen';

The 'antiquarian craze'

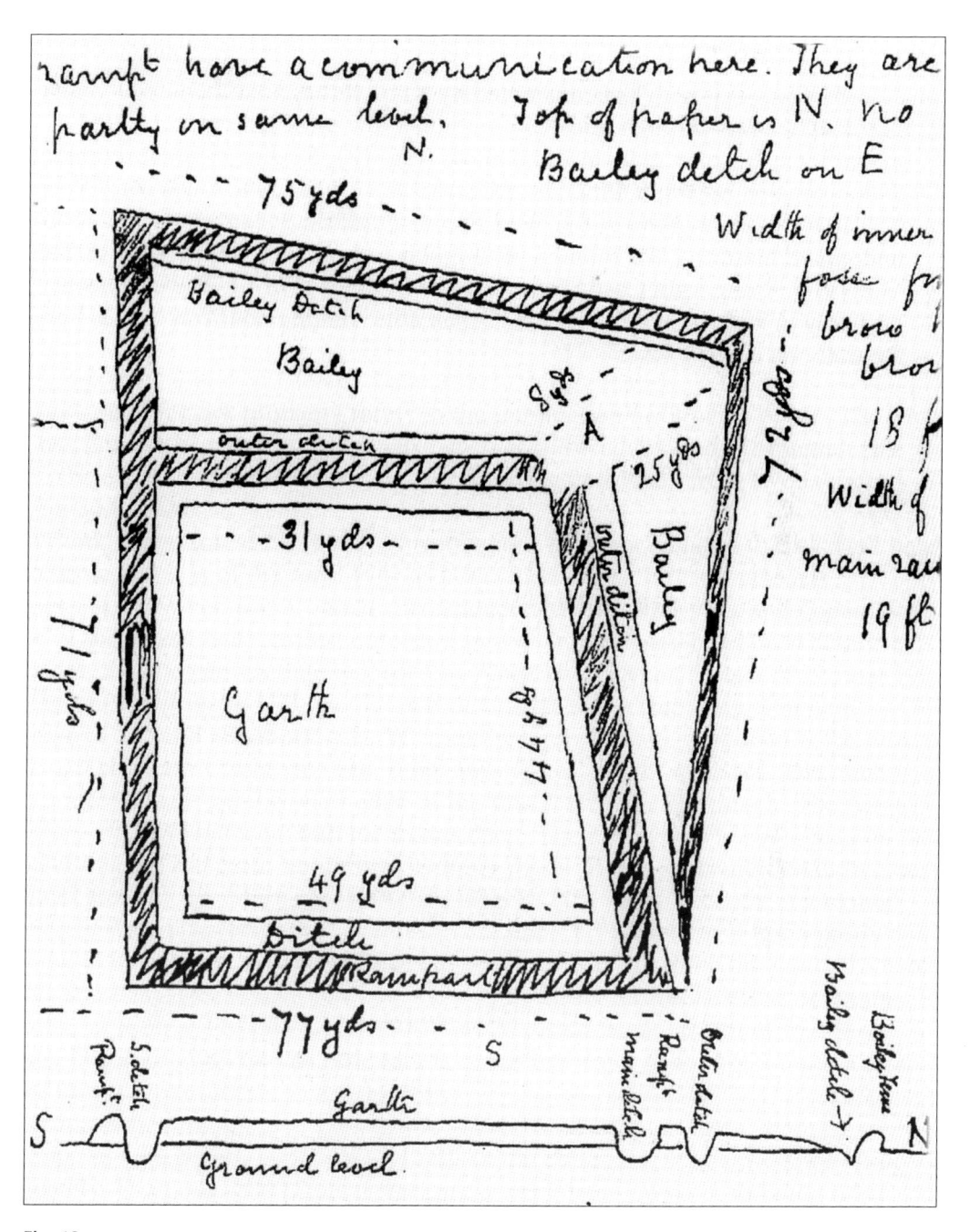

Fig. 13.
Page from Knox's notebook in which he has copied Lyons' drawing of an earthwork at Runnamoat, Co. Roscommon, presumably a medieval moated site.

Plate 75.
One of two photographs c.1913 of Rathgorgin Castle in which Lyons draws our attention to 'new work between two towers bonded by one stone on each side. Originally two separate towers' and notes that Orpen considers it to resemble Bunratty Castle on a smaller scale. (See also Plate 76).
Photo: Lyons Collection, N.U.I.Galway.

'2.7.1912: In excavation of the Well Fort at Tulsk on S side Mr. Orpen found undoubted masonry. We found a rectangular fort near Clooneyquin N of Tulsk';

'3.6.1914: Rathgorgin Castle is in Rathgorgin (Plates 75-6). The castle was probably in style of Bunratty. G.H. Orpen after visiting confirms this as being like Bunratty on a small scale';

'7.6.1914: A plan of Kilcolgan burgess found by Orpen is being made. He found also lower story of Ballinacourty Manor House close to the church'.[48]

In 1910 Orpen published 'The Mote of Castlelost, County Westmeath' which he illustrates with a photograph taken by James Tuite but attributes the description to Lyons: 'Castlelost is the name of a parish in the barony of Fartullagh, County Westmeath. Mote and castle are about a mile north of Rochfortbridge. To the east of the mote is a slightly raised bailey, 61 by 46 yards, and on the edge of this bailey, about 18 yards from the mote, the castle was built with its door facing the mote. It is conjectured that the earthwork was formed out of an esker knoll, that

Plate 76.
Rathgorgin Castle c.1913.
Photo: Lyons Collection, N.U.I.Galway.

---

the eastern part of the knoll was cut away to about the height of 6 feet, and that the material thus obtained was used to form the mote, while the denuded part served as a raised bailey. There are traces of another enclosure to the north, and when the stone castle was built, another bailey was added to the south. The road from Rochfortbridge has cut into the mote at one side, and the opposite side has been mutilated, so that the space on the summit, probably originally circular, is now about 23 by 13 yards. The mote rises about 16 feet above the raised bailey. The church, about 400 yards to the north-east, appears to have been semi-fortified. There are some curious sculptured stones here in the arch of the east window, which ought to be examined and described. Others were removed, and have been built into the new chapel at Meedian, where they are preserved. I owe the above notes to Sergeant Lyons of Ballyhaunis'.

In his notebook Knox quotes from Lyons' letter of 16 September 1907: 'I have just paid a short visit to Westmeath. I was at Castlelost – of which a description hereafter' and on 27 March 1908 records the receipt of photographs of the mote and castle; as Orpen's paper was published some 2-3 years after Lyons' first recorded visit, continuing correspondence and awareness of the each others archaeological endevours is implied.[49]

In the 1915-6 *Journal of the Galway Archaeological and Historical Society* Orpen published 'The mote of Oldcastle and the castle of Rathgorgin' in which he acknowledges that 'the appearance and character of the work can be judged from the accompanying photographic reproduction, the blocks for which have been kindly presented by Mr. H.T. Knox'. The photograph which accompanies this paper is one of three photographs of Rathgorgin castle which are included in the Lyons Collection in N.U.I.Galway.[50]

In his letter to Goulden Lyons mentions that his 30 years of correspondence with Orpen overlapped with the 22 years of his letters to Knox. Orpen does not refer to Lyons in any of his papers written after 1916. However, it is evident from the Orpen Papers (archived in the National Library of Ireland) that their correspondence continued until at least December 1931. Two short letters are dated January 1918 and January 1919 (while Lyons was serving in the R.I.C. barracks in Newport) and describe Lyons' attempts to find details of inscriptions and in both of which he notes that 'Miss R[eddington] has again broken one of her wrists'. The remaining 24 letters were written in 1931 (during Lyons' retirement in Clonmel) and are very different in character. They consist of rambling reflections on politics, church and state relations, reminiscences and criticisms of the change in police methods and comments on personal and place-names; the letters commence with phrases such as 'I again presume to write without having anything to say worth saying' and evoke a lonely scholar wishing to continue sharing his speculations and reminiscences with an appreciative mind.

Knox's notebooks end inconclusively on 29 October 1918 with the entry 'Glassymoo (Doagh & Ballyglanna rock scribings will be photoed [sic.] again. "Ballymonach (mote ? HTK) is about 1 mile from Lissaghow. Last year I found a small rectangular fort South of the latter"[...].' The paucity of transcriptions from Lyons' letters in the years 1917-18 and their sporadic nature indicate Knox's failing health; however, it seems clear that Lyons was still painstakingly measuring and photographing field monuments and forwarding the results to Knox together with his observations and speculations. The four notebooks record the meticulously detailed work of Patrick Lyons during the years from 1905 to 1918 without which none of the papers written by Knox in theses years could have been attempted. In the wealth of their recorded detail, therefore, it is possible that Knox's notebooks bear unique testimony to a remarkable phase of archaeological fieldwork in the west of Ireland in the early years of the twentieth century.

Chapter 4

Lyons in Clonmel

Having resigned from the Royal Irish Constabulary, it is probable that Lyons returned immediately to his birth-place, Clonmel; in his letters and notes there is no mention of correspondence or visits with family or friends (with the exception of the letter to Goulden in 1953). As was happening throughout the countryside, Tipperary in the 1920s was in the throes of violence. Thurles was a strong Republican centre and it was believed that the Royal Irish Constabulary there belonged to the Orange Order and had been transferred from Northern Ireland. In the week before Lyons' resignation the *Clonmel Nationalist* reports a 'Reign of Terror following the Oola battle, where two soldiers were shot dead and three wounded. Tipperary town, which hitherto had been congratulating itself on its immunity from disturbances, has been in a regular ferment'; a week later in Clonmel, two ex-service men were fired on by soldiers in a military lorry and, what may have been more personally worrying for Lyons, 'Twenty R.I.C. men on temporary duty in Tipperary returned to their stations traveling in civilian clothes and without arms [...] they were instructed to dress in civilian clothes to avoid trouble on the railways'. The necessity of anonymity for Lyons must have been intense, as is further evidenced by a report that 'a man in plain clothes, who is said to have been a member of the R.I.C. is reported to have been fired at at Ballydine, near Dundrum, Co. Tipperary. The man made his escape in the darkness. There is an unconfirmed report that he was subsequently conveyed to Tipperary military hospital'. Presumably Lyons could not keep in contact with any of his colleagues in Mayo or Galway and one wonders what his thoughts might have been on reading that 'a party of seventeen R.I.C. under District Inspector-Stevenson, were ambushed at Carrowkennedy, near Westport, last night by one hundred men. District-Inspector Stevenson, a

Plate 77.
Photograph c.1910 which Lyons describes as 'Figure on E gate pier of Relig Vreedha, Thurles. About 15 inches in height'. *The Archaeological Inventory of Co. Tipperary* records that St. Briget's church site and graveyard is situated in the townland of Garryvicleheen, outside the walled town. In the S wall of the graveyard there is a large stone pier into which are inserted several architectural fragments and carved stones, most of which are of recent date.

Photo: Lyons Collection, N.U.I.Galway.

sergeant and four constables were killed. Four constables were seriously wounded. All arms and ammunition were taken and the tenders and one touring car burnt'.

Throughout 1922 Clonmel came under attack: in February, some seven months after the signing of the Truce and the establishment of the Irish Free State (after which the police in Clonmel carried no arms), a daring night raid lasting two hours, was made on the Royal Irish Constabulary barracks in Clonmel 'probably the largest police station in the South of Ireland [... which] during the recent evacuation of outlying stations on the disbanding of the Black and Tans was made the repository of such stores as these contained [...] the garrison at present is mostly comprised of the old R.I.C. men from the surrounding closed-up stations'; in July, following 'the burning of buildings at the north side of Clonmel Military Barracks' rail and postal services were suspended. The utter isolation of Clonmel is thus completed'; in August, 'Clonmel, the centre of Irregular activity and their chief supply base for months, was captured very easily on Wednesday evening by National troops and the hearty, enthusiastic welcome extended to them by the people showed how intensely they felt the relief from the harrowing conditions prevailing in the town and district for a painfully long period'. But Civil War hostilities were not yet over; 'the Free State troops, little more than schoolboys, occupied the town. The Republicans or "the Diehards" as they were popularly called, took over the lower slopes of the Comeraghs, overlooking the town and machine-gun fire kept both sides busy, without much damage to either side, except tragically to a young civilian, a boy, who was killed outside the Post Office by a stray bullet.' Sporadic fighting became a feature of life in Clonmel for the remaining months of 1922; 'there was heavy sniping in Clonmel throughout the nights of Wednesday-Thursday [14-5 Dec]. Several houses in the centre of the town were struck by bullets'.[1]

The earliest date at which we have evidence of Lyons' presence in Clonmel is 6 November 1929, when he was living at 3 Parnell Street. On that day he forwarded Knox's Notebooks to the Royal Society of Antiquaries of Ireland for safe-keeping; his comment that at his death they were 'likely to fall into Philistine hands' may suggest ill-health or perhaps the continuing pressures of life as an ex-policeman anxious to preserve his anonymity; it might also explain why Lyons' name does not appear in newspaper reports of the visit of the Royal Society of Antiquaries of Ireland to Clonmel for their summer meeting and a tour of the historic sights of the surrounding area, even though Lyons had been a Fellow of the Society for eight years. Other letters in the Knox/Lyons collection in the library of the Royal Society of Antiquaries of Ireland indicate that Lyons was living at 38 Lower Irishtown in 1930 and at 8 O'Neill Street from 1932-7; in their 1931 *Journal*, a list of Members and Fellows records Lyons' address as 4 Dillon Street. Lyons' letter to Goulden in 1953 is addressed from Post Office Lane, which address is also recorded in his obituary.[2]

ANTIQUARIAN WORK IN CLONMEL

During the 1930s Lyons published many articles on antiquities in Clonmel and on field-monuments in the surrounding area in the *Journal of the Royal Society of Antiquaries of Ireland*. In 1936 Curtis acknowledged the depth of Lyons' local knowledge in his paper 'Rental of the Manor of Lisronagh 1333': 'I have received many helpful and voluminous notes from Mr. Patrick Lyon [sic.] (ex-R.I.C.), now over seventy years of age, who was born in Newchapel parish adjacent, and has a unique knowledge and interest in the history and antiquities of the Vale of Clonmel, and whose traditions and memory of the same go back a long way. He has studied on foot all the country in and about Lisronagh, and provided me with a valuable map with the identifications marked'. Lyons' contributions to the

Journal of the Royal Society of Antiquaries of Ireland continued throughout the 1940s and early 1950s; his last paper, published just two years before his death was a description of 'The Irish Quern'. In the 1946 *Journal of the Cork Historical and Archaeological Society* Lyons published 'The Stone of Formach' describing a cross-inscribed pillar-stone at Tooracurra, Ballymacarbry, Co Waterford. In the 1950s he published articles in the *Journal of the Clonmel Historical and Archaeological Society*.[3]

ASSOCIATION WITH THE CLONMEL HISTORICAL AND ARCHAEOLOGICAL SOCIETY

The Historical and Archaeological Society of Clonmel and District was founded on 2 January 1944 and within a few months became embroiled in controversy following the discovery of a carved figure at Blue Anchor Lane, about which some members 'expressed the opinion that the figure is a pagan stone known as a "Sighle na gcioch" stone but others believe it to be another type of pagan goddess' (Plate 78). The controversy appears to have begun when a member of the Society, Charles Tinsley, in a letter to the editor of the *Clonmel Nationalist* wrote: 'I regret that I was not present at the meeting of the Historical and Archaeological Society of Clonmel at which Mr. McCarthy [Chairman] propounded his views about this interesting relic, declaring it (very confidently) to be of Indian origin. He builds up quite a pretty, if imaginative, story as to how it managed to hop from India to rare Clonmel [...] but what I really want to stress in this letter is the undue haste with which Clonmel people seem to be parting with this interesting piece of sculpture'. After an exchange of letters to the editor in the following weeks 'Mr. Tinsley suggested a "peace conference at the conclusion of hostilities" [... it was decided to] write to Dr. J. Raftery, Director of the National Museum, requesting a detailed report on the "Idol", noting any differences between the figure and the form of "Sigle na gCioc" generally, with an explanation of such peculiarities'. However, when the report was received, it 'was thought most unsatisfactory by the members present. The feeling of the meeting was that we must await a further report'. At the next meeting Mr. Tinsley and Mr. McCarthy again disagreed: Mr. Tinsley proposed that 'no further communication be addressed by the Society to Dr. Raftery as that gentleman had expressed his opinion that the figure in question was fundamentally similar to that of the sigle na gcioc type' while Mr. McCarthy, seemingly still more comfortable with the idea of a pagan Indian goddess than an Irish Sheela-na-gig, insisted that 'Dr. Raftery admitted that his letter to the Society was unsatisfactory and incon-

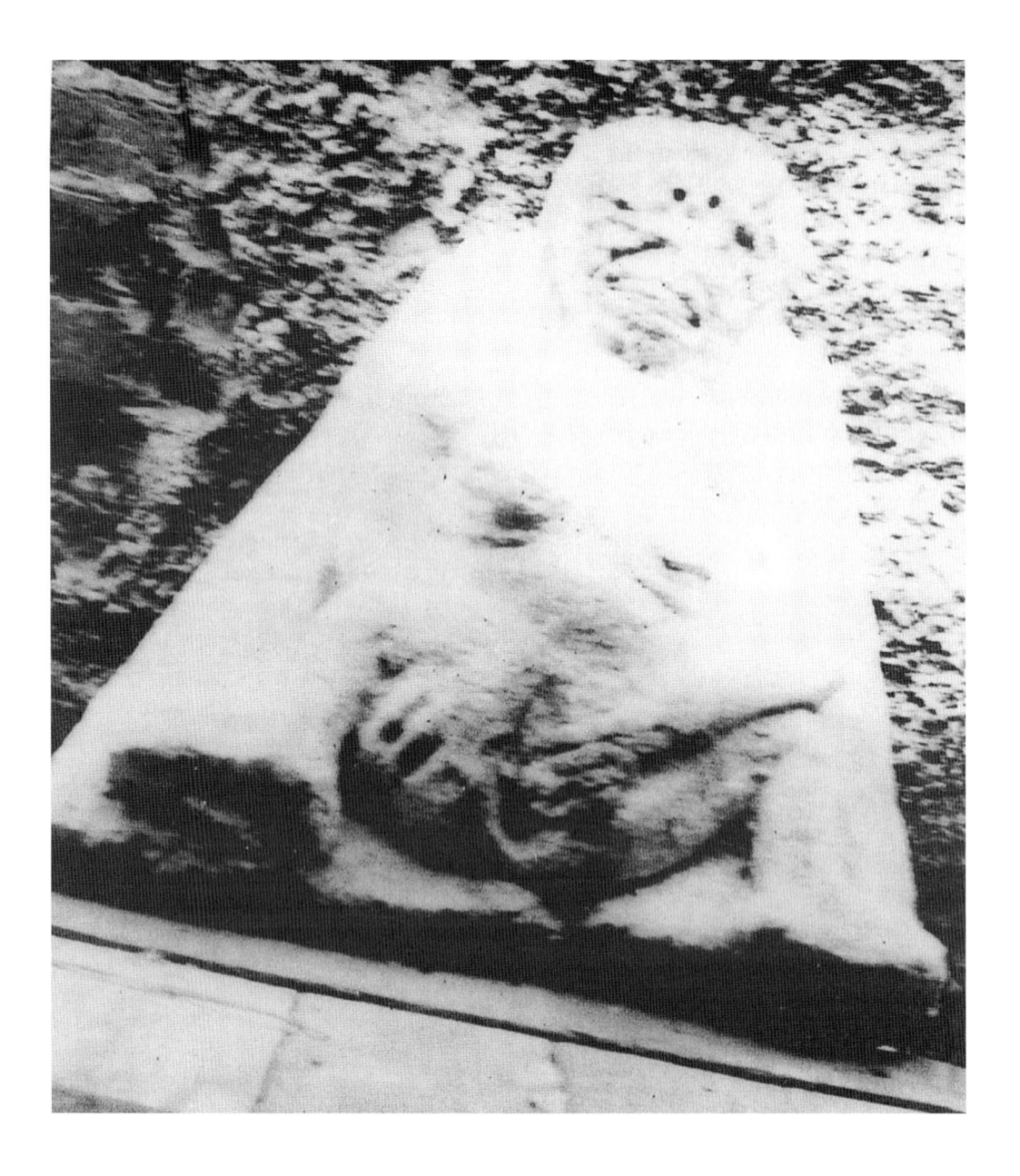

Plate 78.
Photograph by Lyons in April 1944 of the 'Idol of Blue Anchor Lane' after it had been taken down from a wall in a lane off O'Connell St, Clonmel. The sculpture is now in the care of the National Museum.

Reproduced courtesy of the Tipperary South County Museum, Clonmel.

clusive*. He suggested a second letter be addressed to Dr. Raftery requesting a definite expression of opinion. After further discussion it was agreed that if a copy of the Irish Archaeological Society's [sic.] journal containing Dr. Edith Guest's report on figures of the sigle na gcioc type could be made available for the next meeting of the Society it might help clear up the point at issue'. Unfortunately, the minutes of the next meeting are not recorded in the *Minute Book* and no further reference is made to "the Idol" at later meetings.⁴ The monument is now in the care of the National Museum.**

Lyons' work in archaeology was first mentioned at a meeting of the Clonmel Historical and Archaeological Association in June 1944; 'Dr P. O'Connell, in suggesting the area [Inishlonagh] as a venue for an excursion for the Society pointed out that Mr. P. Lyons had already completed most important research in the location of the old stream-bed, in the Scottish burials in the old abbey and on the inscription which puzzles many. Mr. Leask had also been in this area. It was unanimously agreed to invite Mr. P. Lyons to lead the expedition'. O'Connell, a native of Cavan who had contributed frequently to *Seanchas Breifne*, was Principal of Clonmel Technical School in the 1940s; his public lectures on the pre-history and history of the area were often reported in the local press *e.g.* 'A Learned Lecture – "Some Glimpses of Ireland in the Celtic and Early Christian Periods" illustrated with 72 lantern slides showing a variety of Ireland's early monuments and antique treasures'. The friendship between Lyons and O'Connell continued until Lyons' death, during which time 'O'Connell revised his [Lyons] manuscripts for publication'.⁵

In the 1946 edition of the *Journal of the Cork Historical and Archaeological Society* Lyons published 'The Stone of Formach' describing a cross-inscribed pillar-stone at Tooracurra, Ballymacarbery, Co. Waterford (Fig. 14). The stone 'mentioned by Rev. Canon Power in his "Waterford and Lismore" (p. 232) is 4ft. 5in. x 1ft. 3in. x 1ft. The upper figure in relief is 10 inches in diameter. The incised cross, beneath, apparently a Christianising device, is 9 inches long […] the writer assumes that the circular figure is a representation of the sun, used as an emblem of pagan worship

---

* McCarthy's attribution of reticence to Rafftery is puzzling as there is no doubt about the identification.

** Eamon P. Kelly includes a photograph of this figure in *Sheela-na-gigs: origins and functions* (1996, 33). [He considers that the vast majority of sheela-na-gigs found in Ireland appear to date to the period after the Norman invasion and they occur, predominantly, in areas where there was heavy Anglo-Norman settlement].

Fig. 14.
The Stone of Formach, Tooracurra, Ballymacarbery, Co. Waterford. Patrick Lyons to right of stone – as published in the 1946 edition of the *Journal of the Cork Historical and Archaeological Society*.

[...] The Stone of Formach seems to have a close analogy with the sun-emblem-inscribed cross on the Rock of Cashel [...] These pillar stones seem to be documentary mementos of the struggle between Christianity and heliolatry – of which, if the writer's suggestion above is accepted, the incorporation of a circle with the Celtic Cross is a more cogent and general reminder'. In April 1947 'a committee meeting of the Clonmel Historical and Archaeological Association was called to consider a letter received from the Secretary, Cork Historical and Archaeological Society, addressed to Mr. P. Lyons, stating that the members of that society had proposed to visit the district during the period 24th –26th May, making Clonmel their headquarters [...] it was of the opinion of members that the Corporation of Clonmel should afford official recognition to the visitors'. But when this event was reported in the local press Lyons' name is not mentioned. Lyons' paper on 'The Stone of Formach' was read at the November meeting of the Society : 'Attention was drawn to a pillar stone at Tooracurra, Ballymacarbery displaying a circular figure and incised cross described by Mr. P. Lyons [...] A photo of the stone was examined. The dexter side was a mutilated ogham inscription which has been interpreted by Prof[essor] Macalister'.[6]

From 1946-1954 Lyons regularly contributed papers on wide-ranging topics which were read at meetings of the Clonmel Historical and Archaeological Society and his membership of the Royal Society of Antiquaries of Ireland was always attributed to him; 'the members congratulated Mr. Lyons on his election to life membership of the Royal Society of Antiquaries [... he] is a very distinguished historical scholar'. Lyons' obituary, as published in the *Journal of the Clonmel Historical and Archaelogical Society* records that 'an instance of the high repute in which he was held amongst archaeologists was provided two years ago. When the members of the Royal Society of Antiquaries [sic.], meeting at Glendalough, discovered that Clonmel delegate, Very Rev. T.A. Murphy, P.P., Ardfinnan, was a friend of Mr. Lyons, they were awed by the fact that he knew a man who was regarded as almost a legendary figure and clamoured for information about him'.[7] Despite this, Lyons was never elected as a member of the Clonmel Historical and Archaeological Society; presumably an ex-policeman who served under British rule was deemed too ambiguous a qualification for membership.

TERCENTENARY OF THE SIEGE OF CLONMEL

In 1649 Parliamentary forces in England, under the leadership of Oliver Cromwell, were successful in their rebellion against the Crown, which culminated in the execution of Charles 1. In August of that year Cromwell, as Lord Lieutenant and Commander of the English army in Ireland, landed in Dublin. His mission was to re-establish English rule, suppress all royalist support and avenge the massacres of Protestant settlers in the 1641 rebellion. After this successful rebellion of the Gaelic Irish of Ulster (who had combined forces with some Norman and Anglo-Irish lords), the Confederate Catholics set up a parliamentary assembly in Kilkenny in 1642, with a Supreme Council which performed the functions of a government. Cromwell's Irish campaign proceeded rapidly: he successfully besieged Drogheda in September, Wexford and [New] Ross in October and Carrick-on-Suir in November. In January 1650, the towns of Fethard and Cashel surrendered without a fight; in February, the castle at Cahir also surrendered; in March, Kilkenny town managed to withstand a siege for six days. On 19 March Cromwell arrived at Clonmel and offered quarter on immediate surrender. As this was not accepted, Cromwell ordered his cannons to be placed in position and bombardment of the town began on 27 April. However, Cromwell was not prepared for surprise attacks on his forces on the approach roads to Clonmel. At the same time, within the town defensive works were being strengthened, but by 16 May a substantial breach had been made in the north wall. The following day Cromwell stormed Clonmel. In *The Golden Vale of Ivowen* Ó Néill (who bases his description on the accounts of eyewitnesses and participants from both sides) describes the scene: 'three times the attackers seemed to have gained a foothold and three times they were driven back until finally they broke and fled'. Cromwell reorganized his troops and both infantry and cavalry mounted the breach; meeting no resistance, they rushed through the empty streets. 'Suddenly, a strong party of defending musteteers and pike men rushed to the breach from either side, cutting it off and preventing any more entering, at the same time preventing the escape of those inside who tried to get out [...] within an hour it was all over. The breach was held, a thousand [Cromwellians] were slaughtered [within the walls] and Clonmel had withstood a protracted siege with 1,500 troops against 15,000'.

Among those taking part in the tercentenary celebrations in 1950 were Col. Eoghan Ó Néill (author of *The Golden Vale of Ivowen*) and members of the 13th Infantry Battalion, stationed at Kickham Barracks, Clonmel; 'the events of the siege of Clonmel [were re-enacted] before large audiences, with a lifesize mockup of a portion of the walls, and with a cast of about 600 in all, in costume, carrying the weapons of the time (many, especially mounted men, being local

MR. PATRICK LYONS, F.R.S.A.I.; born at Lisronagh, near Clonmel; associated with the late Sir John Rhys of Oxford University in the study of Ogham inscriptions; discovered four Ogham-inscribed monuments; assisted the late H. T. Knox, the historian of Co. Mayo, in his researches; collaborated with the late Dr. Goddard H. Orpen in the exploration of earthworks; contributed to many historical journals, including the *Journal of the Royal Society of Antiquaries* and the *Journal of the Cork Historical Society*.

Fig. 15.
Lyons in 1950 (aged 89). As published in *Siege of Clonmel Tercentenary Souvenir Record*.

civilians). This created such excitement amongst the local population and the officers and men of the battalion that we collected much surviving folklore, particularly during the rehearsal period. I had personally heard many of these traditions, and I had been a friend since boyhood of Mr. Patrick Lyons F.R.S.A.I., with whom I had some discussions on the ground'.

Lyons' knowledge of place-names and folklore proved to be of great assistance in tracing the events of the Cromwellian siege. Unfortunately, no photograph or documentation of the re-enactment is extant: the 13th Infantry Batallion was demobilized in 1956 and no memorabilia remains in the Military Museum, Kickham Barracks. A paper by Lyons, presumably documenting his work, 'The Cromwellian Assault on Clonmel', was published in *Siege of Clonmel Tercentenary Souvenir Record*; Lyons' work also features in another article in this volume, 'Cluain Meala or Cliu Mel', in which O'Connell quotes Lyons paper 'The Norman Burgh of Clonmel' (which had been read at the Clonmel Historical and Archaeological Society meeting in Autumn 1946) 'Mr. Lyons has argued, very convincingly, that in pre-Norman times, before the foundation of the parish church of old St. Mary's, the ancient parish of Rathronan extended southwards to the Suir, and included the present district of Clonmel'. The Tercentenary Souvenir Record concludes with biographies and photographs of contributors, including Lyons (Fig. 15).[8]

In March 1950, as part of the tercentenary commemeorations, many articles on Clonmel history were published in the *Clonmel Nationalist* including "Clonmel in Early and Mediaeval Times" by Mr. Patrick Lyons, F.R.S.A.I., Clonmel' which begins by stating that 'it seems obvious that if the Suir had not changed its course from its old channel at the mountain-base, Clonmel would now occupy the site of the southern capital' and continues by tracing Clonmel's story: its geological development; the arrival of the Cistercians 'who made a canal across the raised moraine [at Inishlounaght] to make their Abbey accessible'; the Danes whose 'colony was probably established in the tenth century'; the Normans whose 'determinants in the choice of the burgh-site seem to have been port facilities' and whose 'stockaded rampart remained until AD 1314 when under the terror inspired by the Bruce invasion it was replaced by the stone structure, portions of which survive'.

DISCOVERIES IN CLONMEL

In 1951 a medieval sculpture was discovered in a yard near the Franciscan Friary of which two faded photographs taken by Lyons are archived in Tipperary South County Museum at Clonmel; these photographs 'were kindly presented to the [Clonmel Historical and Archaeological] Society by Mr. P. Lyons, F.R.S.A.I. Clonmel'. The sculpture 'is a rectangular stone slab 21 inches in height and approximately 11 inches square at the base. On what is clearly the face of the slab is depicted a female figure in raised relief. From a photograph of the stone Mr. H. Leask, of Dublin has identified this as a "Pieta" – the Virgin holding the dead Saviour (Plate 79). The opposite face of the stone displays the vine-leaf ornamentation characteristic of the ecclesiastical symbolism of the 15th and early 16th centuries. The sides display armorials: one of the Butler's arms, probably entitled the Ormonde or Carrick families and the other seems to be a Fitzgerald or Geraldine shield – suggesting a Butler husband and a Geraldine wife. That the stone is only part of a larger shaft is shown by the niche-head below the vine leaves. It may have formed one of the supports to an altar tomb of the Butler's in the old Friary cemetery. Attention was drawn to the monument by Mr. David Condon and Mr. P. Lyons and it has since been removed to the precincts of the Franciscan cemetery'. Lyons sent copies of his photographs to Fr. T.A. Murphy, P.P. Ardfinnan 'with whom he corresponded regularly' mentioning that he was also sending copies 'to Mr. Leask with a view to contact with the Herald'. A week later, when Leask had made his report, Lyons wrote to Fr. Murphy: 'Mr. Leask

Plate 79.

Photograph taken by Lyons in 1951 of the 'Pieta' (Virgin Mary holding the dead body of Christ) discovered near the Franciscan Friary, Clonmel. He considers that it may have formed one of the supports to an altar tomb of the Butler family in the old Friary cemetery.

Reproduced courtesy of Tipperary South County Museum, Clonmel.

---

identified the shield as Butler [...] suggests that it is conjugal [...] Kindly cancel my incorrect attributions on the backs of the photographs'.[9]

During the 1950s it was usual for items of interest to be exhibited at meetings of the Clonmel Historical and Archaeological Society and Lyons' contributions were recorded: 18 May 1951 'some 18th century coins presented by Mr. D. Condon and Mr. P. Lyons'; 8 Nov 1951 'a "States of Jersey" coin, dated 1933, found near Clonmel presented by Messrs P. Lyons and David Condon' and 'Early 18th century powder horn presented by Messrs D. Condon and P. Lyons'; 10 Jun 1952 'two objects, one of metal and the other of stone found in the old town wall – presented by David Condon and P. Lyons. Their purpose is uncertain'.[10]

PUBLICATIONS IN THE CLONMEL NATIONALIST

Papers contributed to the *Journal of the Clonmel Historical and Archaeological Society* were usually reported by the *Clonmel Nationalist*; in this form Lyons' work in archaeology became public knowledge. Publication of his papers continued to within two months of his death when a long article, 'The Town that "Stands Between Two Worlds"' was published in three instalments. It begins 'Clonmel Burgh has a peculiarity of situation not shared by many other towns, for it is no wild exaggeration to say that it stands between two worlds – to the north the carboniferous (or limestone) world, seven or eight hundred millions of years old, while to the south is the Devonian world of brown rock, many millions of years older' and continues to explore how the plants and animals of these neighbouring worlds were interpreted in the Heraldic Arms of Clonmel Burgh; the Palatinate and its origins is then discussed, after which, possible origins of the name Suir are proposed, noting that 'the Sanskrit name of a river is "Suyarn" (Ecc. Ency. Brit. 11th Ed. Article, Herat)'; then follows, commencing with the Glacial Epoch, but not continuing in any sequential order, a more detailed version of the article 'Clonmel in Early and Medieval Times' (which he wrote for the tercentenary celebrations of the siege of Clonmel in 1950); the article concludes with the claim that 'the Bronze Age earthwork at Ballingarrane is probably unique in Ireland in its display of Norman adaptive fortification [...] The ancient moats (or motes) of South County Tipperary deserve careful archaeological exploration which would reveal many of the secrets of their construction'.[11]

CRITICISM OF LYONS' PAPERS

In 1954 the first issue of the *Journal of Clonmel Historical and Archaeological Society* was reviewed in *Irish Historical Studies* and Lyons' papers were chosen for comment: 'it includes two useful contributions by Patrick Lyons entitled 'Ancient Road Systems of South Tipperary' (p.10-17) and 'Church of St Nicholas and its precinct' (p. 23-30). They are an impressive indication of the wealth of exact knowledge which has survived locally. This is too often overlooked and sometimes unprocurable in studies exclusively based upon written documents. If however the local experts can be induced to indicate the sources of their knowledge it usually leads to a substantial addition to general information. Without such citation the important work of analyzing source material can hardly be begun. R.D.E.'.

Lyons' attempts to make connections between the various topics in which he was interested, without taking due cognizance of other works, often led him into dispute with other scholars, one of which was reported in the *Clonmel Nationalist*, a year after his death, as a discussion between correspondents concerning the position of the Old North Gate in Clonmel. 'Dr. Crean [...] advances the suggestion that [the Old North Gate] stood in Gladstone St. at the junction of Kickham St. and Morton St. In support of this view he refers to the ridge which until recent years was visible in Mary St. and which he presumes was a trace of the town wall'. Lyons had previously published 'Norman Antiquities of Clonmel Burgh' (to which he appended a map locating the possible site of the North Gate at the junction of Gladstone Street with Catherine Street) stating the 'no trace of this structure seems to remain'. A correspondent (un-named) to the newspaper accepts Lyons' identification of the location as that of 'a skilled archaeologist and a native of the district' and as confirmation mentions that 'in a later paper, published a few years ago in the *Clonmel Nationalist*, Mr. Lyons refers to excavations made at the William St.- Catherine St. junction about 60 years ago when many human skulls were unearthed – presumably those of the Siege victims who were buried in the ditch alongside the town wall'; Dr. Crean replied 'I have no hesitation in saying that the idea was a wrong one [...] I did not realize until now the extent to which this wrong idea as to the whereabouts of the North Gate had gained credence and regret that, not foreseeing the present unfortunate outcome, I did not trouble to expose the fallacy when Mr. Lyons first suggested it'. Crean had, in fact, previously questioned many of Lyons 'identifications' of details of the Cromwellian siege of 1650.[12]

DEATH OF PATRICK LYONS

Lyons died on 30 August 1954 in his ninety-fourth year and is buried in an unmarked grave in Powerstown Cemetery, Clonmel*. A special meeting of the Clonmel Historical and Archaeological Society was convened to pass a vote of sympathy with Lyons relatives [though none is mentioned by name, nor was any relative named at the obsequies which their *Journal* records as 'representative'; neither was there any mention of the Royal Irish Constabulary]. The *Minutes* of the special meeting record that Lyons' death 'deprived the Society of a staunch friend and valued contributor [...] He was a voluminous writer on archaeological

---

* In 1994, a project undertaken by Clonmel Joint Cemeteries Committee in association with Fás produced an Index of Clonmel Gravestone Inscriptions in which no gravestone bearing the name Patrick Lyons is listed.

subjects [...] always ready when requested to contribute a paper. His knowledge of the history and topography of Co. Tipperary was vast, and he continued his researches until a week before his death. Most of his active life was spent in Co. Mayo, where his work on ogham inscriptions is acknowledged in the *Journal of the Royal Society of Antiquaries of Ireland* as early as the period 1900-1910'. Lyons' obituary which appeared in the *Journal of the Royal Society of Antiquaries of Ireland*, to which he was elected an Honorary Fellow in 1953 (to mark his long participation in the work of the Society and his services to archaeology and local history), notes that 'while his calling in life as a member of the Royal Irish Constabulary was doubtless prosaic enough, his deepest and most abiding interests were the remains of the past in Ireland, its history and folklore'. Leask 'remembers with gratitude much assistance given by Mr. Lyons [...] A generous, extremely modest and retiring man, Mr. Lyons deliberately kept out of the public eye, contenting himself with researches in his chosen fields and – surprisingly – in the acquisition, self-taught and at a quite advanced age, of the languages of Greece and Rome in which he read a great deal'. Surprisingly, no obituary of Lyons appears in the *Journal of the Galway Archaeological and Historical Society*; this omission may have occurred due to the reorganization of the *Journal* which occurred in the mid 1950s when, instead of each volume containing more than one issue e.g. Volume 1, Number 2, a single volume was published for each year; 'Volume XXVI (1954-56) was published in two numbers. The following Volume XXVII, appearing as a single volume carried 1956 over into 1957'.[13]

So ended Patrick Lyons' long and active life. His membership of the Royal Irish Constabulary, during which he spent 34 years stationed in barracks in the west of Ireland, seemingly allowed him ample time and freedom to develope his life-long interest in the recording and photographing of archaeological monuments. He seems to have had a voracious thirst for knowledge; his acquaintance with Knox which commenced c.1898 would have brought archaeological and historical literature to his notice but his interests were more wide-ranging. To satisfy this need, he became a subscriber to the *London Times* in 1905 (at which time he was serving as a member of the Royal Irish Constabulary in Ballyhaunis, Co. Mayo); several of Knox's transcriptions from Lyons' letters refer to articles which Lyons found interesting in the *Times Literary Supplement*. Lyons remained a subscriber until a year before his death, when, as he explained in a letter to his friend Fr. Murphy: 'after a subscription period of 48 years, failing sight compels me to cease subscription to the *London Times* and to severely limit my reading. This sad necessity is rendered more regretful by the fact that it deprives you of the pleasure of reading this great review. For this deprivation I ask your kind forgiveness'[14].

In his letter to Goulden (written just 18 months before his death) Lyons shows his pride in the fact that he is 'the only man living who has found 4 Ogham inscriptions' and in his correspondence with Rhys and Orpen who acknowledged his work in their papers. Yet, for some unexplained reason, in February 1906 Lyons requested Knox not to refer to him by name in the papers on which they collaborated and so we are limited to tantalizing references to 'my colleague', 'my friend the field antiquary' etc. The Knox notebooks clearly show the extent of Lyons' patient work on Knox's behalf; they also reveal a quiet, retiring man with a fertile mind constantly striving to reconstruct the past.

REFERENCES

CHAPTER 1: *Early Life*

1. Cochrane (1898, 400-5); Rhys (1898, 396; 1901, 176-8; 1907, 61-8); Orpen (1910, 227); Macalister (1916-7, 81); Westropp (1919, 167); Curtis (1936, 58); Waddell (1985-6, 132).
2. See Appendix 1 for details of the collection of Lyons' photographs archived in the Hardiman Library, N.U.I.Galway; Appendix 2 for details of Lyons' published papers.
3. Ó Néill. *The Golden Vale of Ivowen* (2001, 172).
4. Ó Néill (*pers.comm.*).
5. Ó Néill (2001, 474-97).
6. Empey (1985, 76).
7. O'Connell (1954-5, 39).
8. Ó Néilll (*pers.comm.*).
9. O'Connell (1954-5, 39); Herlihy (1997, 75).

CHAPTER 2: *Career in the Royal Irish Constabulary*

1. Herlihy (1997, 75-9); Ball (1999, 4).
2. Kivlehan, Garda Archive/Museum (*pers. comm.*).
3. *Longford Independent* 10 May 1887; *Westmeath Examiner* 21 Jan 1893.
4. *Longford Independent* 1 Feb 1889; 19 Oct 1889; 15 Aug 1891; 5 Dec 1891.
5. Fennell (2003, 19).
6. Moran (1991, 182, 189).
7. Herlihy (1997, 60); *Longford Independent* 20 Nov 1886; 7 May 1887.
8. *Longford Independent* 15 Oct 1887; 20 Oct 1888; 2 Nov 1889; 7 Dec 1889; 8 Feb 1890; 31 Jan 1891.
9. Raiswell (2001, 106).
10. Sheehan (1978, 9).
11. *Westmeath Independent* 26 Apr 1894; 30 Jun 1894; Herlihy (1997, 80-1); Fennell (2003, 51).
12. *Western People* 17 Nov 1894.
13. Ó Muraile (1982, 27-8).
14. *Western People* 31 Aug 1895; 14 Sep 1895; 23 May 1896; 8 Jul 1898; 27 Apr 1901; 27 Feb 1904; 7 May 1904; 11 Aug 1908; 16 Sep 1909; 2 Oct 1909; 24 Dec 1909; 30 Apr 1910.
15. O'Connell (1954-5, 39).
16. Aalen (1997, 150).
17. *Western People* 20 Jan 1900; 27 Sep 1902; 22 Nov 1902; 23 Apr 1904; 7 May 1904; 2 Jul

1904; 3 Jun 1905; 23 Sep 1905; 9 Mar 1907; 12 Oct 1912; O'Connell (1954-5, 39).
18. *Western People* 4 Apr 1901; 29 Jun 1901; 8 Aug 1901; 14 Sep 1901; 30 Aug 1902; 5 Apr 1913; 3 May 1913; 15 Jun 1913.
19. Malcolm (2006, 97); Ball (1999, 6, 8); O'Connell (1954-5, 39).
20. *Tuam Herald* 4 Oct 1913; 18 Dec 1915; Qualter (undated, 32).
21. *Connaught Tribune* 12 Jul 1913; 30 Jan 1914; Ball (1999, 4).
22. *Connaught Tribune* 21 Feb 1914; 4 Jul 1914; *Tuam Herald* 7 Jul 1914.
23. *Connaught Tribune* 27 Nov 1914; 3 Jul 1915.
24. Kee (1972, 272); *Connaught Tribune* 20 Nov 1915; 27 Nov 1915.
25. Kee (1972, 275); Qualter (undated, 34); Newell (2006, 121); Ó hEochaidh (1975, 2).
26. Harbison (1970, 91).
27. *Mayo News* 1 Apr 1916; Neilan (1966, 324-6).
28. *Mayo News* 13 May 1916; 17 Jun 1916; 12 Aug 1916; 15 Sep 1917; 29 Sep 1917; 12 Jul 1919; 13 Dec 1919; 12 Feb 1920.
29. *Mayo News* 3 Nov 1917; 9 Mar 1918; 16 Mar 1918; 23 Mar 1918.
30. Corlett (2001, 115).
31. Ní Cheanainn (1988, 154); Kee (1972, 96); Herlihy (1997, 105-7).
32. *Mayo News* 10 Apr 1920.
33. *Mayo News* 24 Apr 1920; 15 May 1920; 29 May 1920.

CHAPTER 3 : *The 'antiquarian craze'*

1. Knox's notebooks are archived in the Library of the Royal Society of Antiquaries of Ireland. They comprise two series; a set of two notebooks in which Knox describes 176 ecclesiastical sites and castles (with accompanying negative numbers dating from 5 June 1899 to 4 September 1908); a set of 4 notebooks (herein referred to as K.N.1, 2, 3, 4) in which Knox records transcriptions from Lyons' letters during the period 1905-18. Collections of Lyons' photographs are archived in the Hardiman Library, N.U.I.Galway, the Library of the Royal Society of Antiquaries of Ireland and in the Tipperary South County Museum, Clonmel. Some photographs are in private ownership and are not accessible.
2. de Burca (*pers.comm.*).
3. K.N.1, 1-11.
4. K.N. 2, 15; 77-8.
5. K.N.1, 28; 137; 148-9; K.N. 2, 38; 58-9; 141; K.N. 3, 49-50; Crawford (1913, 158).
6. K.N 1, 41; 59; 130; K.N. 3, 50.
7. Freyne (1978, 28); Macalister (1945, 9); K.N. 2, 130-1.
8. Cribbin et al. (1994, 61-5); McCormick et al. (1995, 89-98); McCormick (1994, 28).
9. Knox (1914a, 45-6); McCormick et al. (1995, 95-6) ; K.N. 2, 52-3.
10. K.N.2, 1; 32; 105; 142; K.N. 3, 96; K.N. 4, 61.
11. K.N. 1, 119; K.N. 2, 131; K.N. 3, 84-5; 148.

12. O'Connell (1954-5, 39); Ó Néill (2001, 10; 181).
13. Anon. (1920, 151); Lough Mask and Lough Carra Tourist Development Association/Fás (1988, 3); Rhys (1898, 396); Cochrane (1898, 400); Knox (1898, 272-3); Macalister (1897, 73).
14. K.N.1, 44-5; 49; 56; 118; 119-20.
15. Lyons (1943, 270).
16. K.N.1, 124; K.N. 2, 7; 93; 95.
17. Rhys (1898, 396; 1901, 176-8; 1907, 61-8).
18. Williams, National Library of Wales (*pers. comm.*).
19. Cochrane (1898, 400-2); Harbison (1991, 210); Macalister (1916-7a, 92; 1945, 7).
20. Irish Folklore Commission (Ms. 1144, 99); Macalister (1945, 112-6).
21. Cribbin (2000, 60).
22. Knox (1904, 5, 140); K.N. 1, 16; 23-5; 47; K.N. 2, 65; 87; K.N. 3, 13; Westropp (1900, 100-80).
23. Flynn (1996, 78-83); Lucas (1953, 8; 34).
24. Knox (1906-7, 265-76); O'Reilly (1902-4, 57); K.N. 1, 6; 12; 15; 30; 37; 61; Westropp (1906-7, 276).
25. Corlett (2001a, 7).
26. K.N. 1, 28; Rhys (1907, 61-8); Orpen (1910, 227); Macalister (1916-7a, 81); Westropp (1919, 167).
27. Knox (1914a, 50; 1917-8a, 41).
28. Knox (1911, 93; 206); Armitage (1900, 276); Orpen (1911, 267-76); Ashe Fitzgerald (2000, 70-2); Westropp (1902, 584); K.N. 3, 46.
29. Knox (1911, 206; 1911-2, 147; 151-2; 1914a, 1; 26); Orpen (1911, 272).
30. K.N. 2, 66-7; K.N. 3, 23; 53; Waddell (1983, 21; 1988, 16).
31. K.N. 1, 141; Westropp (1919, 167).
32. Knox (1911, 107); K.N. 1, 7; K.N. 3, 60-1; 75-6.
33. Knox (1914b, 348-56); K.N. 3, 90-1.
34. Knox (1915, 290-6).
35. Knox (1915-6a, 1-31); Waddell (1988, 15); Fitzpatrick (2004, 64); K.N. 2, 28.
36. Falkiner (1906, 421-2); K.N. 2, 28; 129-30.
37. Knox (1918, 157-9); K.N. 4, 60-1.
38. Knox (1917-8c, 103-24); K.N. 3, 107-50; K. N. 4, 22; 32; 54-9.
39. Knox (1915-6c, 190-3); K.N. 3, 148; 153; K.N.4, 23; Raftery (1944, 41); Coffey (1904, 14-6); Waddell (1974-5, 10; 1985-6, 131-3).
40. Knox (1917-8b, 71-5); Macalister (1916-7b, 506-8); K.N. 3, 87-9; K.N. 4, 44.
41. Knox (1920, 1-3); Rynne (1987-8, 144-6; 1995, 115); Holland (1987-8, 73); Hardiman (1978, 54); O'Sullivan (1983, 87); Macalister (1913, 198); Anon. (1895, 301); K.N. 3, 87; 100; K.N. 4, 1-2; 11; 12; 16; 17; 18; 58.
42. Obituary - *Journal of Galway Archaeological and Historical Society* 11, (1920, 151-2); *Journal of the Royal Society of Antiquaries of Ireland* 52, (1922, 94).

43. K.N. 1, 1; 12; 54; 60; K.N. 2, 42-4; 53-4; 57-8; K.N.4, 67; Lyons (1920, 61-3); Irish Folklore Commission (Ms. 1127, 110).
44. K.N. 1, 47-8; 77; K.N. 3, 83; 109; 111.
45. K.N. 1, 43; 50-1; 85-6; 87-8; 97-8; 105; K.N. 2, 1; K.N. 3, 136.
46. K.N. 1, 7; 118; 119; 121; 133; 149-50; K.N. 2, 21; 91; 131.
47. Irish Folklore Commission (Ms. 745, 319); Dunlevy (1989, 151).
48. O'Connell (1954-5, 40); K.N. 1, 80; K.N. 2, 13-4; 15; 24; K.N. 3, 79b; K.N. 4, 19.
49. Orpen (1910, 226-8); K.N. 2, 29; 53.
50. Orpen (1915-6, 38).

CHAPTER 4 : *Lyons in Clonmel*

1. Fennell (2003,171); *Clonmel Nationalist* 4 Aug 1920; 11 Aug 1920; 14 Aug 1920; 8 Sep 1920; 4 Jun 1921; 27 Feb 1922; 19 Jul 1922; 12 Aug 1922; 16 Dec 1922; Corbett (1990, 62).
2. *Clonmel Nationalist* 4 Jul 1928; O'Connell (1954-5, 39).
3. See Appendix 2 for published works of Patrick Lyons; Curtis (1936, 58).
4. *Clonmel Nationalist* 8 Apr 1944; 17 May 1944; 24 May 1944; 31 May 1944; Clonmel Historical and Archaeological Society Minutes, 6 Jun 1944; 27 Jun 1944; 25 Jul 1944.
5. Clonmel Historical and Archaeological Society Minutes 6 Jun 1944; *Clonmel Nationalist* 5 Mar 1941; 10 Sep 1954.
6. Lyons (1946, 85); Clonmel Historical and Archaeological Society Minutes 30 Apr 1947; 26 Nov 1947; *Clonmel Nationalist* 28 May 1947.
7. Clonmel Historical and Archaeological Society Minutes 2 Feb 1953; O'Connell (1954-5, 40).
8. Ó Néill (2001, 172-181); *Clonmel Nationalist* 18 Mar 1950; Whelan, Kickham Barracks (pers. comm.); Lyons (1950, 16-8); O'Connell (1950, 82-8).
9. *Clonmel Nationalist* 2 Jun 1951; 10 Sep 1954; Clonmel Historical and Archaeological Society Minutes 18 May 1951.
10. Clonmel Historical and Archaeological Society Minutes 18 May 1951; 8 Nov 1951; 10 Jun 1952.
11. *Clonmel Nationalist* 12 Jun 1954; 19 Jun 1954; 26 Jun 1954.
12. Anon. (1954, 119); *Clonmel Nationalist* 9 Jul 1955; 12 Jul 1955; Lyons (1936, 286); Crean (1937, 125-60).
13. O'Connell (1954-5, 41); Clonmel Historical and Archaeological Society *Minutes* 10 Sep 1954; Leask (1955, 151); O'Halloran (2001, 163).

APPENDIX I

Photographic Collection in Hardiman Library, N.U.I. Galway

Albums are listed in the order in which dated photographs are described in Knox's Notebooks.

UNBOUND ALBUM 3UB

Ref. No.	Location	Monument type	Ref. No.	Location	Monument type
201	None given	Folklife	267	Spaddagh	Folklife
202	Cashel	Church	268	Spaddagh	Folklife
207	Ballyhaunis	Church	269	Coogue North	Megalith (possible)
208	Annagh	Folklife	270	Coogue North	Megalith (possible)
209	Ballyhaunis	Folklife	271	Moate	Earthwork
210	Ballyhaunis	Folklife	272	Moate	Earthwork
211	Ballyhaunis	Folklife	273	Moate	Earthwork
212	Ballyhaunis	Folklife	274	Moate	Earthwork
213	Cullentra	Mill	275	Cashel	Church
214	Cullentra	Mill	276	Cashel	Church
225	Slieve Dart	Cairn	277	Barrinagh/Sheeaunbeg	Earthwork
226	Knockaunbrack	Megalith (possible)			
227	Crucknaroy/Raith	Earthwork	278	Barrinagh/Sheeaunbeg	Earthwork
228	Crucknaroy/Raith	Earthwork	279	None given	Millstone
237	Coogue North	Megalith (possible)	280	None given	?Millstone
238	Killeer	Standing stones	281	Mannin	Sundial (possible)
239	Garrafrauns	Megalith (possible)	282	Kilvine – photo missing	Church
240	Garrafrauns	Megalith (possible)			
241	Garrafrauns	Megalith (possible)	283	Kilvine – photo missing	Church
254	Coolnaha	Millstone			
255	None given	Millstone	284	Doonmacreena	Landscape
256	None given	Millstone	285	Creeveeshal	Devotional site
257	None given	Millstone	286	Cloch-na-dree-deema	Megalith (possible)
258	Tullaghane	Millstone	287	Cloondalgan	Church
259	Tullaghane	Millstone	288	Cloondalgan	Church
260	Tullaghane	Millstone	289	Obliterated	Obliterated
261	None given	Millstone	290	Obliterated	Obliterated
264	None given	Millstone			
265	None given	Millstone			
266	Lisduff	Folklife			

164

Appendix 1: Photographic Collection in Hardiman Library, N.U.I.Galway

UNBOUND ALBUM 4UB

Ref. No.	Location	Monument type
295	None given/? Kilgarriff	Folklife
296	Kilgarriff	Earthwork
297	Lisnadhine	Earthwork
298	Kilgarriff	Millstone
299	Kilgarriff	Earthwork
300	Kilmannin	Ogham stone
301	Kilmannin	Ogham stone
302	Kilmannin	Ogham stone
303	Kilmannin	Ogham stone
304	Dhine	Millstone
305	None given/?Dhine	Millstone
306	None given/?Dhine	Millstone
307	Tooraree	Cross
308	Tooraree	Cross
309	Lisnadhine	Earthwork
310	Moate	Earthwork
311	Moate	Vernacular building
312	Moate	Earthwork
313	Moate	Earthwork
314	Moate	Earthwork
315	Laghtawohoo/Feamore	Souterrain
316	Laghtawohoo/Feamore	Souterrain
317	Laghtawohoo/Feamore	Souterrain
318	Cashelbarnagh	Cashel
319	Cashelbarnagh	Cashel
320	Knockadoon	Devotional site
321	Garrafrauns	Earthwork
322	Carrowneden	Earthwork
323	Lough Caheer	Crannóg (possible)
324	Lough Caheer	Landscape
325	Lough Caheer	Landscape
326	Lough Caheer	Landscape
327	Kilmannin	Landscape
328	Castle Bog	Millstone
329	Cloonbonniff	Millstone
330	Cloonbonniff	Millstone

Ref. No.	Location	Monument type
331	Coolnaha	Folklife
332	Lecarrow	Earthwork
333	Lecarrow	Earthwork
347	Tubbercrunnieve	Folklife
348	Dunmore	Castle
349	Dunmore	Castle
350	Dunmore	Castle
351	Dunmore	Landscape
352	Ballymoat	Earthwork
353	Ballymoat	Earthwork
354	Graigue/Lissaghow	Enclosure
355	Carrownbiggaun	Earthwork
356	Carrownbiggaun	Earthwork
357	Aghamore	Church
358	Aghamore	Church
358a	Aghamore	Devotional site
359	Boleybeg	Enclosure
360	Mountain in Common	Megalith (possible)
361	Mountain in Common	Megalith (possible)
362	Mountain in Common	Megalith (possible)
363	Tooreen	Cairn
364	Raith	Castle
365	Raith	Castle
366	Raith	Castle
367	Carrowneden	Earthwork
368	Cartron North	Earthwork
369	Crossbeg	Earthwork
370	Aghamore	Megalith (possible)
371	Coolnaha	Earthwork
372	Coolnaha	Earthwork
373	Killeenaghir	Ecclesiastical site
374	Kilmannin	Ogham stone
375	Raith	Castle
376	Raith	Castle
377	Raith	Castle
378	Raith	Castle
379	Raith	Castle
380	Temple Saum	Church
381	Temple Saum	Church
382	Knockadoon	Megalith (possible)

Ref. No.	Location	Monument type	Ref. No.	Location	Monument type
383	Knockadoon	Megalith (possible)	423	Knock	Bullaun stone
384	Knockadoon	Megalith (possible)	424	Woodstock	Earthwork
385	Knockadoon	Megalith (possible)	425	Bellmount	Earthwork
386	Scardaun	Pillar stone	426	Bellmount	Cashel
387	Carrowneden	Folklife	427	Emlagh	Cross
388	Doonmacreena	Landscape	428	Emlagh	Cross
389	Doonmacreena	Devotional site	429	Emlagh	Devotional site
390	Bohola	Earthwork	430	Clooneyvindon	Devotional site
391	Cashelbarnagh	Cashel	431	Clooneyvindon	Devotional site
392	Cashelbarnagh	Cashel	432	Clooneyvindon	Devotional site
393	Cashelbarnagh	Cashel	433	Cloonkeen	Pillar stone
394	Cashelbarnagh	Cashel	434	Cloonkeen	Pillar stone
395	Cashelbarnagh	Cashel	435	Island/Ballyhaunis	Folklife
396	Cashelsheenachan	Cashel	436	Island/Ballyhaunis	Folklife
397	Faheeris	Megalith (possible)	437	None given/	
398	Faheeris	Megalith (possible)		? Carnfree	Megalith (possible)
399	Bohola	Church	438	None given/	
400	Killeenrevagh	Pillar stone		? Carnfree	Megalith (possible)
401	Lough Caldragh	Megalith (possible)	439	Carnfree	Pillar stone
402	Sheeaunbeg/		440	Carnfree	Pillar stone
	Barrinagh	Earthwork	441	Carnfree	Pillar stone
403	Sheeaunbeg/		442	Thubber Illiva	
	Barrinagh	Earthwork		(or Nelliva)	Church
404	Sheeaunbeg/		443	Thubber Illiva	Church
	Barrinagh	Earthwork	444	Kilruddhaun	Church
405	Ballyglass	Pillar stones	445	Ballyglass	Pillar stones
406	Killeenrevagh	Pillar stone	446	Ratra	Earthwork
407	Brookhill	Megalith (possible)	447	Thubber Illiva	Church
408	Cloonconnor	Graveyard	448	Milltown	Pillar stone
409	Shanaghy	Enclosure	449	Carnfree	Cairn
410	Shanaghy	Enclosure	450	Ratra	Enclosure
411	Shanaghy	Enclosure	451	Ratra	Earthwork
412	Crucknamannaun	Enclosure	452	Thubber Illiva	Church
413	Crucknamannaun	Enclosure	453	Ballyglass	Pillar stones
414	Dunmore	Castle	454	Kilruddhaun	Inscribed grave
415	Dunmore	Castle			slab
416	Knockadoon	Cairn	455	Lynn	Church
417	Knockadoon	Cairn	456	Carrick	Church
418	Aghamore	Megalith (possible)	457	Castlelost	Church
419	Aghamore	Ecclesiastical site	458	Castlelost	Church
420	Raith	Folklife	459	Castletown-	
421	Knock	Bullaun stone		Geoghegan	Motte & Bailey
422	Knock	Bullaun stone			

Appendix 1: Photographic Collection in Hardiman Library, N.U.I.Galway

Ref. No.	Location	Monument type	Ref. No.	Location	Monument type
460	Castletown-Geoghegan	Motte & Bailey	499	Loughmore	Church
461	Castletown-Geoghegan	Motte & Bailey	500	Cappagh	Megalith (possible)
462	Castletown-Geoghegan	Motte & Bailey	501	Kilrooaun	Bullaun stone
			502	Turlough	Megalith (possible)
			503	Castletown-Geoghegan	Motte & Bailey
463	Castlelost	Castle	504	Castletown-Geoghegan	Motte & Bailey
464	Castlelost	Castle			
465	Clogher	Church	505	Donoughmore	Church
466	Carnabreckna	Earthwork	506	Kilsheelan	Earthwork
467	Carnabreckna	Earthwork	507	Kiltinan	Church
468	Tober Mucknoo	Devotional site	508	Tullamain	Motte
469	Carrowkeel	Devotional site	509	Poulakerry	Castle
470	Carrowkeel	Devotional site	510	Tullamain	Motte
471	Cappagh	Megalith (possible)	511	Tullamain	Motte
472	Cappagh	Megalith (possible)	512	Castlebar	Megalith (possible)
473	Coolnaha	Pillar stone	513	Cloonturriff	Togher/road
474	Coolnaha	Pillar stone	514	Castleknock	Castle
475	Annagh	Castle	515	None given/ ? Castleknock	Motte
476	Erriff	Megalith (possible)	516	None given/ ? Castleknock	Motte
477	Ballintubber	Cross base			
478	Ballintubber	Castle			
479	Mullaghadooey	Earthwork	517	None given	Obliterated
480	Ratra	Earthwork	518	Cloncurry	Church
481	Ratra	Earthwork	519	Cloncurry	Church
482	Ratra	Pillar stone	520	None given -photo missing	Obliterated
483	Knocknalegan	Pillar stone			
484	Red City	Church	521	Ballintubber	Cross base
485	Kilsheelan	Church			
486	Donoughmore	Church			
487	Kiltinan	Inscribed grave slab	ALBUM 1B		
488	Kiltinan	Church	Ref. No.	Location	Monument type
489	Tullamain	Motte	521	Carnabreckna	Earthwork
490	Kilbride	Earthwork	522	Roscommom	Castle
491	Nedin	Church	523	Kilmaclogh	Church
492	Loughmore	Castle	524	Tullamain	Church
493	Loughmore	Castle	525	Clare	Castle
494	Meehaunbwee	Megalith (possible)	526	Clare	Castle
495	Meehaunbwee	Megalith (possible)	527	Oran	Earthwork
496	Loughmore	Castle	528	Oran	Earthwork
497	Donoughmore	Church	529	Oran	Ecclesiastical site
498	Kilmaclogh	Church	530	Oran	Devotional site

Ref. No.	Location	Monument type	Ref. No.	Location	Monument type
531	Oran	Devotional site	574	Carrowndangan	Devotional site
532	Oran	Ecclestiastical site	575	Carrowndangan	Devotional site
533	Oran	Earthwork	576	Killeden	Church & graveyard
534	Ballycaher	Earthwork			
535	Castleplunket	Church	577	Killeden	Church
536	Kilmovee	Ogham stone	578	Cloonagleragh	Landscape
537	Kilmovee	Ogham stone	579	Cloonagleragh	Building
538	Ballyhaunis	Church	580	Carrowcastle	Landscape
539	Ballyhaunis	Church	581	Carrowcastle	Landscape
540	Ballyhaunis	Church	582	Carrowcastle	Earthwork
541	Ballyhaunis	Church	583	Kilsheelan	Landscape
542	Runnamoat	Motte & bailey	584	Kincor	Castle
543	Runnamoat	Motte & bailey	585	Cloghcarrigan	Pillar stone
544	Runnamoat	Motte & bailey	586	Donoughmore	Church
545	Runnamoat	Motte & bailey	587	Clonmel	Building
546	Runnamoat	Motte & bailey	588	Clonmel	Town wall
547	Brittas	Motte & bailey	589	Clonmel	Church
548	Tullamain	Motte	590	Clonmel	Church
549	Tullamain	Motte	591	Clonmel	Town wall
550	Tullamain	Motte	592	Clonmel	Graveyard
551	Loughmore	Castle	593	Fethard	Building
552	Loughmore	Castle	594	Kiltinan	Church
553	Donoughmore	Church	595	Clonkeen	Devotional site
554	Kilsheelan	Church	596	Graigue/Lissaghow	Enclosure
555	Kilsheelan	Church	597	Graigue/Lissaghow	Enclosure
556	Bagnelstown	Mill	598	Graigue/Lissaghow	Enclosure
557	Eskermorley	Enclosure	599	Graigue/Lissaghow	Enclosure
558	Eskermorley	Enclosure	600	Ballyhaunis	Church
559	Island	Earthwork	601	Ballyhaunis	Church
560	Island	Earthwork	602	Oran	Earthwork
561	Ballyhaunis	Church	603	Carrowcastle	Earthwork
562	Tavnane	Pillar stone	604	Ballymoat	Earthwork
563	Cauraun	Earthwork	605	Ballymoat	Earthwork
564	Cauraun	Earthwork	606	Ballymoat	Earthwork
565	Carrick	Church	607	Doonbally	Castle
566	Mote Park	Earthwork	608	Cruckaunnagann-Farnane	Landscape
567	Mote Park	Earthwork			
568	Thubberaher	Church	609	Lagganore	Earthwork
569	Monastereden	Megalith (possible)	610	Lagganore	Earthwork
570	Tubberkevna	Inscribed rock	611	Knockbrit	Earthwork
571	Bohola	Earthwork	612	Ballyboc	Earthwork
572	Bohola	Earthwork	613	Ballyboc	Earthwork
573	Bohola	Earthwork	614	Kilsheelan	Motte

Appendix 1: Photographic Collection in Hardiman Library, N.U.I.Galway

Ref. No.	Location	Monument type	Ref. No.	Location	Monument type
615	Carrownahaun	Souterrain	658	Lakefield	Building
616	Carrownahaun	Souterrain	659	Lakefield	Building
617	Cullnacleha	Folklife	660	Lakefield	Building
618	Tulsk	Earthwork	661	Aughnakilleen	Earthwork
619	Tulsk	Earthwork	662	Aughnakilleen	Earthwork
620	Cashlaun/Tulsk	Earthwork	663	Lisduff	Building/Folklife
621	Cashlaun/Tulsk	Earthwork	664	Cashel	Rock of
622	Eskermorley	Earthwork	665	Cashel	Rock of
623	Eskermorley	Earthwork	666	Killedrimona	Earthwork
624	Eskermorley	Earthwork	667	Logboy	Folklife
625	Thurles	Castle	668	Ballyhaunis	Earthwork
626	Thurles	Castle	669	Ballyhaunis	Earthwork
627	Thurles	Graveyard	670	Ballyhaunis	Earthwork
628	Thurles	Graveyard	671	Ardmayle	Motte & bailey
629	Pass/Rathbrit	Earthwork	672	Ardmayle	Motte & bailey
630	Carrownahaun	Earthwork	673	Ardmayle	Motte & bailey
631	Carrownahaun	Earthwork	674	Ardmayle	Motte & bailey
632	Carrownahaun	Earthwork	675	Ardmayle	Castle
633	Carrownahaun	Earthwork	676	Ardmayle	Castle
634	Cashlaun/Tulsh	Earthwork	677	Ardmayle	Landscape
635	Rathcroghan	Earthwork	678	Patrickswell	Church
636	Rathmore	Earthwork	679	Patrickswell	Church
637	Rathbeg	Earthwork	680	Patrickswell	Church
638	Rathcroghan	Earthwork	681	Patrickswell	Church
639	Slievenaman	Cairn	682	?Patrickswell	Church
640	Urlare	Earthwork	683	?Patrickswell	Church
641	Urlare	Earthwork	684	?Patrickswell	Church
642	Patrickswell	Cross	685	?Patrickswell	Cross
643	Patrickswell	Cross	686	Slaudagh	Earthwork
644	Ballyhaunis	Earthwork	687	Garrafaddy	Earthwork
645	Corrislustia	Cross	688	Paurkeen Saor	Earthwork
646	Lakefield	Building	689	Paurkeen Saor	Earthwork
647	Slievenaman	Megalith (possible)	690	Paurkeen Saor	Earthwork
648	Slievenaman	Megalith (possible)	691	Aughnakilleen	Earthwork
649	Slievenaman	Megalith (possible)	692	Thurles	Church
650	Slievenaman	Megalith (possible)	693	Coleman	Church
651	Slievenaman	Megalith (possible)	694	Coleman	Church
652	Slievenaman	Cairn	695	Coleman	Church
653	Holywell	Church	696	Coleman	Church
654	Slievenaman	Folklife	697	Kilsheelan	Church
655	Slievenaman	Folklife	698	Kilconnell	Castle
656	Fethard	Building	699	Kilconnell	Castle
657	Fethard	Town wall	700	Clonmel	Building

Ref. No.	Location	Monument type	Ref. No.	Location	Monument type
701	Baptist Grange	Landscape	751	Brees	Castle
702	Castleblake	Castle	752	Brees	Castle
703	Rathdrum	Castle	753	Brees	Castle
704	Ballintemple	Church	754	Brees	Castle
705	Mora	Church	755	Portaghard	Earthwork
706	Mora	Church	756	Portaghard	Earthwork
707	Mora	Church	757	Portaghard	Earthwork
708	Cloghatumpaun	Castle	758	Portaghard	Earthwork
709	Cloonkeen	Church	759	Portaghard	Earthwork
710	Cloonkeen	Devotional site	760	Balla	Devotional site
711	Cloonkeen	Devotional site	761	Rathmore	Earthwork
712	Cloonbard	Enclosure	762	Rathmore	Earthwork
713	Baslick	Church	763	Rathscrigg	Earthwork
714	Baslick	Church	764	Carnlough	Earthwork
715	Cloonbard	Earthwork	765	Carnlough	Earthwork
716	Island	Folklife	766	Meelick	Inscribed grave slab
717	Corrislustia	Pillar stone			
718	Coogue North	Megalith (possible)	767	Brackloon	Cashel
719	Tubberkevna	Devotional site	768	Onnyhill	Earthwork
722	Ardeery	Folklife	769	Carrowkeel	Earthwork
728	Carnlough	Earthwork	770	Kilmore	Cross
729	Kilvine	Castle	771	Kilmore	Cross
730	Ratra	Earthwork			
731	Rathbeg	Enclosure		ALBUM 2B	
732	Rathnadharriv	Earthwork			
733	Cauraun	Earthwork	Ref. No.	Location	Monument type
734	Cauraun	Earthwork	772	Kilmovee	Devotional site
735	Rathcroghan	Earthwork	773	Coolnaha	Enclosure
736	Rathcroghan	Earthwork	774	Ballinphuill	Earthwork
737	Rathcroghan	Earthwork	775	Balla	Devotional site
738	Rathcroghan	Earthwork	776	Currykilleen	Earthwork
739	Rathcroghan	Earthwork	777	Currykilleen	Earthwork
740	Cauraun	Earthwork	778	Currykilleen	Earthwork
741	Rathmore	Earthwork	779	Knockaunakill	Castle
742	Rathmore	Earthwork	780	Kilcolman	Devotional site
743	Brees	Castle	781	Carnakit	Earthwork
744	Brees	Castle	782	Grallagh	Earthwork
745	Brees	Castle	783	None given	Folklife
746	Brees	Castle	784	None given	Folklife
747	Brees	Castle	785	Lismeegaun	Cist
748	Brees	Castle	786	Lismeegaun	Cist
749	Brees	Castle	787	Glenballythomas	Megalith (possible)
750	Brees	Castle			

Appendix 1: Photographic Collection in Hardiman Library, N.U.I.Galway

Ref. No.	Location	Monument type
788	Glenballythomas	Megalith (possible)
789	Slevin	Earthwork
790	Slevin	Earthwork
791	Rathcroghan	Earthwork
792	Rathcroghan	Earthwork
793	Rathcroghan	Earthwork
794	Rathcroghan	Earthwork
795	Rathcroghan	Earthwork

ALBUM GII

Ref. No.	Location	Monument type
49	Templemartin	Church
50	Athenry	Church
51	Athenry	Church
52	Athenry	Church
53	Moyode	Castle
54	Moyode	Castle
55	Moyode	Castle
56	Athenry	Devotional site
57	Athenry	Town wall
58	Athenry	Town wall
59	Athenry	Town wall
60	Athenry	Town wall
61	Derrydonnell	Megalith (possible)
62	Derrydonnell – photo missing	Megalith (possible)
63	Derrydonnell	Castle
64	Templegal	Church
65	Shanaclogh	Castle
66	Moyveela	Castle
67	Moyveela	Castle
68	Ballygurrane	Earthwork
69	Athenry	Church
70	Athenry	Church
71	Athenry	Church
72	Athenry	Church
73	Athenry	Church
74	Athenry	Church
75	Ballydavid	Castle
76	Ballydavid	Church
77	Lackafinna	Castle

Ref. No.	Location	Monument type
78	Lackafinna	Castle
79	Wallscourt	Castle
80	Wallscourt	Castle
81	Kilcooly	Castle
82	Kilcooly	Castle
83	Kilcooly	Castle
84	Kilcooly	Castle
85	Kilcooly	Church
86	Kilcooly	Church
87	Finnure	Church
88	Fartamore	Castle
89	Fartamore	Castle
90	Athenry	Church
91	Athenry	Church
92	Athenry	Church
93	Rathgorgin	Castle
94	Rathgorgin	Castle
95	Rathgorgin	Castle
96	Cruckawootha/ Rathgorgin	Castle

ALBUM GIII

Ref. No.	Location	Monument type
97	Cruckawootha/ Rathgorgin	Castle
98	Cruckawootha/ Rathgorgin	Castle
99	Cruckawootha/ Rathgorgin	Castle
100	Killora	Church
101	Killora	Church
102	Lavallyconnor	Castle
103	Lavallyconnor	Castle
104	Moycola	Castle
105	Seefin	Earthwork
106	Cloghastookeen	Castle
107	Killogilleen	Church
108	Killogilleen	Church
109	Killogilleen	Church
110	Cregg	Castle
111	Cregg	Castle

Ref. No.	Location	Monument type
112	Gortnahowna – photo missing	Urn
113	Gortnahowna	Cist
114	Strongford	Castle
115	S. Cleran's	Castle
116	Riverville	Castle
117	Carrigeen	Meggalith (possible)
118	Carrigeen	Meggalith (possible)
119	Mannin	Castle
120	Mannin	Church
121	Gortnahowna	Cist
122	Gortnahowna – photo missing	Cist
123	Gortnahowna – photo missing	Cist
124	Athenry	Church
125	Athenry	Church
126	Athenry	Church
127	Ballygurrane	Earthwork
128	Athenry	Church
129	Athenry	Church
130	Athenry	Church
131	Athenry	Church
132	Athenry	Cross
133	Lisronagh	Motte
134	Lisronagh	Motte
135	Lisronagh	Motte
136	Lisronagh	Motte
137	Killerk	Castle
138	Killerk	Castle
139	Slaudagh	Earthwork
140	Slaudagh	Earthwork
141	Carnaun	Castle
142	Carnaun	Castle
143	Carnaun	Castle
144	Kilnamraw	Church

ALBUM IV

Ref. No.	Location	Monument type
145	Cloran	Earthwork
146	Cloran	Earthwork
147	Athenry	Castle
148	Athenry	Castle
149	Athenry	Castle
150	Athenry	Castle
151	Abbeyknockmoy	Church
152	Abbeyknockmoy	Church
153	Abbeyknockmoy	Church
154	Abbeyknockmoy	Church
155	Athenry	Castle
156	Athenry	Castle
157	Athenry	Castle
158	Athenry	Castle
159	Athenry	Castle
160	Athenry	Town wall
161	Athenry	Town wall
162	Athenry	Town wall
163	Athenry	Town ditch
164	Athenry	Town ditch
165	Kilcornan	Building
166	Kilcornan	Church
167	Athenry	Town wall
168	Cloonkeenkerrill	Church
169	Cloonkeenkerrill	Church
170	Cloonkeenkerrill	Church
171	Cahercrin	Enclosure
172	Cahercrin – photo missing	Enclosure
173	Carheennascovoge	Enclosure
174	Carheennascovoge	Enclosure
175	Carheennascovoge	Enclosure
176	Athenry	Earthwork
177	Killaclogher	Castle
178	Killaclogher	Castle
179	Killeely	Church
180	Killeely	Church
181	Kilcornan	Church
182	Dunmore	Castle
183	Derrydonnell	Earthwork
184	Templemoyle	Church

Appendix 1: Photographic Collection in Hardiman Library, N.U.I.Galway

Ref. No.	Location	Monument type
185	Templemoyle	Church
186	Templeawalla	Church
187	Templeawalla	Church
188	Athenry	Castle
189	Castle Ellen	Castle
190	Baunmore	Folklife
191	Baunmore	Folklife
192	Baunmore	Folklife

ALBUM V

Ref. No.	Location	Monument type
1	Carnfree	Earthwork
2	Carnfree	Earthwork
3	Carnfree	Earthwork
4	Carnfree	Earthwork
5	Carnabreckna	Earthwork
6	Carnabreckna	Earthwork
7	Carnabreckna	Earthwork
8	Carnabreckna	Earthwork
9	Doogara	Earthwork
10	Doogara	Earthwork
11	Doogara	Earthwork
12	Doogara	Earthwork
13	Doogara	Earthwork
14	Clooncah	Earthwork
15	Clooncah	Earthwork
16	Skeaghavarta	Earthwork
17	Baunmore	Folklife
18	Baunmore	Folklife
19	Baunmore	Folklife
20	Garbally	Castle
21	Garbally	Castle
22	Baunmore or Cahermorrissey	Castle
23	Baunmore or Cahermorrissey	Castle
24	Oldcastle	Earthwork
25	Oldcastle	Earthwork
26	Lavally – photo missing	Megalith (possible)
27	Lavally – photo missing	Megalith (possible)
28	Killeeneen	Church
29	Athenry	Church
30	Mount Shaw	Earthwork
31	Mount Shaw	Earthwork
32	Lady's Well	Devotional site
33	Killogilleen	Earthwork
34	Killogilleen – photo missing	Castle
35	Killogilleen	Castle
36	Creggymulgreny	Castle
37	Creggymulgreny	Castle
38	Creggymulgreny	Castle
39	Creggymulgreny	Castle
40	Carnfree	Earthwork
41	Carnfree	Earthwork
42	Corker	Earthwork
43	Corker	Earthwork
44	Corker	Earthwork
45	Corker	Earthwork
46	Sheegeera	Earthwork
47	Glennamacaul	Megalith (possible)
48	Carnfree	Pillar stone

ALBUM VIII

Ref. No.	Location	Monument type
1	Creeve	Earthwork
2	Gortnalon	Earthwork
3	Gortnalon	Earthwork
4	Tample	Earthwork
5	Laragh	Castle
6	Ballybride	Earthwork
7	Ballybride	Earthwork
8	Ballybride	Earthwork
9	Ballybride	Devotional site
10	Dunmore	Earthwork
11	Dunmore	Earthwork
12	Rathmoyle	Earthwork
13	Knockbrack	Earthwork

Ref. No.	Location	Monument type
14	Cloonkeenkerrill – photo missing	Church
15	Cloonkeenkerrill – photo missing	Church
16	Castlebin	Earthwork
17	Masonbrook – photo missing	Megalith (possible)
18	Turoe	Pillar stone
19	Streamford – photo missing	Enclosure
20	Bauvin – photo missing	Castle
21	Ballyglass	Earthwork
22	Tullaghane	Earthwork
23	Knockair	Souterrain
24	Knockair	Souterrain
25	Woodlawn – photo missing	Earthwork
26	Feerwore	Cist/enclosure
27	Turoe/Knocknadaula	Earthwork
28	Galbooley	Castle
29	Galbooley	Castle
30	Bullaun	Earthwork
31	Turoe	Pillar stone
32	Roo	Enclosure
33	Roo	Enclosure
34	Aggardmore	Earthwork
35	Cappanshruhaun	Earthwork
36	Woodlawn	Enclosure
37	Boreenard/Athenry	Togher/road
38	Lisnagranshy	Souterrain
39	Gortroe/Liscorn	Souterrain
40	Gortroe/Liscorn	Souterrain
41	Gortroe/Liscorn	Souterrain
42	Poulnagorragh	Enclosure
43	Newport	Landscape
44	Knocknalegan	Megalith (possible)
45	Rossbeg	Megalith (possible)
46	Kilmeena	Devotional site
47	Brockagh	Castle
48	Brockagh	Castle

UNBOUND ALBUM 1UB

Ref. No.	Location	Monument type
1	Mannin	Building
2	Island	Ogham stone
3	Island	Ogham stone
4	Tullaghane	Ogham stone
5	Tober Mucknoo	Devotional site
6	Straide	Church
7	Aghamore	Church
8	? Near Aghamore	Cross
9	Kilmullen	Church
10	Kilcronan	Landscape
11	Coogue North	Devotional site
12	Greenwood	Megalith (possible)
13	Straide	Church
14	Straide	Church
20	Bekan	Megalith (possible)
38	Feamore/Laght-a-wohoo	Megalith (possible)
39	Feamore/Laght-a-wohoo	Megalith (possible)
40	Slieve Goley	Enclosure
41	Aghnacliff	Megalith (possible)
42	Cleenrath	Megalith (possible)
43	Lassiney	Enclosure
44	Kiltiernan Demesne	Building
45	Kiltiernan Demesne	Building
54	Burrishoole	Church
55	Shanaghmrel	C.B.G.
56	Barnayanig	Pillar stone
57	Barnayanig	Pillar stone
58	Bekan	Church
59	Corrislustia	Megalith (possible)
60	Raith	Castle
61	Derrycastle	Castle
62	Slievenaman	Cairn
63	Finnstable	Megalith (possible)
64	Ballygurrane	Souterrain
66	Ballygurrane	Souterrain
103	Kilnamannin	C.B.G.
104	Carrowneden	Megalith (possible)
105	Cashels	Megalith (possible)
106	Island	Crannóg

Appendix 1: Photographic Collection in Hardiman Library, N.U.I.Galway

Ref. No.	Location	Monument type
135	Carrickmiclear	Landscape
136	Foxhall	Church
137	Killare	Earthwork
138	Cashel	Cashel

UNBOUND ALBUM 2UB

Ref. No.	Location	Monument type
177	Roo	Bullaun stones
180	Doon	Earthwork
181	Ardygommon	Pillar stone
182	Lough Feagh	Earthwork
194	Cahergal	Devotional site
195	Ballinsmalla	Church
196	Ballinsmalla	Church
197	Ballinsmalla	Church
198	Knockfarnaght	Earthwork
199	Burrishoole	Landscape
200	Burrishoole	Landscape
201	Tubber Marean	Devotional site
202	Tubber Marean	Church & graveyard
203	Newport	Folklife
204	Newport	Folklife
205	Newport	Building
206	Cloonkeenkerrill	Church
224	Kildun	Devotional site
225	Kildun	Devotional site
226	Drumgallagh	Megalith (possible)
227	Mulrany	Landscape
228	Tallagh	Megalith (possible)
229	Drumslide	Folklife
230	Drumgallagh	Megalith (possible)
231	Drumslide	Megalith (possible)
232	Tallagh	Megalith (possible)
233	Drumgallagh	Megalith (possible)
234	Rathsowny	Earthwork
235	Doon	Earthwork
236	Doon	Earthwork
236a	None given	Megalith (possible)
237	Doon	Earthwork

Ref. No.	Location	Monument type
237a	None given	Megalith (possible)
238	Doon	Earthwork
238a	Murrisk	Church
239	Ivymount	Church & graveyard
239a	None given/ Croagh Patrick	Landscape
240	Rosgallive	Pillar stone
241	Rosgallive	Pillar stone
243	Kilmeena	Church
246	Ballyhaunis	Folklife
247	Newport	Folklife
248	Newport	Landscape
249	Newport	Landscape
252	Ballinglass	Rock art
253	Ballinglass	Rock art
254	Ballinglass	Rock art
255	Newport	Church

ENVELOPE 'VARIOUS SITES'

Ref. No.	Location	Monument type
1	Newport	Folklife
2	Killower	Cairn
3	Ballybrit	Megalith (possible)
4	Ardnamaol	Megalith (possible)
5	Shanra	Earthwork
6	Castlebin	Earthwork
7	Shanra	Earthwork
8	Ballygurrane	Souterrain
9	Ballygurrane	Cashel
10	Ballygurrane	Cashel
11	Cunnicaire	Earthwork
12	Clamperpark	Enclosure
13	Castlebin	Earthwork
14	Castlebin	Earthwork
15	Caherdrineen	Enclosure
16	Caherdrineen	Enclosure
17	Caherdrineen	Enclosure
18	Kiltiernan	Church
19	Kiltiernan	Church
20	Kiltiernan	Church

Ref. No.	Location	Monument type
21	Kiltiernan	Church
22	Kiltiernan	Church
23	Kiltiernan	Church
24	Kiltiernan	Church
25	Kiltiernan	Church
26	Kiltiernan	Church
27	Kiltiernan	Church
28	Kiltiernan	Church
29	Church Island	Inscribed grave slab
30	Church Island	Ecclesiastical site
31	Church Island	Church
32	Church Island	Church
33	Ardrahan	Castle
34	Ardrahan	Castle
35	Lisheenawalla	Ecclesiastical site
36	Lisheenawalla	Graveyard
37	?St. Andrew's	Building
38	?St. Andrew's	Building
39	?St. Andrew's	Building
43	Lisnamottaun	Castle
45	Ballygurrane	Cashel
46	Ballygurrane	Cashel
47	Woodlawn	Castle

ENVELOPE 'VARIOUS PHOTOGRAPHS'

Ref. No.	Location	Monument type
1	Parknaree	Megalith (possible)
2	Blasket Islands	Folklife
3	Blasket Islands	Folklife
4a	Mason?? Island	Holt and others on board ship
4b	Mason?? Island	Folklife
5	Moyne	Church
6	Tory Island	Round tower
8	nr. Lough Swilly	Earthwork/ ? smelting place
9	Ballynamanagh	Building
10	Rosserk	Church
11	Erren	Church
12	Ballynacloghy	Devotional site
13	Ardfry	Castle
14	Blasket Islands	Folklife
15	Valentia Island	Ogham stone
16	Ardfry	Castle
17	Gurraun/ Ballynacourty	Megalith (possible)
18	Garraun/ Ballynacourty	Megalith (possible)
19	Ballynacourty	Devotional site
20	Ballynacourty	Church
21	Ballynacourty	Church
22	Ballynacourty	Building
23	Ballynamanagh	Building
24	Killeeneen	Church
25	Oilean	Landscape
26	Valentia Island	Megalith (possible)
27	Creganna	Castle

APPENDIX 2

Published works of Patrick Lyons

1920   'Straw Head-dresses', *Journal of the Royal Society of Antiquaries of Ireland* 50, 61-3;

1934   'Forts etc near Clonmel', *Journal of the Royal Society of Antiquaries of Ireland* 64, 260-1;

1935   'Alignment at Reanadampaun, Ballymcarbery, Co. Waterford', *Journal of the Royal Society of Antiquaries of Ireland* 65, 148-9; 'Brugh Da Derga' (Henry Morris with note by Lyons), 297-312;

1936   'Norman Antiquities of Clonmel Burgh', *Journal of the Royal Society of Antiquaries of Ireland* 66, 285-94; 67,125-6;

1937   'Three-ringed Fort at Clonacody, Co. Tipperary', *Journal of the Royal Society of Antiquaries of Ireland* 67, 126-7; 'Sheela-na-Gig at Kilmacomma, Co. Waterford', 127-8; 'Norman Antiquities at Lisronagh, Co. Tipperary', 242-9;

1938   'Earthwork and Castle at Powerstown, Clonmel', *Journal of the Royal Society of Antiquaries of Ireland* 68, 152-5; 'Prehistoric Grave near Clonmel', 161; 'Neville's Fort', 288-90; 'Some surnames', 290-1;

1939   'The Placename Clonmel', *Journal of the Royal Society of Antiquaries of Ireland* 69, 221-2; 'Norman-French Survivals', 225-6;

1940   'Harvest Lore', *Béaloideas* 10, 291; 'The Irish Spade', 292-3;

1942   'Creagh's Pond', Clonmel', *Journal of the Royal Society of Antiquaries of Ireland* 72, 71-3;

1943   'Stick Fencing (in Co. Tipperary)', *Béaloideas* 13, 269; 'The Crow's Advice', 270; 'Shee Boo', 270; 'Faction Fighting', 270-1; 'Shellika-Boork', 271-2;

1945   'The Deardaol', *Béaloideas* 15, 283; 'The May Bush', 283; 'An early Tea Party', 284; 'Old Inn sign', 284; 'The Ragwell, near Clonmel', (Told by P.

Condon) 285; 'Ruined Wall-tower at NE angle of Clonmel Burgh', *Journal of the Royal Society of Antiquaries of Ireland* 75, 258; 'Staircase Towers (?) in Clonmel', 259;

1946 'The Stone of Formach', *Journal of the Cork Historical and Archaeological Society* 51, 85-6;

1948 'Double bullaun at Park, Parish of Rathgormack, Co. Waterford', *Journal of the Royal Society of Antiquaries of Ireland* 78, 178;

1949 'Clonmel Gleanings', *Béaloideas* 19, 189-92;

1950 'Kilfeakle and Knockgraffon Motes, Co. Tipperary', *Journal of the Royal Society of Antiquaries of Ireland* 80, 263-8; 'The Cromwellian Assault on Clonmel', in P. O'Connell and W.C. Darmody (eds.) *Siege of Clonmel Tercenterary Souvenir Record*, 16-8;

1952 'The Irish Quern', *Journal of the Royal Society of Antiquaries of Ireland* 82, 183;

1952-3 'Ancient Road Systems of South Tipperary', *Journal of the Clonmel Historical and Archaeological Society* 1, No. 1, 10-7; 'Church of St. Nicholas and its precinct', 23-30;

1953-4 'Some local entries in the Annals of Innishfallen', *Journal of the Clonmel Historical and Archaeological Society* 1, No. 2, 14-5; 'The Manor of Kiltinane', 16-20; 'Parish of Clerihan' 34-42;

1954-5 'The Burgh of Clonmel', *Journal of the Clonmel Historical and Archaeological Society* 1, No.3, 20-6; 'Pre-Norman Clonmel', 28-3.

BIBLIOGRAPHY

Aalen, F.H.A. 1997. 'Buildings' in F.H.A. Aalen, K.Whelan, M.Stout (eds.), *Atlas of the Irish Rural Landscape*, 150. Cork University Press, Cork.

Anon. 1895. 'Excursions', *Journal of the Royal Society of Antiquaries of Ireland* 25, 299-301.

Anon. 1920. Obituary – Hubert T. Knox, *Journal of the Galway Archaeological and Historical Society* 11, 151-2.

Anon. 1922. Obituary – Hubert T. Knox, *Journal of the Royal Society of Antiquaries of Ireland* 52, 94.

Anon. 1954. Short Notices. *Irish Historical Studies* 9, 119.

Anon. 1982. *Arresting Memories: Captured Moments in Constabulary Life*. Royal Ulster Constabulary Diamond Jubilee Committee, Coleraine, Co. Derry.

Armitage, E. 1900. 'Anglo-Saxon Burghs and Early Norman Castles', *Proceedings of the Royal Society of Antiquaries of Scotland* 34, 260-88.

Ashe Fitzgerald, M. 2000. *Thomas Johnson Westropp (1860-1922): An Irish Antiquary*. Department of Archaeology, U.C.D., Dublin.

Ball, S. (ed.) 1999. *A Policeman's Ireland – Recollections of Samuel Waters, RIC*. Cork University Press, Cork.

Clonmel Historical and Archaeological Society (Minutes): 6 Jun 1944; 27 Jun 1944; 25 Jul 1944; 30 Apr 1947; 26 Nov 1947; 18 May 1951; 8 Nov 1951; 10 Jun 1952; 2 Feb 1953; 10 Sep 1954.

Clonmel Joint Cemeteries Committee/Fás. 1994. *Clonmel Gravestone Inscriptions: an alphabetical index*, Co. Tipperary Joint Libraries Committee, Clonmel, Co. Tipperary.

Clonmel Nationalist: 4 Aug 1920; 11 Aug 1920; 14 Aug 1920; 8 Sep 1920; 4 Jun 1921; 27 Feb 1922; 19 Jul 1922; 12 Aug 1922; 16 Dec 1922; 4 Jul 1928; 5 Mar 1941; 8 Apr 1944; 17 May 1944; 24 May 1944; 31 May 1944; 28 May 1947; 18 Mar 1950; 2 Jun 1951; 12 Jun 1954; 19 Jun 1954; 26 Jun 1954; 10 Sep 1954; 9 Jul 1955; 12 Jul 1955.

Cochrane, R. 1898. 'Ogam inscriptions discovered in Ireland in the year 1898', *Journal of the Royal Society of Antiquaries of Ireland* 28, 399-408.

Coffey, G. 1904. 'On the excavation of a tumulus near Loughrea, Co. Galway', *Proceedings of the Royal Irish Academy* 1904b, 25C, 14-20.

Connaught Tribune: 12 Jul 1913; 30 Jan 1914; 21 Feb 1914; 4 Jul 1914; 27 Nov 1914; 3 Jul 1915; 11 Nov 1915; 20 Nov 1915; 27 Nov 1915.

Corbett, Rev. P.A. 1990. 'Tans, Staters and Diehards' in *The "Nationalist" Centenary*

Supplement, 1890-1990, 62. Clonmel Nationalist, Clonmel, Co. Tipperary.

Corlett, C. 2001a. 'Milling around Bagnelstown', Archaeology Ireland 15, No. 3, 7; 2001b. Antiquities of West Mayo, Wordwell Ltd., Bray, Co. Wicklow.

Crawford, H.S. 1913. 'A descriptive list of early cross-slabs and pillars (Connacht)', Journal of the Royal Society of Antiquaries of Ireland 43, 151-69.

Crean, T.J. 1937. 'Clonmel Antiquities', Journal of the Royal Society of Antiquaries of Ireland 67, 125-6.

Cribbin, G. (et al.) 1994. 'A Destroyed Late Iron-Age Burial from Kiltullagh, Ballyglass Middle td., Co. Mayo', Emania 12, 61-5.

Cribbin, G. 2000. 'Seargant [sic.] Patrick Lyons R.I.C. (Ballyhaunis) 1894', Annagh, 59-61, Western People, Ballina Co. Mayo.

Curtis, E. 1936. 'Rental of the Manor of Lisronagh 1333', Proceedings of the Royal Irish Academy 43, 58-62.

Dunlevy, M. 1989. Dress in Ireland. B.T.Batsford Ltd., London.

Empey, C. A. 1985. 'The Norman Period, 1185-1500', in W. Nolan (ed.) Tipperary: History and Society, 76. Geography Publications, Dublin.

Falkiner, W.F. 1906. 'Earthworks, Rathnarrow, County Westmeath', Journal of the Royal Society of Antiquaries of Ireland 36, 421-2.

Farrelly, J. and O'Brien, C. 2002. Archaeological Survey of Co. Tipperary. Vol 1: North Tipperary. Dublin.

Fennell, T. 2003. The Royal Irish Constabulary. University College Dublin Press, Dublin.

Fitzpatrick, E. 2004. Royal Inauguration in Gaelic Ireland c. 1100-1600: a cultural landscape study. Boydell and Brewer Ltd. Woodbridge.

Flynn, M. 1996. Harvest: a history of grain growing, harvesting and milling in Ireland from earliest times to the 20th century. Heritage House, Macroom, Co. Cork.

Freyne, B. 1978. 'Ballyhaunis – B.C. and A.D.' Annagh, 28-30, Western People, Ballina, Co. Mayo.

Harbison, P. 1970. Guide to National Monuments. Gill and Macmillan, Dublin; 1991. Pilgrimage in Ireland. Barrie and Jenkins, London.

Hardiman, R. (ed.) 1978. A Chorographical Description of West or h-Iar Connaught, written A.D. 1684 by Roderick O'Flaherty, Esq. Kenny's Bookshops and Art Galleries Ltd., Galway.

Herlihy, J. 1997. The Royal Irish Constabulary – a short History and Genealogical Guide. Four Courts Press, Dublin.

Holland, P. 1987-8. 'The Anglo-Normans in Co. Galway: the process of colonization', Journal of the Galway Archaeological and Historical Society 41, 73-89.

Holt, E.W.L. 1909-10. 'Notes on Ordnance Survey letters relating to the Barony of Dunkellin', Journal of the Galway Archaeological and Historical Society 6, 129-69; 1911-12. 'Notes on Ordnance Survey letters relating to the Barony of Dunkellin iii Ballynacourty Parish', *Journal of the Galway Archaeological and Historical Society* 7, 205-50.

Irish Folklore Commission. Ms. 745, 301-19; Ms. 879, 43-58; Ms. 1127, 64-441; Ms. 1144, 97-101; Ms. 1145, 29-36, 101.

Kee, R. 1972. *The Green Flag* (Volume 2, *The Bold Fenian Men*; Volume 3, *Ourselves Alone*). Penguin Books, London.

Kelly, E.P. 1996. *Sheela-na-gigs: origins and functions*. Town House and Country House, Dublin.

Knox, H.T. 1898. 'Note in reference to the Breastagh Ogham stone', *Journal of the Royal Society of Antiquaries of Ireland* 28, 272-3;

1904. *Notes on the Diocese of Tuam, Killala and Achonry*. Hodges Figgis and Co. Ltd. Dublin;

1906-7. 'Notes on gig-mills and drying kilns near Ballyhaunis, County Mayo', *Proceedings of the Royal Irish Academy* 26, 265-76;

1911. 'The Croghans & some Connaught raths and motes', *Journal of the Royal Society of Antiquaries of Ireland* 41, 93-116; 206-41; 301-42;

1911-2. 'Seven Mayo Earthworks', *Journal of the Galway Archaeological and Historical Society* 7, 147-65;

1914a. 'Ruins of Cruachain Ai', *Journal of the Royal Society of Antiquaries of Ireland* 44, 1-50;

1914b. 'Dumha Brosna', *Journal of the Royal Society of Antiquaries of Ireland* 44, 348-57;

1915. 'Rath Brenainn', *Journal of the Royal Society of Antiquaries of Ireland* 45, 289-98;

1915-6a. 'Carnfree and Carnabreckna', *Journal of the Galway Archaeological and Historical Society* 9, 1-32; 65-79;

1915-6b. 'Some Rath Caves in and near the Barony of Dunkellin', *Journal of the Galway Archaeological and Historical Society* 9, 178-90;

1915-6c. 'The Turoe Stone and Rath of Feerwore', *Journal of the Galway Archaeological and Historical Society* 9, 190-3;

1915-6d. 'The Mound at Tample', *Journal of the Galway Archaeological and Historical Society* 9, 206;

1917-8a. 'Caher and Rath Caves of Galway and Meath', *Journal of the Galway Archaeological and Historical Society* 10-11, 1-48;

1917-8b. 'The Masonbrook Rings and Mound', *Journal of the Galway Archaeological and Historical Society* 10-11, 71-96;

1917-8c. 'Ballygurraun and Raheen Group of Works in Earth and Stone', *Journal of the Galway Archaeological and Historical Society* 10-11, 101-24;

1918. 'Cruachain Ai Roads and Avenues', *Journal of the Royal Society of Antiquaries of Ireland* 48, 157-63;

1919. 'St. Marcan's Loch and Ruins', *Journal of the Royal Society of Antiquaries of Ireland* 49, 89-91;

1920. 'Notes on the Burgus of Athenry: its First Defences, and its Town Walls', *Journal of the Galway Archaeological and Historical Society* 11, 1-26.

Leask, H.G. 1955. 'Obituary – Patrick J. Lyons', *Journal of the Royal Society of Antiquaries of Ireland* 85, 151.

Longford Independent: 20 Nov 1886; 7 May 1887; 10 May 1887; 28 May 1887; 15 Oct 1887; 20 Oct 1888; 1 Feb 1889; 19 Oct 1889; 2 Nov 1889; 7 Dec 1889; 8 Feb 1890; 31 Jan 1891; 15 Aug 1891; 5 Dec 1891.

Lough Mask and Lough Carra Tourist Development Association/Fás. 1988. *The Treasures of South Mayo*. Ballinrobe, Co. Mayo.

Lucas, A.T. 1953. 'The horizontal mill in Ireland', *Journal of the Royal Society of Antiquaries of Ireland* 83, 1-35.

Lyons, P. 1920. 'Straw Head-dresses' *Journal of the Royal Society of Antiquaries of Ireland* 50, 61-3;

1936. 'Norman Antiquities of Clonmel Burgh', *Journal of the Royal Society of Antiquaries of Ireland* 65, 284-94;

1946. 'The Stone of Formach', *Journal of the Cork Historical and Archaeological Society* 41, 85-6;

1950. 'The Cromwellian Assault on Clonmel' in P. O'Connell and W.C. Darmody (eds.) *Siege of Clonmel Tercenterary Souvenir Record*, 16-8. Clonmel Nationalist, Clonmel, Co. Tipperary.

Macalister, R.A.S. 1897. *Studies in Irish Epigraphy*. David Nutt, London.

1913. 'The Dominican church at Athenry', *Journal of the Royal Society of Antiquaries of Ireland* 43, 197-222;

1916-7a. 'Notes on certain Irish inscriptions', *Proceedings of the Royal Irish Academy* 33, 81-92;

1916-7b. 'A report on some excavations recently conducted in Co. Galway', *Proceedings of the Royal Irish Academy* 33, 505-10;

1945. *Corpus Inscriptionum Insularum Celticarum*. Stationery Office, Dublin.

Malcolm, E. 2006. *The Irish Policeman, 1822-1922*. Four Courts Press, Dublin.

Mayo News: 1 Apr 1916; 13 May 1916; 17 Jun 1916; 12 Aug 1916; 21 Apr 1917; 15 Sep 1917; 29 Sep 1917; 3 Nov 1917; 9 Mar 1918; 16 Mar 1918; 23 Mar 1918; 12 Jul 1919; 13 Dec 1919; 12 Feb 1920; 10 April 1920.

Moran, G. 1991. 'Politics and electioneering in Co. Longford' in R. Gillespie and G. Moran (eds.) *Longford: Essays in county history*, 180-9. Lilliput Press, Dublin.

McCormick, F. 1994. 'New light on burial practice' *Archaeology Ireland* 8, No.3, 28.

McCormick, F. (et al.) 1995. 'A Pagan-Christian Transitional Burial at Kiltullagh', *Emania* 13, 89-98.

Neilan, M. 1966. 'The Rising in Galway' in Henry, Fr. (ed.) *The Capuchin Annual*, 324-6. Dublin.

Newell, U. 2006. 'The Rising of the Moon: Galway 1916', *Journal of the Galway Archaeological and Historical Society* 58, 114-35.

Ní Cheanainn, A. 1988. *The Heritage of Mayo*. Western People, Ballina, Co. Mayo.

O'Connell, P. 1950. 'Cluain Meala or Cliu Mel' in P. O'Connell and W.C. Darmody (eds.) *Siege of Clonmel Tercentenary Souvenir Record*, 82-8. Clonmel Nationalist, Clonmel, Co. Tipperary.

1954-5. 'Death of Mr. Patrick Lyons, F.R.S.A.I.', *Journal of the Clonmel Historical and Archaeological Society* 1, No. 3, 39.

O'Halloran, J. 2001. 'By time everything is revealed: the Galway Archaeological and Historical Society, 1900-1999', *Journal of the Galway Archaeological and Historical Society* 53, 163.

Ó hEochaidh, E. 1975. *Liam Mellowes*. Liam Mellows Cumann of Sinn Fein, Dublin.

Ó Muraile, N. 1982. 'An Outline History of County Mayo' in B. O'Hara (ed.) *Mayo*, 10-35. The Archaeological, Historical and Folklore Society, Regional Technical College, Galway.

Ó Néill, E. 2001. *The Golden Vale of Ivowen*. Geography Publications, Dublin.

Orpen, G.H. 1910. 'The Mote of Castlelost, County Westmeath', *Journal of the Royal Society of Antiquaries of Ireland* 40, 226-8;

1911. 'Croghans and Norman motes', *Journal of the Royal Society of Antiquaries of Ireland* 41, 267-76;

1915-6. 'The Mote of Oldcastle and the Castle of Rathgorgin', *Journal of the Galway Archaeological and Historical Society* 9, 33-44.

O'Reilly, J.A. 1902-4. 'Some further Notes on Ancient Horizontal Water Mills, Native and Foreign', *Proceedings of the Royal Irish Academy* 24, 55-84.

O'Sullivan, M.D. 1983. *Old Galway*, Kenny's Bookhops and Art Galleries Ltd., Galway.

Qualter, A. (undated). *Athenry – History from 1780. Folklore recollections*. Galway County Libraries, Galway.

Raftery, J. 1944. 'The Turoe Stone and the Rath of Feerwore', *Journal of the Royal Society of Antiquaries of Ireland* 74, 23-52.

Raiswell, M. (ed.) 2001. 'Private Notes of George McKee, Royal Irish Constabulary, Castlebar 1880-1915', *Cathair Na Mart* 18, 106.

Rhys, J. 1898. 'Newly Discovered Ogams in Mayo and Antrim, with readings of some undescribed in Cork and Waterford', *Journal of the Royal Society of Antiquaries of Ireland* 28, 396;

1901. 'The Tullaghane Ogam-Stone, Co. Mayo', *Journal of the Royal Society of Antiquaries of Ireland* 31, 176-8;

1907. 'The Kilmannin Ogam, Co. Mayo', *Journal of the Royal Society of Antiquaries of Ireland* 37, 61-8.

Rynne, E. 1987-8. 'Meiler de Berimngham's Tombstone', *Journal of the Galway Archaeological and Historical Society* 41, 44-7;

1995. 'Athenry' in A. Simms and J.H. Andrews (eds.) *More Irish country towns*, 106-118. Mercier Press, Dublin.

Sheehan, J. 1978. *South Westmeath: Farm and Folk*. Blackwater, Dublin.

Tuam Herald: 4 Oct 1913; 10 Jan 1914; 7 Jul 1914; 18 Dec 1915.

Waddell, J. 1974-5. 'The Bronze Age Burials from County Galway', *Journal of the Galway Archaeological and Historical Society* 34, 5-20;

1983. 'Rathcroghan – a Royal site in Connacht', *Journal of Irish Archaeology* 1, 21-46;

1985-6. 'Knocknagur, Turoe and Local Enquiry', *Journal of the Galway Archaeological and Historical Society* 40, 130-3;

1987-8. 'J.R.W. Goulden's excavations on Inishmore, Aran, 1953-1955', *Journal of the Galway Archaeological and Historical Society* 41, 37-59;

1988. 'Rathcroghan in Connacht', *Emania* 5, 5-18.

Western People: 17 Nov 1894; 31 Aug 1895; 14 Sep 1895; 23 May 1896; 21 Aug 1897; 8 Jul 1898; 20 Jan 1900; 4 Apr 1901; 20 Apr 1901; 27 Apr 1901; 29 Jun 1901; 8 Aug 1901; 14 Sep 1901; 30 Aug 1902; 27 Sep 1902; 22 Nov 1902; 27 Feb 1904; 23 Apr 1904; 7 May 1904; 2 Jul 1904; 3 Jun 1905; 23 Sep 1905; 9 Mar 1907; 11 Aug 1908; 16 Sep 1909; 2 Oct 1909; 24 Dec 1909; 30 Apr 1910; 12 Oct 1912; 5 Apr 1913; 3 May 1913; 15 Jun 1913.

Westmeath Examiner: 21 Jan 1893.

Westmeath Independent: 26 Apr 1894; 30 Jun 1894.

Westropp, T.J. 1900. 'Churches of County Clare and the origin of the Ecclesiastical Divisions in that county', *Proceedings of the Royal Irish Academy* 22, 100-80;

1902. 'The Ancient Forts of Ireland; being a contribution towards our knowledge of their types, affinities and structural features', *Transactions of the Royal Irish Academy* 31, 579-726;

1919. 'Notes on several forts in Dunkellin and other parts of southern Co. Galway', *Journal of the Royal Society of Antiquaries of Ireland* 49, 167.

Index

Page numbers of plates and illustrations are given in bold print.
A county location for places mentioned in Knox's notebooks is not always possible.

A
Aghataharn, 50
Annagh, Co. Mayo, 60
Armitage, E., 79, 80, 85
Athenry, Co. Galway, 78, 107-21
    Boreenard, **29**
    Castle, 107, 116, **117, 118, 119**
    Dominican Priory, **112, 113, 114, 115**, 116
    foundation and development of town, 107, 110-1
    map of medieval town, **108**
    Market Cross, 117, **121**
    St. Mary's Collegiate Church, 116, **119**
    town walls and gates, 107, **109**, 110, 111, 116, **120**
Aughamore, Co. Mayo, 45, 68-9, 123

B
Bagnelstown, Co. Carlow, **77**
Balla, Co. Mayo, 68, 83, 84
Ballaghdorragher, 45
Ballinacourty, Co. Galway, 140
Ballyboy, Co. Mayo, 93
Ballybride, Co. Roscommon, **56**
Ballyglanna, 142
Ballyglass, Co Mayo, 50-4, **51, 52, 53**
Ballygurraun, Co. Galway, 97, **106**
Ballyhaunis, Co. Mayo, 18, **19**, 40, 69, 84, **125**
Ballyhowley, Co. Mayo, 83
Ballymonach, 142
Ballyveel, Co. Mayo, 138
Baptist Grange, Co. Tipperary, 5, 48
Barrettstown, Co. Tipperary, 84
Barrinagh, 138
Baunmore, Co. Galway, **131**, 132-3
Belmullet, Co. Mayo, 28

Bohola, Co. Mayo, 99, **100**
Boleybeg, Co. Mayo, 69
Boleyboy, 133
Bonese's Cross, Co. Mayo, 69
Bracklaghboy, Co. Mayo, 63, **64, 65**
Breastagh, Co. Mayo, 59
Brees, Co. Mayo, 82, 83

C
Cahergal, Co. Mayo, **70**
Caherroyan, Co. Galway, 99
Cappagh, Co. Mayo, 69, 93, 130
Carnbreckna, Co. Roscommon, 87, **89**, 90-4,
Carnfree, Co. Roscommon, 87, 90-4, **94**
Carroll, Sgt. E., 28, 40-1
Carrowgarve, Co. Roscommon, **92**, 93-4
Carrowkeel, Co. Mayo, **26**, 83
Carrowkennedy, Co. Mayo, 144
Carrownedin, Co. Mayo, 45, 46, 69, 136
Cartron, Co. Mayo, 69
Cashels
    Ballyboy, Cappagh, Co. Mayo, 93
    Carnabreckna, Co. Roscommon, 90
    Cashelgal, 45
    Coolnaha, Co. Mayo, 85
    Kiltabo, Co. Mayo, 45
Cashelgal, 45
Cashelmore, 49
Castlebar, Co. Mayo, 34, 39, 126
Castlelost, Co, Westmeath, 136, 140-2
Castletown-Geoghegan, Co. Westmeath, 17
Castles
    Annagh, Co. Mayo, 60
    Athenry, Co. Galway, 107, 116, **117, 118, 119**

Ballinacourty, Co. Galway, 140
Ballyveel, Co. Mayo, 138
Brees, Co. Mayo, 82, 83
Currykilleen, Co. Mayo, 82, 83
Dunmore, Co. Galway, **31**, 99
Island, Co. Mayo, 46, 84
Kilcolgan, Co. Galway, 78, 140
Kilconnell, Co. Tippperary, 54
Lea, Co. Laois, 54
Lisronagh, Co. Tipperary, 54, 57, **58**
Rathgorgin, Co. Galway, **140**, **141**, 142
Tooloobaun, Co. Galway, 78

Cauraun, 99

Churches
Aughamore, Co. Mayo, 45, 123
Baptist Grange, Co. Tipperary, 48
Carnabreckna, Co. Roscommon, 90
Holywell, Co. Mayo, 130
Kilmannin, Co. Mayo, **59**, 60
Kilmovee, Co. Mayo, 62
Meedian, 142
St. Faraunan's, Donoughmore, Co. Tipperary, 47, 48
St. Marchan's, Newport, Co. Mayo, 78

Civil War, 37-41, 144-6
Cloghvoley, Co. Mayo, 130
Clonmel, Co. Tipperary
'Idol of Blue Anchor Lane', 147-9, **148**
Clonmel Historical and Archaeological Society, 147-51
Condon, D., 127, **154**, 155
discovery of medieval sculpture 154, **155**
Lyons' antiquarian work in, 5, 146-51
Lyons' residences in, 146-7
Murphy, Rev. T.A., 151, 154, 159
O'Connell, P., 149, 153
re-enactment of the Siege of Clonmel, 5, 151-4
Cloonboyoge, Co. Roscommon, 132
Clooncan, Co. Mayo, 69, 71
Clooneyquin, Co. Roscommon, 140
Cloonfad, 45
Cloonpatrick, 68
Cloonroe, Co. Mayo, 69
Cochrane, R., 4, 12, 48, 58, 64, 72, 78
Coffey, G., 99-100, 101, 103
Condon, D., 127, 154, 155
Coolnaha, Co. Mayo, **61**, 62, 85

Corlett, C., 35, 77
Corraun, Co. Roscommon, 95,
Crannogs, 46, 138
Crawford, H.S., 48
Creeve, Co. Roscommon, 95, **96**, 99
Cribbin, G., 50, 67
Cromwellians, 57, 111, 113, 151-2
Crossbeg, Co. Mayo, 69, 85-6
Cullentra, Co. Mayo, **73**
Currykilleen, Co. Mayo, 82, 83
Curtis, E., 4, 146

D
Derrydonnell, Co. Galway, 30
Dhine, Co. Mayo, **75**
Donoughmore, Co. Tipperary, 47, 48
Dooagh, 142
Drumbaun, 45
Drumgollagh, Ballycroy, Co. Mayo, **38**
Dunmore, Co Galway, **31**, 99,

E
Earthworks
Altered Dumha', **92**, **93**, **94**
'Dumha Selca', **92**, **93**, **94**
'dumha', 87-8
Balla, Co. Mayo, 83, 84
Ballaghdorragher, 45
Ballybride, Co. Roscommon, **56**
Ballygurraun, Co. Galway, 97, **106**
Ballyhowley, Co. Mayo, 83
Ballymonach, 142
Barrettstown, Co. Tipperary, 84
Barrinagh, Sheeaunbeg, 138
Bohola, Co. Mayo, 99, **100**
Boreenard, Athenry, Co. Galway, **29**
Brees, Co. Mayo, 82, 83
Caherroyan, Co. Galway, 99
Carnabreckna, Co. Roscommon, 87, **89**, 90-4
Carnfree, Co. Roscommon, 87, 90-4, **94**
Carrowkeel, Co. Mayo, 83
Carrownedin, Co. Mayo, 45, 46, 136
Castlelost, Co. Westmeath, 136, 140-2
Castletown-Geoghegan, Co. Westmeath, **17**

Clooneyquin, Co. Roscommon, 140
Corraun, Co. Roscommon, 95,
Creeve, Co. Roscommon, 95, **96**, 99,
Crossbeg, Co. Mayo, 85-6
Currykilleen, Co. Mayo, 82, **83**
Dunmore, Co. Galway, 99
Feerwore, Co. Galway, 55, 99-104, **102**
Killedmond, 81
Kilsheelan, Co. Tipperary, **8**
Kiltinan, Co. Tipperary, 55, 107
Knockadoo-Brosna, 88
Knockbrackboy, 134
Knockfarnaght, Co. Mayo, 95, **97**
Lismurtagh/Carrowgarve, Co. Roscommon, **92**, 93, **94**
Lisronagh, Co. Tipperary, 54
Lissaghow, 142
Masonbrook, Co. Galway, 87, 99, 104-5
Moate, Co. Mayo, **137**, 138
Mount Shaw, Co. Galway, 99
Mullaghadooey, Co. Roscommon, 138
Oldcastle, Co. Galway 142
Oran, Co. Roscommon, 84
Portaghard, Co. Mayo, **82**, 83
Raha, Co. Mayo, 83
Raheen, Co. Galway, 97
Rathbeg, Co. Roscommon, 86
Rathbrennan, Co. Roscommon, 88-90, **91**, 93
Rathbrit, Co. Tipperary, 54
Rathcroghan, Co. Roscommon, 2, 4, 55, 78, 81, 83, 86, 87, 90, 93, **96**, 98, 104
Rathmore, Co. Roscommon, **86**, 87
Rathnarrow, Co. Westmeath, 93
Rathra, Co. Roscommon, **137**, 138
Rathscrigg, Co. Roscommon, 95
Runnamoat, Co. Roscommon, 84, 138, **139**
Tulsk Fort, Co. Roscommon, **24**
Well Fort, Tulsk, Co. Roscommon, 140
Easter Rising 1916, **33**, 34
Ecclesiastical sites
Holywell, Co. Mayo, 130
Kilmovee, Co. Mayo, **66**, 67
Kiltullagh, 48
Lady's Well, Baunmore, Co. Galway, **131**, 132-3

Laghty, 45
Linnabaustia, Brackloon, Co. Mayo, 45
Meelick, Co. Mayo, 48, **49**
Relig Vreedha, Thurles, Co. Tipperary, **145**
St. Cronan's Well, Co. Mayo, 45
St. Dominic's Well, Co. Mayo, **70**
St. Marchan's Lough, Co. Mayo, 78
St. Mobhi's Well, Co. Mayo, **66**, 67
Thubbercoghlan, Co. Mayo, 130, 132
Thubber-Muira, Co. Roscommon, 132
Thubber-na-Bachaille, Co. Mayo, 62
Thubber–na-Crush-Neeve, Co. Galway, 130, 131
Thubbernaneeve, 130
Tubberkevna, Co. Mayo, **70**
Tully, Co. Roscommon, 45
Erritt, Co. Mayo, 69
Evictions, **15**, 16, 20
Excavations, 50-4, 99-105

F

Falkiner, W. F., 47, 93
Feerwore, Co. Galway, 55, 99-104, **102**
Fenians, 7, 15
Fitzpatrick, E., **92**, 93, **94**
Flaskagh, 45
Folklife and lore, 123-133
  'ancient boat' (Island), 134
  'Mummers', 126-7
  'The Spinner', **124**
  'tinkers', 127-9, **128, 129**
  'Wren Boys', **19**, 123-7, **125**
  bonfires, 123, 126
  devotional practices, 130-3, **131**
  ethnology, 129-30
  faction fights, 132
  Inishkea Islands, Co. Mayo, 55
  John Carney at St. Patrick's Stone, **26**
  Lady's Well, Co. Galway, **131**, 132-3
  marriage practices, 126-7
  pillar stones at Ballyglass/Kiltullagh, Co. Roscommon, 50-4, **51, 52, 53**
  threatening notice at Lisduff, Co. Mayo, **42**
  typical cottage, **21**
Fortwilliam, Co. Tipperary, 9, 57,

Foxhall, Co. Longford, 14
Freyne, B., 50

G
Galway Archaeological and Historical Society, 4, 121-2
Glassymoo, 142
Goulden, letter to, 3-4 , 18, 28, 41, 44, 55, 56, 57, 136, 142, 144, 146, 159
Granard, Co. Longford, 12, 16, 129

H
Holt, E., 85, 176
Holywell, Co. Mayo, 130
Home Rule Act, 32

I
Illaun-nan-Yach, 46
Inishkea Islands, Co. Mayo, 55
Insurrection 5-9
Irish Folklore Commission, 66, 127, 136
Island, Co. Mayo, 46, 58, 60, 63, **64, 65,** 69, 84, 134, 135

K
Kelly, E.P., 149
Kilcolgan, Co. Galway, 78, 140
Kilconnell, Co. Tipperary, 54
Kildun, Co. Mayo, **68**
Kilerr, 99
Kilgarriff, C. Mayo, **75**
Kilkelly, Co. Mayo, 69
Killedmond, 81
Killaunagher, Co. Mayo, 69
Kilmannin, Co. Mayo, **59, 60,** 63
Kilmovee, Co. Mayo, **62, 66,** 67
Kilruddhaun, Co. Mayo, 68-9
Kilsheelan, Co. Tipperary, **8**
Kiltaboe, Co. Mayo, 45
Kiltimagh, Co. Mayo, 68
Kiltinan, Co. Tipperary, 55, 107
Kiltullagh, Co. Mayo, 48, 50-4, **51, 52, 53,** 55
Knockadoo- Brosna, 88
Knockbrackboy, 134

Knockfarnaght, Co. Mayo, 95, **97**
Knockinn, Co. Mayo, 123
Knox, H.T.
  'Ballygurraun and Raheen Group of Works in Earth and Stone' 97-9, 130
  'Carnfree and Carnbreckna', 90-4
  'Cruchain Ai Roads and Avenues', 93-5, **96**
  'Dumha Brosna', 87-8
  'Notes on gig-mills and drying kilns near Ballyhaunis, County Mayo' , 71-6
  'Notes on the Burgus of Athenry', 78, 107-110, 122
  'Rath Brenainn', 88-90
  'Seven Mayo Earthworks', 81-3
  'The Croghans and some Connaught Raths and Motes' , 79-81, 85
  'The Ruins of Cruachain Ai', 83-4
  birth, 1
  collaboration with Lyons, 1, 2, 4, 57-9, 67-79, 85, 159
  criticism by Orpen, 80-1
  notebooks, 4-5, 44-6, 60, 67, 69, 73, 90, 98, 99, 122, 123, 135, 143, 146, 158
  Notes on the Diocese of Tuam, Killala and Achonry, 67-9, 71
  obituaries, 58, 78, 107, 121-2,
  origin of mottes, 79-85,
  racial theories regarding builders of earthworks, 79, 97-9
  residences, 57-8
  sepulchral or ceremonial nature of earthworks, 79, 85-96

L
Lady's Well, Baunmore, Co. Galway, **131,** 132-3
Laght-a-Wohoo, Feamore, Co. Mayo, **47,** 48, 50
Laghty, 45
Land Acts, 25-7, 28
Land League, 16-7, 19-20, 26-7, 28
Lauralea, 133
Lea, Co. Laois, 54
Leask, H.G., 149, 154, 158
Licensing Acts, 22-5

Linnabaustia, Brackloon, Co. Mayo, 45
Lisduff, Ballyhaunis, Co. Mayo, **42**
Lismurtagh, Co. Roscommon, **92**, 93, **94**
Lisnadhine, 49
Lisnamaneegh, Co. Mayo, 70
Lisronagh, Co. Tipperary, 1, 5, **6**, 54, 57, **58**, 146
Lissaghow, 142
Lough Caheer, Co. Mayo, 46, 133, 134
Lough Caldra, 132
Lough Coghlan, Co. Mayo, 131, 132
Lough Mannin, Co. Mayo, 45
Lough O'Flynn, 138
Lough Roe, 50
Lough Urlaur, 50
Loughanoge, Co. Mayo, 69
Lyons, P.
    assistance with antiquarian activities by R.I.C. colleagues, 55-6, **56**
    association with H.T. Knox, 1, 2, 57-9, 67-79, 85, 159
    association with Goddard Orpen, 136-42
    at Fortwilliam, 9, 57
    birth, 1, 5
    career in Royal Irish Constabulary, 1, 9-12, 20, 28, 41
    correspondence with antiquarians, 46-8, 67,
    criticism, 156-7
    excavations, 50-4, 99-105
    interest in folklife, 41-3, **42**, 60, 123-133
    obituaries, 22, 151, 157
    preservation of artefacts, 133-5
    retirement in Clonmel, 2, 5, 145-57
    use of local information, 49-54
Lyons Photographic Collection, N.U.I.Galway, 4, 41, 46, 48, 52, 67, 76, **77**, 80, 83, 84, 93, 95, 100, 104, 107, 110, 124, 132, 138, 142

M
Macalister, R.A.S., 4, 12, 50, 59, 66, 67, 78, 104-5, 112, 113, 151
Malcolm, E., 28
Masonbrook, Co. Galway, 87, 99, 104-5
McCormick, F., 50-4

McKee, G, 17
Meedian, 142
Meehaunbwee, Co. Roscommon, 54
Meelick, Co. Mayo, 48, **49**,
Megaliths
    Aghataharn, 50
    Cappagh, Co. Mayo, 93, 130
    Derrydonnell, Co. Galway, 30
    Drumgollagh, Co. Mayo, **38**
    Knockfarnaght, Co. Mayo, 95, **97**
    Knockinn, Co. Mayo, 123
    Laght-a-Wohoo, Feamore, Co. Mayo, **47**, 48, 50
    Meehaunbwee, Co. Roscommon, 54
    Slieve Dart, Co. Mayo, 45
Mellowes, L., **32**, **33**
Mills and millstones
    Bagnelstown, Co. Carlow, **77**
    Cullentra, Co. Mayo, **73**
    Dhine, Co. Mayo, **75**
    Kilgarriff, Co. Mayo, **75**
    milling artifacts, 76
    millstones, , **75**, 107
Moate, Co. Mayo, **137**, 138
Mount Shaw, Co. Galway, 99
Mullaghadooey, Co. Roscommon, 138
'Mummers', 126-7
Murphy, Rev. T.A., 151, 154, 159

N
Newport, Co. Mayo, **125**, 127
'Normanisation', 84, 85-6, **91**, 138

O
O'Connell, P., 149, 153
O'Reilly, J.A., 72-3
Ó Néill, E., 6, 57, 152-3
Ogham Stones
    Bracklaghboy, Co. Mayo, 63, **64**, **65**
    Breastagh, Co. Mayo, 59
    Island, Co. Mayo, 58, 60, 63, **64**, **65**
    Kilmannin, Co. Mayo, **59**, **60**, 63
    Kilmovee, Co. Mayo, **62**, **66**, 67
    Rusheen West, Co. Mayo, **61**, 62, 66, 67
    Tullaghan, Co. Mayo, 45, 50, 60, 63
Oldcastle, Co. Galway, 142

Oran, Co. Roscommon, 84
Orpen, G., 4, 47, 48, 78, 79, 85, 90, 116, 136-42, 159

P
Petrie, G., 48
Pillar stones
   Ballyglass/Kiltullagh, Co. Roscommon, 50-4, **51**, **52**, **53**, 55
   Carnabreckna, Co. Roscommon, 90
   Coolnaha, Co, Mayo, **61**, **62**
   Kildun, Co. Mayo, **68**
   Rosgallive, Mallaranny, Co. Mayo, **35**
   St Patrick's Stone, Carrowkeel, Co. Mayo, **26**
   Stone of Formach, Tooracurra, Co. Waterford, 147, 149, **150**, 151
   Turoe, Co. Galway, **101**, 102-3
Portaghard, Co. Mayo, **82**, 83,

R
Raftery, J., 102-3, 147, 149
Raha, Co. Mayo, 83
Raheen, Co. Galway, 97
Raith, Co. Mayo, 69
Rathbeg, Co. Roscommon, 86
Rathbrennan, Co. Roscommon, 88-90, **91**, 93
Rathbrit, Co. Tipperary, 54
Rathcroghan, Co. Roscommon, 2, 4, 55, 78, 81, 83, 86, 87, 90, 93, **96**, 98, 104
Rathgorgin, Co. Galway, **140**, **141**, 142
Rathmore, Co. Roscommon, **86**, **87**, 88
Rathnarrow, Co. Westmeath, 93
Rathra, Co. Roscommon, **137**, 138
Rathscrigg, Co. Roscommon, 95
Redington, M., 1, 85, 103, 107, 116, 142
Rhys, Sir J., 3, 4, 12, 44, 56, 58, 60, 62-4, 78, 159
Rosgallive, Mallaranny, Co. Mayo, **35**
Royal Irish Constabulary
   agitation against Land Acts, , 25-7, 28, 41-3, **42**
   Athenry barracks, 12, 28
   Ballyhaunis barracks, 4, 12, 18, 27, 158
   Court of Inquiry, 12, 35-7, 122
   daily keeping of law and order, 13-4, 17, 28
   Defence of the Realm Regulations, 32
   disapproval of Lyons' antiquarian activities,1, 2, 4, 44, 55, 77-8
   evictions, **15**, 16, 20
   Longford No. I barracks, 12
   Lyons' career in, 1, 9, 11, 13, 20, 28, 41
   Lyons' court appearances, 20-5
   Moate barracks, 18
   More Pay Movement, 29
   Newport barracks, 2, 33, 142
   organisation of, 11
   political meetings, 16-7, 25-7, 30-1, 32, 38-9
   regulations, 10, 18
   semi-military role of, 11, 16, 40
   service record, 13
   Streamstown barracks, 18
   training, 11
Royal Society of Antiquaries of Ireland
   Knox/Lyons collection, 4-5, 44, 71, 72, 105-7
   Lyons' membership of, 3, 4, 67, 84-5, 127, 146-7, 151, 158
   visit to Athenry, Co. Galway, 113
   visit to Clonmel, Co. Tipperary, 151
Runnamoat, Co. Roscommon, 84, 138, **139**
Rusheen West, Co. Mayo, **61**, 62, 66, 67
Rynne, E., **108**, 116, 117, 118, 121,

S
Sheeaunbeg, 138
Slieve Dart, 45, 68
Spaddagh, Co. Mayo, **128, 129**
St. Marchan's Lough, Co. Mayo, 78
Stokes, Miss, 47-8
Streamstown, Co. Westmeath, 18

T
Thubbercoghlan, Co. Mayo, 130, 132
Thubber-Mhuira, Co. Roscommon, 132
Thubber-na-Bachaille, Co. Mayo, 62,
Thubber-na-Crush-Neeve, Co. Galway, 130, 131
Thubbernaneeve, 130

Thurles, Co. Tipperary, **145**
'Tinkers', 127-9, **128**, **129**
Tooloobaun, Co. Galway, 78
Tooracurra, Co. Waterford, 147, 149, **150**, 151
Tubberkevna, Co. Mayo, **70**
Tullaghan, Co. Mayo, 45, 50, 59, 60, 63
Tully, Co. Roscommon, 45
Tulsk, Co. Roscommon, **24**, 140
Turoe, Co. Galway, 99-104, **101**,

U
Urlaur, Co. Mayo, 69

V
Volunteers, 30-1, 32, 33, 34, 38-40

W
Waddell, J., 3, 83, 90-2, 103
Waters, S., 28
Well Fort, Tulsk, Co. Roscommon, 140
Westport, Co. Mayo, 33, 38-40
Westropp. T.J., 4, 58, 71, **74**, 76, 78, 79, 85, 106,
'Wren Boys', 123-7

The life, times and work in archaeology of Patrick Lyons R.I.C. (1861-1954)